Dollar and Yen

Dollar and Yen

Resolving Economic Conflict
between the United States
and Japan

Ronald I. McKinnon and
Kenichi Ohno

The MIT Press
Cambridge, Massachusetts
London, England

© 1997 Massachusetts Institute of Technology

All rights reserved. No part of this book may be reproduced in any form by any electronic or mechanical means (including photocopying, recording, or information storage and retrieval) without permission in writing from the publisher.

This book was set in Palatino on the Monotype "Prism Plus" PostScript Imagesetter by Asco Trade Typesetting Ltd., Hong Kong.

Printed and bound in the United States of America.

Library of Congress Cataloging-in-Publication Data

McKinnon, Ronald I.
    Dollar and yen : resolving economic conflict between the United States and Japan / Ronald McKinnon and Kenichi Ohno.
    p. cm.
    Includes bibliographical references and index.
    ISBN 0-262-13335-0 (alk. paper)
    1. United States—Foreign economic relations—Japan. 2. Japan—Foreign economic relations—United States. 3. Foreign exchange rates—United States. 4. Foreign exchange rates—Japan. I. Ohno, Kenichi. II. Title.
HF1456.5.J3M418   1997
337.73052—dc21   97-1584
                                                                           CIP

To Margaret and Izumi

Contents

Preface   ix

1   Introduction: The Syndrome of the Ever-Higher Yen   1

2   Policy Causes and Postwar Origins of Japan–U.S. Economic
     Conflict: Differential Productivity Growth and the Saving
     Shortage in the United States   21

3   Exchange-Rate Fluctuations and Their Consequences: Price
     Diffusion and *Endaka Fukyo*   51

4   Balancing International Competitiveness in the Longer Run:
     Wage Adjustment versus Yen Appreciation   73

5   The Transfer Problem and Macroeconomic Fluctuations: *Endaka
     Fukyo*, Bubbles, and Credit Crunches   93

6   The Exchange Rate and the Trade Balance in Theory: Insular
     versus Open Economies   125

7   The Exchange Rate and the Japan–U.S. Trade Balance in
     Practice: A Critique of the Modern Elasticities Approach   143

8   Monetary and Exchange-Rate Regimes, Inflation Persistence,
     and the Volatility of Long-term Interest Rates   163

9   Price Deflation and Purchasing Power Parity: A Causality
     Analysis of Yen Appreciation and Japanese Monetary
     Policy   177

10 Overcoming the Syndrome: Toward a U.S.–Japan Commercial
   Compact and Monetary Accord   205

11 Is the Syndrome Over? The Fall of the Yen, 1995–96, and Its
   Implications for the Transition   223

   Notes   237
   References   247
   Index   257

Preface

Can yet another tract on the political and economic interaction between Japan and the United States be justified? For more than thirty years, criticisms by Americans of Japan's industrial and exchange-rate policies, and by Japanese of America's anemic saving behavior and excessive litigation, have been all too common. Yet even the wilder accusations of one side about the other occasionally contain a germ of truth.

What perspective does this book bring to resolving economic conflict between the United States and Japan? Because one author teaches at an American university and the other at a Japanese one, jointly we can better assess—and accept—what is valid criticism of either country. Correspondingly, as academics we feel free to reject or simply to ignore the fanciful and often corrosive paranoia that sells so well on airport newsstands—whether in English or in Japanese.

More positively, we also bring something new to the discussion: an integrated theory of how mercantile disputes influence financial processes and business cycles in each country. Our focus is usually through the lens of the yen-dollar exchange rate and expectations about how it will move in the future. Strengthening the theory required a lot of empirical work, some of it amenable to econometric testing. Thus, we can't promise a completely easy read, but we do offer a systematic approach to defusing trade disputes and improving the macroeconomic performances of the world's two largest economies.

That said, most of the book is not very technical, including chapters 1, 10, and 11, which contain the main arguments. So it will appeal to the wide audience interested in the United States and Japan as well as international economics more generally. Even chapters with equations should be readily accessible to students and teachers of international finance.

We would like to thank our wives, Margaret and Izumi, for being so tolerant of the long transpacific flights necessary to our work on what has

been very much a joint effort. Margaret McKinnon was particularly helpful in editing several chapters. Thanks also to Professor Daniel Okimoto,
director of Stanford University's Asia/Pacific Research Center, for his
unflagging encouragement and financial support.

The staff of The MIT Press, particularly Terry Vaughn, Victoria
Richardson, and Sandra Minkkinen, were most understanding in tolerating
our rewriting of chapters as important events unfolded and as our ideas
continued to coalesce. The Nihon Keizai Shimbun, under whose auspices
the Japanese translation will be published, was similarly patient.

1   Introduction: The Syndrome of the Ever-Higher Yen

The economic interaction between the United States and Japan is an endlessly fascinating subject. From the the mid-1950s, after its remarkable recovery from wartime devastation, through the 1980s, Japan expanded faster than any other major industrial economy. It largely displaced America as the dominant player in worldwide markets for manufactures—first in light industries such as textiles and consumer goods, and then in many areas requiring prime engineering skills, such as automobiles and electrical machinery. Even from 1992 to 1995, when Japan suffered a prolonged economic recession (which is part of the syndrome of the ever-higher yen, to be explained in this chapter), its trade surpluses in high-technology industrial goods remained robust.

Innumerable books, journal articles, and newspaper stories sought to explain Japan's mercantile success—and to determine whether that success constituted a threat to particular American industries or to the American economy in general. In the 1970s and 1980s, many authors linked America's seeming decline in the world economy and its burgeoning trade deficits to "unfair" Japanese industrial, commercial, exchange-rate, and domestic financial practices that, among other things, kept the Japanese market closed to a wide variety of foreign goods.

Rather than reviewing the dynamics of international trade on an industry-by-industry basis, this book focuses on overall macroeconomic and financial interactions between the Japanese and American economies from the early 1950s to the mid-1990s. Given the "problem" of relatively high growth in Japanese industrial productivity and exports, how did wages, overall price levels, and interest rates in the two countries mutually adjust? Did adjustment during the 1950s and 1960s, when the yen-dollar exchange rate was fixed, differ significantly from adjustment after no-par floating began in 1973? For some of the answers, we look at the savings shortage in the United States, the liberalization of foreign access to the

Japanese capital market by the early 1980s, and the huge transfer of capital from Japan to the United States over the past two decades. Macroeconomic instability since 1985—including Japan's asset bubble of the late 1980s, the U.S. credit crunch of 1991–92, and Japan's deflationary slump from 1992 through 1995—is also considered.

But such a potentially sweeping field of inquiry needs a unifying theme to focus the analysis. After staying comfortably at its Bretton Woods dollar parity of 360 yen to the dollar (plus or minus 1 percent) from 1949 to early 1971, the yen rose persistently if erratically at least until mid-1995 (figure 1.1). Even in early 1997, the dollar would buy only about 120 yen. The first distinctive feature of this book is that it links this great yen appreciation against the dollar, and against other major currencies, to mercantile pressure from the United States—pressure arising out of commercial disputes and trade tensions between the two countries. Correspondingly, the fall of the yen from mid-1995 to early 1997—an important episode analyzed in chapter 11—can be linked to a relaxation of U.S. mercantile pressure.

Traditionally, economists separate the study of international finance—the implications of monetary and fiscal policies for exchange-rate determination—from the study of trade flows, commercial policies, and trade disputes. This simplifying dichotomy is valid for most countries most of the time. Nevertheless, to understand the peculiarities of the U.S.–Japan macroeconomic relationship since 1971, we shall argue that the traditional dichotomy is invalid. Commercial tensions, including intermittent threats of a trade war, were an important force in driving the yen upward through at least April 1995. And, on occasions when these threats were relaxed, as in the summer of 1995, the yen fell.

The second unconventional aspect of our approach is that we treat the course of the yen-dollar exchange rate as a forcing variable for Japanese monetary policy, rather than assuming that monetary policy independently determines the exchange rate. This was obviously true in the 1950s and 1960s, when the Bank of Japan (BoJ) subordinated domestic credit expansion to maintaining the fixed yen-dollar exchange rate (Suzuki 1986). Less obviously, however, we hypothesize that the deflationary course of the BoJ's monetary policy since the early 1970s, relative to the rate of inflation independently determined by the U.S. Federal Reserve System, has been conditioned by the yen's appreciation, as demonstrated econometrically in chapters 7 and 9.

These two important, if little recognized, causal chains—from mercantile pressure to the yen-dollar rate, and from this exchange rate to Japanese monetary policy—motivate much of the analysis in this book.

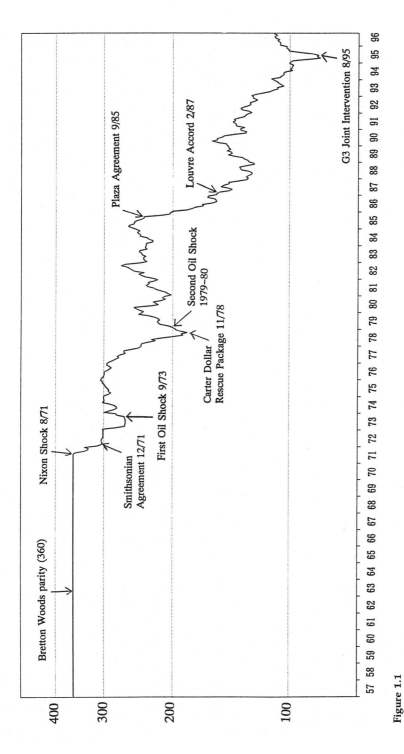

Figure 1.1
Nominal yen-dollar exchange rate, semilog scale. *Source:* IMF, *International Financial Statistics*, CD-ROM, December 1996.

Most authors writing on exchange rates and balance-of-payments adjustment (e.g., Bergsten and Cline 1985; Krugman 1991; Williamson and Henning 1994) treat the nominal exchange rate as an adjusting rather than a forcing variable. Autonomous monetary (and fiscal) policies result in differential rates of national price inflation to which the exchange rate adjusts, or can be made to adjust. In addition, these authors view substantial changes in the real exchange rate to be useful for correcting trade imbalances between countries—that is, for facilitating a warranted net transfer of capital from country A to country B. Thus, they are reluctant to return to fixed par values for nominal exchange rates.

We do not deny the validity of this traditional approach in many important circumstances, particularly for soft-currency countries whose governments depend on the inflation tax for revenue and must continually allow their currencies to depreciate. Even for countries that do not suffer from chronic inflation but that are insular—imperfectly integrated with the outside world by trade and financial flows—chapter 6 shows that exchange-rate adjustments can be useful for controlling the balance of payments.

However, for hard-currency countries, whose goods and capital flows are highly open to world markets, we believe untethered nominal exchange rates, reflecting uncoordinated national monetary policies, to be volatile and disturbing. At the microeonomic level, exchange fluctuations introduce noise into relative goods prices and so reduce investment efficiency (chapter 3). At a more macro level, fluctuations in nominal exchange rates between closely linked economies impede otherwise smooth longer-term adjustment in relative wage growth, interest rates, and price levels (chapter 4), as exemplified by the yen's erratic appreciation for 25 years after 1970. In the intermediate term, exchange overvaluation can cause severe economic downturns (chapters 3 and 5). The smooth transfer of capital from one country to another is more difficult if the future course of the exchange rate is uncertain (chapters 7 and 8). Although these themes were developed more generally by one of the authors in a companion volume (McKinnon 1996), the present case study of Japan and the United States lends much-needed empirical evidence of how costly fluctuating relative currency values can be.

1.1 Commercial Disputes: A Brief Sketch

Since no-par floating began in the early 1970s, commercial disputes between Japan and the United States have been central to determining the yen-dollar exchange rate. Therefore, it is important to understand the political economy of these disputes as it affects the behavior of both governments. Why should commercial tension be, or have been, more intense between Japan and the United States than between other pairs of industrial countries?

The much higher average productivity and output growth since the early 1950s of Japanese manufacturing industries compared to their American counterparts, as documented in chapter 2, created great commercial tension. This growth was highly uneven: more explosive in Japanese industries such as electrical machinery, automobiles, and consumer electronics than in others. The overall Japanese economy, now the world's second largest, grew rapidly: total Japanese exports amounted to only about one-fourth of U.S. exports in 1964, but had risen to well over three-fourths by 1995. Thus, no matter how smoothly the international financial mechanism had functioned, and no matter how assiduously each country's diplomats had sought political harmony, a serious problem of mutual economic adjustment would still exist.

But adjustment was also complicated by unfortunate trends in the political economy of each country, also described in chapter 2. On the Japanese side, the government relied too long on the principle of "developmental authoritarianism" (see definition on page 30), or more simply "developmentalism" (Murakami 1992), for promoting the industrial sector—well past the point when such action might have been needed to support recovery from wartime devastation. For the next several decades, the government consciously targeted the development of particular industries to be internationally competitive, though not always successfully or accurately. To prevent the domestic distribution of income from being unduly skewed by such favoritism, the government then used a complex regulatory apparatus to cosset or shield many other "disadvantaged" industries—often those outside the manufacturing sector—from the rigors of both international and domestic competition.

To foreigners trying to sell in Japan, this concerted regulatory power of the various ministries, often operating through industrywide trade associations of Japanese business firms, appeared to be a formidable barrier and a possible shield for collusive behavior in international markets as well. Whence the proliferation of books on Japan being an "unfair" international competitor. Upscale in this genre, Laura Tyson, President Clinton's principal economic advisor in 1992–96, published the book *Who's Bashing Whom? Trade Conflict in High-Technology Industries* (1992). After several chapters documenting the extreme regulatory hurdles facing American producers of semiconductors, cellular telephones, supercomputers, and other high-technology goods who were trying to sell in the Japanese market, and the intense political confrontations arising out of those disputes, Tyson concludes, "The[se] cases of U.S.–Japan trade competition ... provide compelling historical evidence of the persistence of structural and policy impediments to the Japanese market. Although formal protection has been phased out, primarily in response to American *gaiatsu* [pressure], the peculiar features of Japanese capitalism impede access to foreign suppliers to shape competition to the advantage of their Japanese rivals" (p. 266). Similarly, in a more extensive review of industry studies covering Japanese manufacturing, primary products, and services in their book *Reconcilable Differences? United States–Japan Economic Conflict* (1993), C. Fred Bergsten and Marcus Noland conclude:

In Japan there is scant evidence of significant tariffs and quotas outside of agriculture. Nevertheless, it is widely believed that the Japanese market is effectively closed to manufactured imports. The methods of import control include discriminatory networks of affiliated firms (*keiretsu*); administrative guidance on the part of government officials to intimidate importers; misuse of customs procedures and product standards, testing, and certification procedures to discourage imports; incomplete enforcement of patent and trademark rights; government procurement procedures that advantage domestic suppliers; and restrictions on the distribution channels for imported products, to name a few. (P. 72)

But airport newsstands sport plenty of downscale versions of how Japan Inc. was conspiring to undermine the American economy through collusive trading practices. Although Japan lowered many of its more restrictive regulatory barriers to foreigners selling in the Japanese market —for example, opening large-scale discount retailers (OECD 1995)—the idea of an overly intrusive Japanese bureaucracy persists in the minds of foreign protagonists in trade disputes.

On the American side, there is an equally pernicious hangover from the past—what Jagdish Bhagwati (1993) calls "the diminished giant syndrome." In the 1950s and 1960s, the United States dominated world markets in high-tech manufactures on the one hand, and was the free world's bulwark against the advance of communism on the other. With the initiation of the General Agreement on Tariffs and Trade in 1947, the Marshall Plan in 1948, and the Dodge Plan in 1949, the United States overcame domestic parochial and protectionist interests to fashion a new, multilateral world trading order based on the principle of liberal economies with open markets. In order to enlist the cooperation of Europeans and Japanese in this great crusade, the United States was willing in the 1950s to allow some transitional trade discrimination against American goods to encourage Western European countries to buy from each other and to allow Japan to follow (transitional) covert protectionist practices for a surprisingly long time. For example, it was not until 1964 that Japan formally accepted full current-account convertibility under the International Monetary Fund's Article 8, and not until the early 1980s was there more or less full convertibility on capital account.

However, the very success of the great crusade inevitably led to the diminished giant syndrome. As some European countries and Japan grew to achieve, more or less, technical parity with the United States, America's old dominance of markets for sophisticated manufactures inevitably declined. The parallel with Britain at the end of the nineteenth century is striking.

The dimunition in Britain's preeminence in the world economy led to a rise in protectionist sentiments and demands for an end to Britain's unilateralist embrace of free-trade principles. And the United States has followed the same path. The present-day sentiments in the United States have been aimed pointedly at newly successful rivals, just as their nineteenth-century counterparts' were. The United States and Germany were to Britain what the Pacific nations—Japan in particular—are to the United States today. (Bhagwati 1989, pp. 48–49)

Although not threatened militarily as Britain was, America showed one further trait of a diminished giant. Just as world financial markets became effectively open in the 1980s and 1990s, the relative decline in America's exports was exacerbated by the fall in American savings rates (chapter 2). The resulting need to import capital from the rest of the world created huge U.S. current-account and trade deficits, thus speeding the decline of America's share in various world markets for manufactures.

The American government's concern with mercantile pressure from its faster-growing political allies goes back a long way. As early as 1956, the United States put pressure on Japan to impose a "voluntary" export restraint (VER) on Japanese cotton textiles entering the American market.[1] In 1966, a number of European countries and Japan were persuaded to impose a VER on steel exports to the United States, a restraint that spread to specialty steels in the 1970s. In 1968, U.S. television producers filed antidumping suits against Japanese producers, and in 1971 the U.S. government imposed substantial antidumping duties on imports of Japanese televisions. In the late 1960s, severe measures to protect all manufacturing industries were introduced in the U.S. Congress. These ultimately failed but nevertheless put pressure on the American government to "do something" to help American manufacturing industry (Robert Baldwin 1988).

As long as the Bretton Woods system of par values for exchange rates was firmly in place and the U.S. current account showed a surplus, as was generally the case in the 1950s and 1960s (see chapter 7), the dollar's exchange rate was unaffected by protectionist pressure. This was one of the great strengths of the par value system. However, the protectionist pressure intensified when inflation in the United States increased after 1968 and U.S. wholesale prices began drifting upward relative to those in Germany and Japan (chapter 4). In August 1971, President Nixon insisted that the dollar be devalued against other major currencies. The devaluation, by about 17 percent against the yen, occurred the following December. Although not fully understood at the time, this move effectively ended America's commitment to stable par values for exchange rates.

But the one-time dollar depreciation did not end protectionist pressure. In the late 1970s, the United States government introduced trigger prices on steel imports, which, when VERs expired, were (and are) associated with a variety of antidumping suits filed by American steel companies, against foreign steel producers in general and against Japanese in particular, throughout the 1980s and into the 1990s. And the mercantile concerns of the American government increasingly focused on Japan as it made its way up the ladder from simple to more complex industrial goods. Voluntary restraints on Japanese exports to the American market proliferated, affecting televisions beginning in the 1970s, machine tools in the 1970s and 1980s, and automobiles in the 1980s. The U.S. Commerce Department made it increasingly easy for American firms to prove allegations of dumping against foreigners (Krueger 1995), particularly those from countries with appreciating currencies,[2] like Japan.

Before the mid-1980s, government-to-government negotiations to relax mercantile pressure on the United States resulted in ad hoc "voluntary" export restraints. These were certainly outside the spirit of the GATT but were not inconsistent with any of its specific articles. Similarly, private antidumping suits were potentially consistent with the antidumping articles of the GATT. However, the procedures used by the U.S. Department of Commerce in evaluating "fair" foreign prices for selling in the U.S. market, the incredible bookkeeping costs imposed on foreign firms victimized by antidumping suits (whether successful or not), and the ever-weaker standards for determining material injury to American producers, are not (Krueger 1995).

By the late 1980s, however, the retreat of international communism as an organized economic and military threat to the United States made it even more difficult for the American president to suppress domestic protectionist interests, which had always been heavily represented in Congress. By 1988, aggressive unilateralism outside the rules of the GATT had become firmly institutionalized in American trade law under what is now popularly called "Super 301." In her book *American Trade Policy: A Tragedy in the Making* (1995), Anne Krueger suggests that

the Omnibus Trade and Competitiveness Act of 1988 extended Section 301 of the Trade Act of 1974 to broaden considerably the scope of the unfair trade procedures and took it well beyond procedures that are consistent with the GATT in principle. In particular, Congress instructed the USTR [United States Trade Representative] to take an inventory of other countries' unfair trading practices ... in a report to Congress by the end of May each year.... The 1988 trade act also instructed the USTR to take retaliatory action against imports from the named country (or countries) in the event that the USTR could not negotiate for the removal of the named practices. (P. 64)

Without requiring reciprocity by the United States, Section 301 cleared the way for the USTR to demand unilaterally that other countries take action to open their national markets to American goods. One result has been to specify specific shares in foreign markets through so-called voluntary import expansions (VIEs). The first VIE was negotiated in 1986, in semiconductors, to assure foreign producers (imagined to be mainly American) 20 percent of the Japanese market; it contained riders for keeping Japanese prices sufficiently high that American producers could compete more easily at home and in third markets. There have been recriminations and subsequent renegotiations into the 1990s over whether or not the Japanese were violating those riders (Itoh 1994).

Krueger notes that Super 301 was not renewed by the Bush Administration when it expired at the end of 1990. But she also notes that

by the winter of 1994, however, bilateral trading relations with Japan had deteriorated under the Clinton Administration's pressure for "quantitative targets." In March 1994, President Clinton reinstituted Super 301 by executive decree. He insisted that the bilateral trade balance with Japan, and even the magnitude of Japanese imports of individual items, were legitimate subjects for bilateral bargaining. He threatened retaliation (presumably punitive tariffs) if Japan did not address to the satisfaction of the United States, the "unfair trading practice" of a large bilateral trade imbalance. (P. 67)

The reinstituted Super 301 was the basis for acrimonious discussions during the first four months of 1995 about opening Japanese markets to American automobiles and components. After a cliff-hanging settlement process, during which the U.S. negotiators threatened to impose a 100 percent U.S. tariff on imports of Japanese luxury cars (without clearance from the World Trade Organization) and the yen rose sharply in the foreign exchanges, the two governments finally concluded in June 1995 a weak agreement to promote Japanese imports of American automobiles and components. (The exchange-rate consequences of the subsequent relaxation of commercial pressure on Japan are taken up in chapter 11.)

We conclude that, despite the completion of the Uruguay Round in 1994, which created the World Trade Organization (WTO) to supersede the GATT, institutionalized bilateral tension over commercial policy between Japan and the United States may well continue. What, then, have been—and could well continue to be—the financial consequences?

1.2 The Syndrome of the Ever-Higher Yen

As defined by the tenth edition of *Merriam Webster's Collegiate Dictionary*, a *syndrome* is (1) a group of signs and symptoms that occur together and characterize a particular abnormality; or (2) a set of concurrent things (as emotions or actions) that usually form an identifiable pattern.

Since 1971, the interactions of the American and Japanese governments in their conduct of commercial, exchange-rate, and monetary policies have resulted in what we call the *syndrome of the ever-higher yen*. In addition to contributing to a generation of political discord, the erratically appreciating yen undermines microeconomic efficiency in trade between the two economies and has led to serious macroeconomic disturbances in Japan.

Because of its large size and its history as the center country in the world payments system, the United States has generally exercised monetary independence, whereas Japan has been forced to follow a surprisingly dependent monetary policy, despite the fact that no-par floating was advertised (and is still advertised; see Obstfeld 1995) as a device for securing national macroeconomic autonomy. The U.S. government has generally been the initiator of actions—whose consequences it does not fully understand—that promote the syndrome. Nevertheless, the Japanese government has been very slow to learn how its own reactions support or validate the yen's continual appreciation. Thus the two countries have been trapped in a mutual interaction, the "syndrome," that is distinctly suboptimal for both of them.

What mechanism propagates the syndrome? When President Nixon closed the gold window in August 1971, he also imposed a surcharge on imports of manufactured goods, which would remain in place until trading partners in Europe and Japan appreciated the dollar value of their currencies. Because of Japan's persistent trade surpluses since then, the United

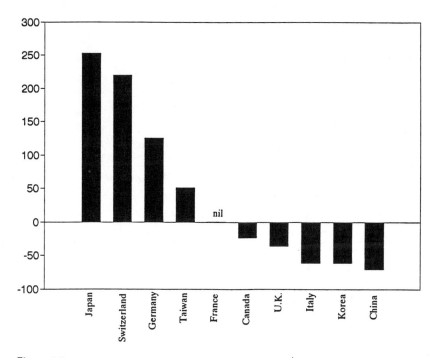

Figure 1.2
Nominal appreciation against the dollar, cumulative percent change in 1970–94. *Sources:* IMF, *International Financial Statistics*, and Bank of Japan, *Economic Statistics Monthly*, various issues.

States has pursued a similar policy of coupling protectionist threats with demands, implicit or explicit, for yen appreciation. (The major exceptions were the strong-dollar policy of the first Reagan administration, from 1981 to 1984, and the dramatic relaxation of mercantile pressure on Japan leading to the fall of the yen after April 1995 and analyzed in chapter 11.) Figure 1.2 shows that the yen's 250 percent appreciation against the dollar from 1970 to 1994 was the greatest among U.S. trading partners.[3] So the exchange-rate cum mercantile-dispute problem was mainly one between Japan and the United States.

No matter how much the dollar fell, at least some U.S. government officials typically looked at the Japanese trade surplus and saw further room for yen appreciation. Since the Nixon shock in 1971, various Secretaries of the Treasury—notably Blumenthal in 1977, Baker in 1985–87, and Bentsen in 1993—have suggested that the dollar was too high against the yen. Often these attempts to talk the dollar down were accompanied by intense trade negotiations aimed at forcing the Japanese to open or share this or that market. Taking a short-run view of what would improve American competitiveness vis-à-vis Japan, foreign-exchange traders see in a lower dollar a way of ameliorating—or perhaps forestalling—protectionist threats from the United States. For example, in the first four months of 1995, when the U.S. Trade Representative tried to force Japan to set numerical targets for buying American automobiles and components, the dollar fell particularly sharply, from 100 to 80 yen (figure 1.1).

But talk is cheap. Why should it force the yen up in the near term? Although the exchange rate is a forward-looking asset price, the (forward) fundamentals are difficult for foreign-exchange traders or econometricians to define, let alone to model. Thus, under certain circumstances, talk about exchange rates by Treasury secretaries, and the commercial disputes themselves, can affect people's perceptions of future economic policies, and thus diminish the eagerness of Japanese investors to add to their portfolios of dollar assets in the near term.

The markets see the U.S. government behaving as if it were populist in two senses. First, the loss of shares in manufactures in world markets (particularly to Japan) makes the government more receptive to domestic industrial lobbies—a symptom of America's diminished giant status. These lobbyists petition to reduce the competitiveness of Japanese producers, whether through so-called voluntary export restraints, arbitrary calculations of foreign costs in antidumping suits, punitive sanctions to force foreigners to import more American goods, or other means. They see the yen's appreciation, albeit myopically, as just another technique for reducing Japanese competitiveness in the short run.

Second, populist behavior by the American government has been aided and abetted by economists—perhaps the majority of them—who espouse an exchange-rate doctrine based on the elasticities model of the balance of trade. They have convinced American policy makers that devaluing the dollar will, by itself, reduce the U.S. trade or current-account deficit, and that exchange-rate changes can be treated as a rather clean and acceptable instrument of economic policy. And because Japan has had the biggest current-account surpluses—until 1994, about the same size as the U.S. deficit (figure 1.3)—the yen-dollar rate becomes the focus of attempts by the American government to reduce the trade deficit by talking the yen up.

But when applied to industrial economies that are financially open and would otherwise be stable, this elasticities approach for correcting a trade

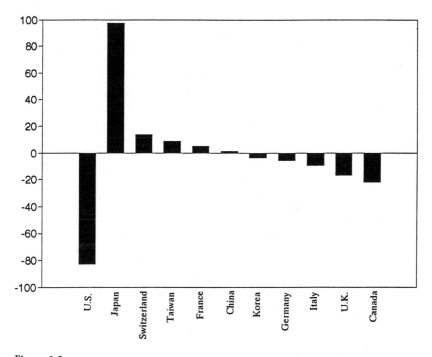

Figure 1.3
Current-account balance, 1990–94 average, in billions of dollars. *Sources:* IMF, *International Financial Statistics*, and the Bank of Japan, *Economic Statistics Monthly*, various issues.

imbalance is misplaced (Komiya 1994). As shown in chapter 2, the persistent current-account imbalance between the two countries reflects Japan's saving surplus on the one hand and abnormally low saving by the United States on the other. Chapter 6 demonstrates theoretically that, for a *financially open* economy, simply changing the exchange rate has no predictable effect on the trade balance in the short and intermediate terms after price effects and expenditure repercussions are taken into account; this outcome is unlike what the elasticities model would claim. Chapter 7 demonstrates the inevitable long-run tendency for nominal yen appreciation to be offset by relative deflation in Japan so as eventually to leave the real exchange rate unchanged. Figure 1.4 shows the increase in the U.S. wholesale price index (WPI) relative to the Japanese WPI since floating began in 1971.

Therefore, the markets, in contrast to the populist American government, have also come to realize that yen appreciation alone will not reduce Japan's saving surplus as reflected in its current-account surplus.

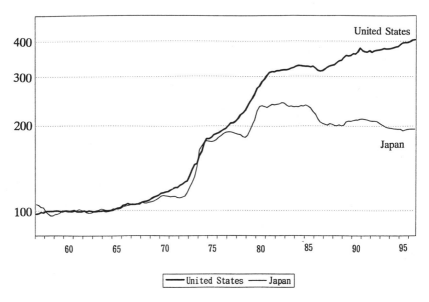

Figure 1.4
Price level of tradable goods (WPI), semilog scale, 1960:Q1 = 100. *Note:* Each graph is taken from line 63 of IMF, *International Financial Statistics*, CD-ROM, December 1996. In 1985, the U.S. WPI was merged into a series on the U.S. producer price index (PPI).

After any one episode when the yen is run up and the American government is (temporarily) mollified, forward-looking international investors project that the Japanese current-account surplus and the American current deficit will continue in the future. They foresee that populist political agitation in the United States will eventually reappear as people complain about "unfair" Japanese competiton, that the American government will again threaten sanctions unless Japan "does something" about its trade surplus, and that, in the future, the yen is likely to rise further. Private Japanese investors in dollar assets get a bit more nervous, and there is no tendency for the yen—having risen in the near term—to regress in the long term.

But how does such populist pressure in the foreign-exchange market affect the long-run monetary fundamentals and thus sustain itself? An important aspect of the syndrome is the asymmetry in the conduct of monetary policies in the two countries. Because of its role at the center of the world's monetary system, the United States traditionally has had the freedom to determine its own monetary policy independently of other countries' official interventions in the foreign exchanges (McKinnon 1996). And, unlike Japan's internal price level, the American one is relatively invariant to exchange-rate fluctuations (chapter 3). Thus, in determining the rate of price inflation in the United States, the Federal Reserve System has been able to act without paying much heed to other countries' inflation rates or monetary policies.

Then, according to how much the yen appreciates in the face of mercantile pressure from the United States, the course of future Japanese monetary policy becomes relatively deflationary. If the yen ratchets up in the short run, the markets project that the Japanese government will tolerate a higher value of the yen in order to avoid the wrath of American protectionists. Even if the Bank of Japan were able to do so, it hesitates to flood the foreign or domestic financial markets with liquidity to bring the yen down. True, in episodes of particularly sharp yen appreciations—as in 1971–73, 1977–78, 1985–87, and 1993 to mid-1995—the BoJ typically responds by easing Japanese monetary policy in order to dampen the yen's upward momentum, as we show in chapter 9. But in extreme cases where Japanese short-term interest rates are already close to zero (the liquidity trap discussed in chapters 3 and 5), the BoJ may be pretty well helpless to bring the yen down even if it wants to.

The upshot of a number of such episodic yen appreciations is that Japan is forced into relative deflation in the longer run. Athough the BoJ may resist particularly sharp appreciations in the short run, as we show in chapter 9, that resistance is insufficient to prevent secular (relative) deflation. As shown in figure 1.4, since the mid-1970s, the Japanese WPI has risen more slowly than its American counterpart and has actually fallen in absolute terms since 1985.

1.3   Long-term Interest Rates and Exchange Expectations

Although the yen began appreciating in 1971 under mercantile pressure from the United States, the expectations of an ever-higher yen (so central to the syndrome) were not yet, of course, firmly rooted in anybody's mind. In the early 1970s in the aftermath of the breakdown in the Bretton Woods dollar parities,[4] people worried more about the inflationary pressure emanating from the United States into the world economy including Japan's severe price-wage inflation through 1974, so evident in figure 1.4. The great volatility of exchange rates, rather than sustained movement in one direction, seemed to be the more pressing problem.

With the benefit of hindsight, however, it is clear that the speech of U.S. Treasury Secretary Michael Blumenthal in June 1977, in which he intimated that the dollar was again overvalued against the yen (although the dollar was already quite low by the criterion of purchasing power parity), more strongly signaled the emergence of the syndrome in bilateral U.S.–Japan relations—as distinct from American mercantile problems with other trading partners. Together with commercial tension over Japanese industrial policies and emerging U.S. current deficits and Japanese surpluses, the speech contributed to the great run on the dollar in 1977–78. The run was finally halted in November 1978 through massive intervention by all the important central banks, by the Carter dollar rescue package (figure 1.1), and by a sharp increase in both short- and long-term U.S. interest rates. In contrast, Japanese long-term rates fell in nominal terms in 1977–79 and fell even more relative to their American counterparts (figure 1.5). Apparently, expectations of sustained yen appreciation were now in place. Since 1978, Japanese long-term interest rates have averaged 3 to 4 percentage points less than American rates.

As befits a more or less permanent regime change, these expectations of yen appreciation *in the long term* remained remarkably robust despite the ebb and flow of spot movements in the yen-dollar exchange rate in the short and intermediate terms. These expectations of long-term yen appreciation were not upset by the Reagan period of the strong dollar from late 1980 through early 1985, when there was net appreciation of

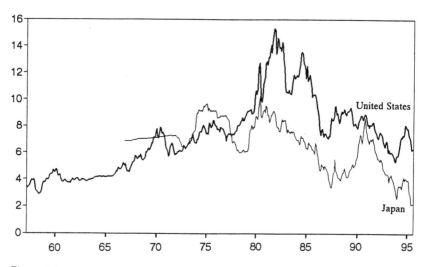

Figure 1.5
Long-term government bond rate, percent. *Source:* IMF, *International Financial Statistics*, CD-ROM, December 1995. *Note:* After World War II, the issuance of Japanese long-term government bonds only began in October 1966.

the dollar against the yen (figure 1.1) and even more against other hard currencies. Although the strong dollar took the markets by surprise, its apparent overvaluation by the purchasing power parity criterion seemed to reinforce the expectation that it would eventually fall against the yen and, at the same time, against other strong currencies like the mark. Indeed, Jeffrey Frankel (1995) attributes part of the very high interest differential favoring the United States from 1981 through 1985 to the markets' perceiving that the dollar had overshot in the foreign exchanges and must come back down.

Similarly, when the dollar rose strongly against the yen from April 1995 through 1996, American nominal interest rates remained 3 to 5 percentage points higher than their Japanese counterparts at various terms to maturity—a puzzle that is discussed in chapter 11. In effect, when the dollar was strong, regressive expectations apparently reinforced the syndrome.

But this regressivity seems asymmetrical. If the dollar is undervalued, expected increases in the yen-dollar exchange rate are weak or absent. When the dollar fell below purchasing power parity against the yen in 1985–87 and in 1993–95 (chapter 9), American long-term interest rates still remained well above Japanese (figure 1.5). If regressive expectations did exist when the yen was unusually high against the dollar, their revealed impact on the long-term interest differential was minimal. In principle, changes in shorter-term interest-rate differentials should reflect these regressive exchange-rate expectations rather better. Their terms to maturity could be selected to better match the time horizons of cycles in exchange rates. In practice, however, short-term interest rates are unclear predictors of future exchange-rate movements (Frankel 1995), if only because of the way they are manipulated by national monetary authorities.

Thus, we hypothesize that expectations in the financial markets associated with the syndrome of the ever-higher yen were firmly in place by 1978, and continued afterward. Expectations in other markets in the Japanese economy were similarly affected by the prospect of relative deflation. Chapter 4 shows that firms and workers anticipated falling prices and, accordingly, adjusted money-wage claims downward relative to their American counterparts—perhaps even substantially below some natural level of productivity growth in Japanese manufacturing.

But to sustain the belief for more than twenty years that the yen was likely to go ever higher, the markets had to believe that the BoJ was also caught up in the syndrome. As American mercantile pressure pushed the yen up in episodic trade disputes, the BoJ would tolerate the relative deflation necessary to sustain an ever-higher yen. Although often unhappy with the deflation, the BoJ—and the Japanese government more generally—accommodated a higher yen in order to placate the Americans and reduce the threat of a costly trade war. Whence the importance of chapter 9 where we present a series of statistical tests showing that changes in the yen-dollar exchange rate preceded changes in the Japanese price level, and these exchange-rate changes not only anticipated Japanese long-run monetary policy but actually caused it.

Does the syndrome matter for macroeconomic stability in both countries? The interested reader will find out only by reading the remaining chapters of this book! However, in the late 1970s and early 1980s era of high expected inflation and high nominal interest rates in the United States, having relative deflation imposed on Japan was an advantage. Indeed, because of its apparently better performance in controlling inflation during that era, the fact that the BoJ was running a dependent monetary policy was not even recognized as such. Only from the mid-1980s into the mid-1990s, when the American price level became more stable but the yen continued to rise, did the fact that the BoJ was being forced into unwanted deflation, with severe attendant problems of macroeconomic management, become clearly evident. Indeed, the Japanese term *endaka fukyo*, meaning "high-yen-induced recession," may find its way into the English language.

1.4   Overcoming the Syndrome

Later chapters bear more directly on the problem of overcoming the syndrome and on the implications of greater exchange-rate stability for the behavior of interest rates. Indeed, chapter 8 discusses how interest-rate volatility has varied historically across exchange-rate regimes.

Chapter 10 focuses on the need for a U.S.–Japan commercial compact to complement a monetary accord. It lays out eight rules of the game for ongoing monetary cooperation that could generate virtual exchange stability so that people come to expect that the yen-dollar rate will remain close to some mutually agreed-on parity in the longer run. Yet, such a new monetary regime would retain enough exchange flexibility to allow the two countries to differentiate their monetary policies in the short and medium terms. But none of this is possible without a commercial compact or understanding that effectively insulates the yen-dollar rate from trade disputes.

Chapter 11 deals with the potentially volatile transition path of escaping from the syndrome into this new, idealized monetary regime with stationary exchange-rate expectations. Because the yen fell from mid-1995 through early 1997, the BoJ could effectively re-expand the Japanese economy to recover somewhat from the *endaka fukyo* of 1992–95. Whether the syndrome is permanently in remission or a resumption has occurred won't be known until after the book is published.

2

Policy Causes and Postwar
Origins of Japan–U.S.
Economic Conflict:
Differential Productivity
Growth and the Saving
Shortage in the United
States

Mutual and accelerating irritation over economic issues in general, and over trade flows in particular, has characterized the bilateral relationship between Japan and the United States, as discussed in chapter 1. Here we analyze some of these issues in greater depth in order to better understand American mercantile pressure on the yen-dollar exchange rate.

The friction stems partly from understandable psychological reactions as one economy grows in size relative to another. But, more fundamentally, it also comes from entrenched policies that each country has pursued for a number of decades. These policies are backed by equally entrenched ideas in the field of international economics. However useful those ideas and policies might have been in another place and time, the set of policies currently implemented by Japan and by the United States are incompatible with the welfare of both countries.

As for Japan, the institutional mechanism—and the national consensus that supported it—for industrial catch-up, which worked so marvelously when Japan was a developing country, should finally be dismantled. That mechanism consisted of the promotion of manufacturing industries by heavy-handed intervention accompanied by the transfer of income from urban to rural populations to protect less efficient farmers and service-sector workers.[1] Whether government intervention was the primary, a supplementary, or an insignificant cause of Japan's economic success is still debated. But we can say at least that government intervention, despite its pervasiveness, did not seriously damage the growth potential of the private sector. This is a remarkable achievement, given the dismal record of official economic intervention around the globe. But as any economy matures, supporting policies must also change. The problem with Japan is that its economy grew so fast that the transformation of its policies—as well as its psychology—lagged far behind. It is generally thought that Japan's catch-up with Western industrial economies in manufacturing was more or less complete by the early 1970s. This implies that systemic transformation from the "catch-up model" is overdue by more than two decades.

The main task for the United States is to sustain the internal vigor of its own economy through forward-looking measures that will boost domestic income while increasing international competitiveness. Although weakened relative to its past status and to its competitors, the United States remains at the hub of the international economic system. Excessively inward orientation by the (weakened) center country contributes significantly to worldwide financial instability and sluggish output. In the macroeconomic sphere, the United States must restore the financial discipline it had years ago, for the sake of itself and all other countries. It should refrain from disproportionate reliance on dollar devaluation and bilateral trade negotiations for reducing trade deficits that are symptomatic of low private saving and a large budget deficit. Economic revitalization would require replacing interest-group politics with the true spirit of the competitive market mechanism. The government can encourage this by offering consistent and farsighted leadership.

2.1 Two Economies at a Crossroads

The relative strengths of the Japanese and U.S. economies have been shifting. One may argue about the speed and extent of the shift, but its general direction is beyond doubt. Quantitative shifts are well known and easy to document. For example, the Japanese economy was 6 percent of the size of the U.S. economy in 1955; the corresponding figure in 1994 was 68 percent. In a sense, Japan's relative growth is unsurprising because the country began its postwar recovery from an extremely low base. But the hallmark of economic dynamism is not mere size, but ability to adapt to and even initiate changes rather than resisting changes imposed by other countries and by external circumstances. By this criterion, Japan was truly a dynamic economy in the 1950s and 1960s, although episodes of *endaka fukyo* have sapped its dynamism in more recent years.

In terms of productivity growth, Japanese manufacturing industries outperformed their U.S. counterparts during the postwar era, often by wide margins. This fact has been confirmed by various studies using different methods of productivity comparison (Jorgenson and Nishimizu 1978; Marston 1987; Jorgenson 1988; Boskin and Lau 1990; Jorgenson and Kuroda 1991; Kuroda 1992). Figures 2.1a and 2.1b show the average annual change in productivity of fourteen industries in Japan and the

United States during 1954–73 and 1974–90, based on the authors' calculations (see the appendix to this chapter for technical information). The concept of productivity adopted here is total factor productivity (TFP) with labor and materials as inputs.[2]

Two features stand out in these figures. (Although measurement of productivity is subject to substantial errors, the following observations are well recognized by many previous studies.) First, for all industries and in both periods, Japanese productivity growth was higher than that of the United States. The remarkable bilateral difference in productivity performance—especially during 1954–73—is largely due to the fact that U.S. technology was already at the level of international best practice while the task of Japan was to catch up (World Bank 1993). Cutting a new technological path is inevitably a slower business than treading an already cleared terrain. Second, for all industries except nonferrous metals and iron and steel in the United States, productivity growth slowed down between the two periods: the average annual productivity growth for all manufacturing industries fell from 6.3 percent to 3.4 percent in Japan, and from 1.1 percent to a dismal −0.7 percent in the United States.[3] (U.S. productivity growth has recovered somewhat in the 1990s.)

As Kuznets (1971) observed, "The acceleration in the rate of growth in per capita product, characteristic of modern economic growth, was accompanied by an equally conspicuous acceleration in the rate of change in production structure" (p. 154). Uneven growth in productivity is the primary cause of such structural change. As high-performing firms and industries underbid and displace less successful rivals, they draw labor, capital, and other resources from the rest of the economy, and expand. This is precisely the process through which comparative advantage and trade patterns change in a dynamic economy.

The results of economic dynamism are apparent in the shifting industrial structure. Figures 2.2a and 2.2b illustrate the real composition of Japanese and U.S. output, respectively, during the postwar period.[4] In Japan, the rapidly expanding manufacturing base and the equally rapidly shrinking agricultural sector, particularly in the early years, are remarkable. By contrast, U.S. manufacturing did not significantly change its share throughout the period. In the United States, visible structural shifts occurred outside manufacturing, with gradual expansion of distributive trade and other services at the expense of primary industries, mining, and construction.

Moreover, considerable transformation was also taking place within the Japanese manufacturing sector. Figure 2.3a, in a similar format, reveals an

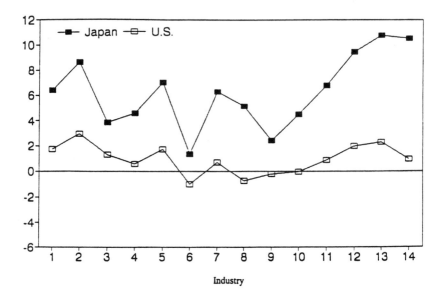

Industry index:

1	Food	8	Iron and steel
2	Textiles	9	Nonferrous metals
3	Wood products	10	Metal products
4	Paper and pulp	11	General machinery
5	Chemicals	12	Electrical machinery
6	Oil and gas	13	Transport machinery
7	Ceramics etc.	14	Precision machinery

Figure 2.1a
Productivity growth: 1954–73, percent per year.

enormous growth of machinery industries and an almost symmetrical decline of food and textile industries in postwar Japan. The performance of the electrical machinery industry, which started from a base of nearly zero, is most impressive. The share of the intermediate materials industry rose initially but has fallen since the mid-1970s. In contrast, structural shifts in U.S. manufacturing industries have been much less dramatic (figure 2.3b).

Are fast productivity changes and structural changes related? More specifically, do industries with relatively high productivity growth tend to grow quantitatively, too? This is intuitively plausible, and can be

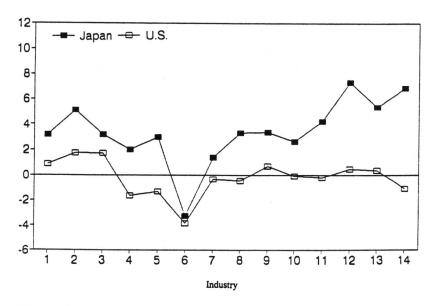

Industry index:

1	Food	8	Iron and steel
2	Textiles	9	Nonferrous metals
3	Wood products	10	Metal products
4	Paper and pulp	11	General machinery
5	Chemicals	12	Electrical machinery
6	Oil and gas	13	Transport machinery
7	Ceramics etc.	14	Precision machinery

Figure 2.1b
Productivity growth: 1974–90, percent per year.

demonstrated statistically as well. In table 2.1, growth rates of real output or real export for fourteen manufacturing industries are regressed on the *difference* in productivity growth rates between Japan and the United States, for each industry.

During Japan's high-growth era (1954–70), which largely coincided with the period of fixed exchange rates, Japanese industries that performed well in productivity (relative to the United States) also tended to be high performers in output and export. However, this result is not universal. In the later period of Japanese low growth (1974–90), and with floating exchange rates, a statistically significant linkage between productivity and industrial expansion (although estimated coefficients on the

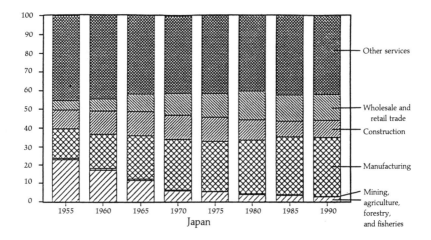

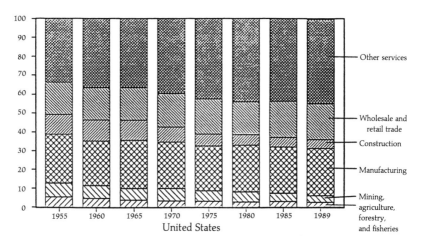

Figure 2.2
(a) Output structure: Japan, evaluated at 1985 prices; (b) Output structure: U.S., evaluated at 1982 prices. *Note:* Excludes government and public-sector enterprises. *Sources:* Economic Planning Agency, *Annual Report on National Accounts,* various issues, and Council of Economic Advisors, *Economic Report of the President,* February 1991.

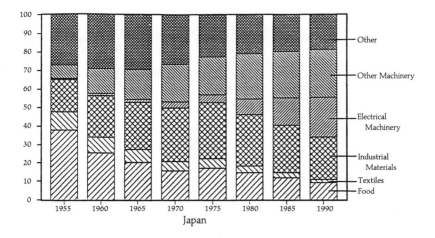

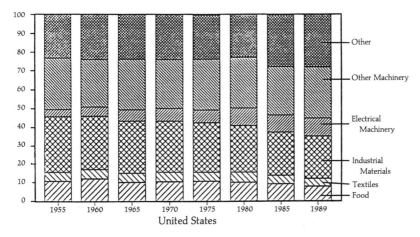

Figure 2.3
Manufacturing output (*a*) Japan, evaluated at 1985 prices; (*b*) United States, evaluated at 1982 prices. *Source:* Economic Planning Agency, *Annual Report on National Accounts*, various issues.

productivity gap remain positive) no longer exists. Also, the base growth that would have been attained *even without a bilateral productivity gap* as measured by the constant term, was significantly positive—11.5 percent for output and 9.0 percent for exports—in the first period, but negative and insignificant in the second period. This confirms the common view that the rapid and dynamic process of catch-up was complete by the early 1970s, when Japan became a mature industrial economy and most of its latecomer's advantages were exhausted.

For the United States, bilateral productivity gaps are unrelated to structural changes, for both indices and periods.[5] Presumably, this is because

Table 2.1
Productivity as a determinant of output and export growth

Dependent variable	Constant	Productivity gap[a]	R^2	SE
Japan				
Output 1954–70	0.115	0.787	0.341	0.034
	(0.014)*	(0.316)*		
Output 1974–90	−0.015	1.062	0.205	0.036
	(0.027)	(0.603)		
Exports 1954–70	0.090	1.915	0.492	0.060
	(0.025)*	(0.561)*		
Exports 1974–90	−0.035	1.214	0.122	0.057
	(0.042)	(0.942)		
United States				
Output 1954–70	—	—	—	—
Output 1973–90	0.002	0.178	0.031	0.017
	(0.013)	(0.287)		
Exports 1954–70	0.049	0.125	0.016	0.031
	(0.013)*	(0.284)		
Exports 1974–88	0.020	−0.102	0.003	0.031
	(0.023)	(0.518)		

Note: $N = 14$; standard errors in parentheses. The asterisk denotes significance at the 5 percent level.
a. The average annual productivity growth of the Japanese industry minus that of the corresponding U.S. industry.

the United States was more mature industrially throughout the postwar period. Like Japan's, however, underlying U.S. export growth (the constant term) slowed down between the two periods, from 4.9 percent to a statistically insignificant 2.0 percent.

2.2   Japan: Delayed Graduation from the Catch-up Model

With remarkable economic growth in the postwar period, Japanese per capita income joined the world's top rank by the early 1970s. Two decades after that achievement, however, the majority of Japanese people do not feel that their daily lives offer material comfort and satisfaction commensurate with the status of one of the richest peoples in the world.[6]

Although this dissatisfaction may be due in part to slow transformation of small-country mentality, not all of it can be attributed to psychological factors. Japanese industrialists and workers have been galvanized, until the recent past, for the pursuit of economic excellence and market dominance with export growth as a performance criterion. This catch-up strategy emphasized upgrading industrial infrastructure and technology at the cost of social amenities such as housing, public parks, comfort in commuting, sewage networks, and urban and rural landscapes.

Similar dualism is present in many facets of the Japanese economy. At the industry level, the Japanese economy includes permanent laggards under government protection side by side with superachievers in the modern manufacturing sector. Inefficient farming coexists with first-class electronic gadgets. In some industries, bureaucratic meddling has bred the kind of overregulation and absurdity often associated with much less developed countries.

To explain this puzzling duality, a historical overview is useful. When a country faces an enormous task of reconstruction from the ashes of military defeat, or from a similar social upheaval, with very limited resources and a hungry population, the selection of industrial growth as the primary national target is indeed reasonable. In a crisis situation, clean air, beautiful scenery, and comfortable public transportation are of secondary importance to many people. Jobs and minimum food and shelter are their immediate concern. When the entire production and distribution systems are paralyzed, the government is expected to play a crucial role in physically rebuilding the country. This generally requires strong leadership, competent bureaucracy, a mechanism to help the poorest among the poor, and popular mobilization for a common cause.

Such a system for staging a nationalistic industrialization drive is called developmental authoritarianism, the developmental state, or simply developmentalism (*kaihatsushugi*). Murakami's (1992) definition of developmentalism, as an alternative to classical economic liberalism, is as follows:

Developmentalism refers to an economic system based on the principles of private property and market economy (i.e., capitalism) with the objective of industrialization (i.e., a continuous increase of per capita output), where the government is permitted, for this purpose, to intervene in the market from a long-term viewpoint. Clearly, a state or a similar political entity acts as the implementing body of developmentalism as a politico-economic system. In many such cases, certain restrictions on parliamentary democracy are imposed—for example, in the form of royalism, party dictatorship, or military dictatorship. (Vol. 2, pp. 5–6)

Together with high-performing East Asian economies today, Japan in the 1950s and 1960s offered a prime example of successfully implemented developmentalism.

According to Murakami, the key instrument of developmentalism is *industrial policy*, which attempts to maintain sufficient market competition in certain industries that exhibit increasing returns to scale.[7] Industrial policy is clearly different from socialist planning. The former preserves, rather than replaces, market competition and private-sector initiative. Ingredients of industrial policy include industry targeting, indicative planning, promotion of technical change, price cartels, protectionism, and subsidies—all of which were present in the postwar policies of Japan's Ministry of International Trade and Industry (Johnson 1982; Komiya, Okuno, and Suzumura 1988; Okimoto 1989).

In addition, developmentalism must be supplemented by income redistribution policy, education, and fair and competent bureaucracy. Redistribution is particularly important to offset an emerging gap between the rich and the poor during the economic takeoff—known as the Kuznets inverted U-curve phenomenon. As Murakami (1992) puts it,

Development of industries targeted by industrial policy will widen the gap between them and untargeted industries, leading to economy-wide problems—frequent bankruptcies and unemployment in the latter industries and eventually social unrest. These problems will likely be worse under industrial policy than without it. Hence another policy—conventionally called distribution policy—will be needed to alleviate the disparity. For this reason, industrial policy requires distribution policy.... Without distributive measures, industrial policy will probably fail. Together, these two policies form one complete set. (Vol. 2, p. 99)

In postwar Japan, many of the disadvantaged industries were in the nonmanufacturing sector. During 1955–93, within a democratic framework, a mild form of political monopoly by the Liberal Democratic Party (LDP) was in place. The most notable shape that its distribution policy took was agricultural support measures coupled with "supportive rural participation" (Kabashima 1993):

"Supportive rural participation"—the overwhelming backing of the LDP by the farmers of Japan—gave the LDP a crucial popular base that enabled it to acquire and maintain power. In return, the farmers have benefitted from various kinds of patronage, and in any case they are thoroughly imbued with a deferential political culture. Hence, while participating actively in politics to the extent of voting, they passively accepted the authoritative decision making by the elite in matters of national policy. This broad-based, supportive rural participation does not fit the citizen-based "town meeting" ideal of democracy. But it helped preserve the democratic system in the period shortly after World War II. It softened the divisiveness and tension among social groups and moderated demands for radical change that accompanied rapid economic development. (P. 248)

Furthermore, quite apart from LDP politics, the uniqueness of Japan's highly homogeneous population, undivided by ethnicity or class, and the positive role it has played in realizing shared growth, can hardly be over-stated. In particular, high labor mobility helped narrow the wage gaps between rural and urban workers as well as across different industries.

Now, more than two decades after the economy's graduation from the catch-up phase, various remnants of developmentalism are still in place in Japan, in part or whole, and only slowly are being replaced by new ideas, policies, and institutions. These remnants include the catch-up mentality itself, uniform value orientation, compulsive work ethic, strong bureaucracy, the heavy hand of the government, economic and political centralization, and overregulation of inefficient industries such as agriculture, construction, transportation, communication, finance, and distribution.

Japan's economic dualism can be illustrated by the configuration of various prices over time and across industries. Through technological progress, export-oriented manufacturing firms have been able to lower their prices while maintaining adequate profit margins. In contrast, protected and less innovative producers have had to raise their prices (relative to those of manufactured goods) in order to survive. Of course, those price increases were made possible by intentional suppression of competition through controlled entry and import restriction.

Internal price divergence is illustrated in figure 2.4, which shows the movement of the consumer price index (CPI) relative to the wholesale

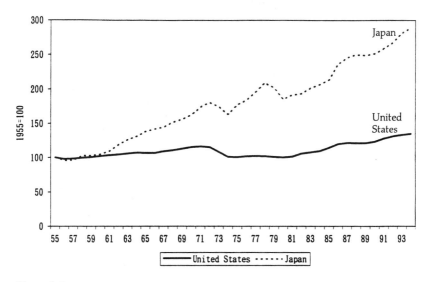

Figure 2.4
Internal price divergence, consumer prices/wholesale prices. *Source:* IMF, *International Financial Statistics*, CD-ROM, June 1995.

price index (WPI). CPI includes food, housing, utilities, clothing, health care, transportation, education, and other categories, which cover a wide spectrum of nontraded or protected industries in Japan. WPI, on the other hand, includes a broad basket of exportable industrial goods. The ratio of CPI to WPI is therefore a rough indicator of how prices of protected items have moved relative to those of manufactured goods. Divergent prices, in turn, reflect the widening productivity gap between the two sectors. Japanese consumer goods have become significantly more expensive (relative to industrial goods) over the past forty years, in a rise punctuated by temporary disturbances due to oil shocks and the asset bubble. The United States CPI, by contrast, shows only a mild tendency to rise relative to WPI. In the United States, the structural duality so prominent in Japan has hardly existed.

International price comparison provides additional evidence on Japan's lopsided price structure. Figure 2.5 shows the hypothetical yen-dollar rate (called *purchasing power parity*, or PPP, and discussed extensively in chapter 9) that would equate the price of a particular bundle of goods or services in Japan with the average of its prices in the countries belonging to the Organization for Economic Cooperation and Development (OECD).

A high PPP rate indicates that the bundle is expensive in Japan compared with the rest of the industrial world. The comparison is based on 1990 prices. The actual yen-dollar rate in that year was 145. The con-

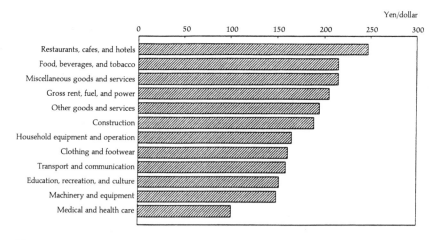

Figure 2.5
Purchasing power parity by expenditure: 1990, Japan against the rest of OECD. *Source:* OECD, *Purchasing Power Parities and Real Expenditures*, Paris 1992 (based on final expenditure on GDP and using the United National International Comparison Project categories).

cept of PPP is closely related to *naigai kakakusa* (international price differentials). For example, PPP for restaurants, cafes, and hotels was 247, implying that Japanese prices for these items were 70 percent higher (247/145 = 1.70) than the OECD average in 1990. (At the 1995 exchange rate of well below 100 when the yen was overvalued in terms of tradable goods (chapter 9), the price gap was far greater.) It is noteworthy that many of the residential and food-related items show high PPP rates— that is, they are expensive in Japan. Medical and health care is the only exception, because the Japanese medical care system reduces the direct financial cost to health care receivers.

Generally, as a country develops economically and attains a higher income, its general price level tends to rise relative to its past and to its neighbors. This phenomenon, called the Balassa-Samuelson effect, results from productivity in the tradable sector (typically manufacturing industries) improving more rapidly than in the nontradable sector during the industrialization process. If exchange rates are determined roughly to equalize tradable prices across countries, then nontradable goods and services in industrial countries will look more expensive than those in underdeveloped countries, as we discuss in chapter 4.

However, Japanese food and service prices are much higher than the Balassa-Samuelson effect would predict. Figure 2.6 shows the relationship between *real* per capita income (i.e., evaluated at PPP) and the general price level (GDP deflator) for twenty-five OECD countries. The data were obtained from OECD *Main Economic Indicators*. As a high-income country, Japan naturally has high prices, but they are in fact much higher than income differences alone would suggest. This is indicated by Japan's position as the largest outlier (49.6 percent) in the upward direction relative to the regression line in figure 2.6. In contrast, the United States lies 29.7 percent below the predicted line, which is another piece of evidence that Japanese domestic industries are overly protected.

Since the late 1980s, we have seen politicization of the problem of international price differentials. Partly, this is the result of *gaiatsu* (foreign pressure) from the United States. But more importantly, as is apparent from the recent political change, the time was also ripe in Japan for reforming the dualistic economic structure that brought recovery and then prosperity to postwar Japan. The old system has become unsustainable for more than one reason.

First, the lower growth rate of the manufacturing sector in recent decades limits the feasibility of continued transfer of income from that sector to the less efficient sectors. Second, Japan in the 1990s, as an advanced

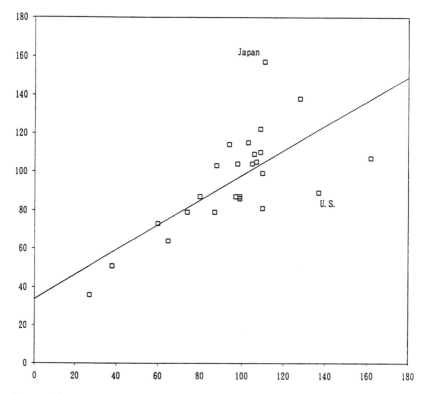

Figure 2.6
Per capita income and price levels: 1994, evaluated at PPP; OECD average = 100. *Source:*
OECD, *Main Economic Indicators*, September 1995.

country, is no longer permitted to pursue developmental policies; rather,
it is expected to contribute significantly to free trade and to the openness
of the world economy. Third, the postwar income transfer was so successful that rural residents in many ways now enjoy higher living standards than their urban compatriots, making further transfer politically
unpalatable.

Japan's historical task is to transform itself into a truly developed country by belatedly replacing the decades-old catch-up model, featuring
heavy doses of protection and regulation, with an open system based
on free markets and free trade. This does not necessarily mean that the
Japanese economy will converge toward the American prototype. Instead,
Japan will probably find a way to become freer and more open without
jettisoning the uniqueness of its society. Indeed, in the 1990s, liberali-

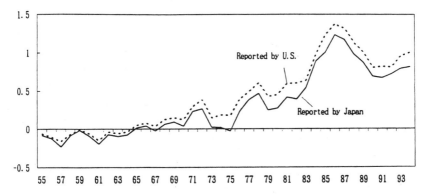

Figure 2.7
Japan–U.S. trade balance in percent of U.S. GDP.

zation in the previously protected sectors has proceeded so that Japan's CPI is no longer rising, and may even be falling relative to its WPI (see chapter 11).

2.3 The United States: Restoring Financial Responsibility

A stable international monetary system is not merely an economic issue; it is also a question of global political leadership. The center country must make a strong commitment to financial stability—including fiscal discipline, price stability, a sound banking system, open financial markets, and promotion of free trade. Countries in the periphery are then willing to give up a large part of their monetary autonomy and peg themselves to the center in order to import economic stability. No international monetary system can remain stable if the center country becomes economically weak, considers its financial responsibilities too onerous, and fails to provide an anchor that others want to emulate.

To evaluate the economic policies of the United States as the center country, we propose to divide the entire postwar period into two: first, the period in which the United States admirably fulfilled its responsibilities as the global financial anchor; and second, the period in which U.S. dominance gradually eroded and its policies became destabilizing to the rest of the world. Although the watershed year cannot be pinpointed, figure 2.7 and figures 1.1 and 1.4 (chapter 1) vividly suggest that the metamorphosis of the United States from a dependable leader to a less impressive large country took place sometime in the late 1960s or early '70s.

How did changing U.S. policies adversely affect the rest of the world in general and Japan in particular? First, the remarkable stability in American wholesale prices during the fixed-rate dollar standard of the 1950s and 1960s, when the U.S. Federal Reserve System alone among central banks had the power to conduct a stable monetary policy, was lost (figure 1.4). Why this should be so was partly doctrinal, the ascendency of Keynesian theory that made it more difficult for politicians to resist expansionist pressures on aggregate demand. But equally important was the failure of American economists to articulate properly the monetary rules of the game for sustaining the highly successful fixed-rate dollar standard: price stability in the United States was the anchor for prices in other countries. In the companion volume (McKinnon 1996), the monetary order for the fixed-rate dollar standard is laid out, along within an analysis of why the world business cycle of the 1970s through 1984 was so virulent: two major cycles of inflation followed by painful disinflations. (In chapter 10 of this volume, we return to the issue of what rules of the game are appropriate for sustaining monetary and exchange stability between the United States and Japan into the twenty-first century.)

Second, and related to the upward creep in the American price level after 1968, protectionist sentiment in the United States surged—as described in chapter 1—from losses of markets to economies like Japan's that not only were growing faster but had more stable price levels. Concern with "unfair" mercantile pressure from foreigners led to the Nixon shock in August 1971 (figure 1.1), with his demand that the dollar be devalued against the currencies of other industrial countries; this was the beginning of the syndrome of the ever-higher yen. More generally, these unilateral (or bilateral) U.S. initiatives to protect American markets at home and abroad (as described in chapter 1) detracted from traditional support by the center country for negotiating trade pacts multilaterally, the hallmark of the old GATT.

Third, the United States changed from being the largest creditor country in the world economy (it ran substantial current-account, though declining trade, surpluses throughout the 1950s and 1960s) to one with growing trade deficits. One can look at this declining trade position bilaterally with Japan or multilaterally with all trading partners.

Excluding services, the bilateral U.S.–Japan trade balance is plotted in figure 2.7 as a percentage of U.S. gross domestic product (GDP). A positive number indicates Japan's recorded surplus with the United States or, equivalently, the U.S. trade deficit with Japan. Although statistical discrepancies prevent these two statistics from matching exactly,[8] they are highly correlated, and their relationship is stable over time. Until the mid-1960s, the bilateral balance favored the United States, and Japan was concerned with (potential) trade deficits. From the early 1970s to the present, however, the United States has recorded large bilateral deficits.

The picture is no better if we look at American current-account deficits on a multilateral basis (figure 1.3). Although not quite as big relatively as in the mid-1980s, in 1996 America's current-account deficit was still more than 2 percent of GDP—a remarkable change from its net creditor status in the 1950s and 1960s. Since 1970, this has been the point of departure for American Treasury secretaries and many academic economists for trying to "talk-up" foreign currencies—especially the yen—against the dollar in order to reduce this trade deficit, and thus has been an important contributor to the syndrome of the ever-higher yen (chapter 1).

2.4   The American Saving Shortage

Rather than an exchange-rate or mercantile problem, as the prevailing views would have it, the persistent bilateral trade imbalance reflects, primarily, the increasing American tendency to overspend and the contrasting Japanese proclivity to underspend their respective incomes. To understand this historical perspective, we must examine the evolution of the saving-investment (SI) and current-account balances in the two countries.

Some Statistical Issues

We start with the familiar accounting identity for any one country:

$$S - I = CA = -FS, \qquad\qquad (2.1)$$

where S is total (i.e., private plus public) gross national saving, I is gross national investment, and CA is the current-account balance.[9] Ignoring any statistical discrepancy, $-CA$ reflects the extent to which the economy is relying on foreign saving, as denoted by FS. Column 5 in table 2.2 shows that American reliance on foreign saving averaged 2.7 percent of GDP in the late 1980s and that, after a sharp fall in 1991, it is again increasing in the mid-1990s.

In principle, gross national saving and investment can be broken down into their private and government components:

Table 2.2
U.S. savings and investment (as percentage of GDP)

	(1) Net personal saving	(2) PLUS: Corporate saving	(3) PLUS: Government saving	(4) EQUALS: Net national saving	(5) PLUS: Foreign saving	(6) PLUS: Statistical discrepancy	(7) EQUALS: Net domestic investment	(8) PLUS: Depreciation	(9) EQUALS: Gross domestic investment[a]	(10) Of which: Plant & equipment
1960–64	4.4	3.4	−0.1	7.8	−0.8	−0.3	6.6	8.6	15.2	9.3
1965–69	4.9	3.6	−0.2	8.3	−0.4	0.0	7.9	8.2	16.1	10.5
1970–74	5.9	2.3	−0.5	7.7	−0.3	0.1	7.5	9.0	16.5	10.7
1975–79	5.0	2.8	−1.1	6.8	−0.1	0.5	7.1	10.4	17.6	11.6
1980–84	5.8	1.4	−2.6	4.6	0.7	0.1	5.3	11.9	17.2	12.6
1985–89	3.6	1.9	−2.4	3.0	2.7	−0.3	5.5	11.1	16.5	11.3
1990	3.2	1.4	−2.5	2.1	1.4	0.1	3.6	10.9	14.5	10.5
1991	3.5	1.3	−3.4	1.4	−0.2	0.4	1.7	11.0	12.7	9.5
1992	3.6	1.8	−4.7	0.7	0.8	0.6	2.1	11.0	13.1	9.2
1993	3.0	1.9	−3.5	1.4	1.5	0.2	3.1	10.9	14.0	9.8
1994	3.0	2.0	−2.0	3.0	2.1	−0.5	4.7	10.6	15.3	10.4

Source: Bureau of Economic Analysis, U.S. Department of Commerce.
Note: Due to rounding, numbers may not add up exactly.
a. Gross domestic investment includes investment in residential structures, changes in inventories, and plant and equipment investment.

$$S = S_P + S_G$$
$$\tag{2.2}$$
$$I = I_P + I_G$$

For Japan, the components of these equations are shown in figures 2.8a and 2.8b. In Japan's national income accounts, the general government's[10] investment is separated from its consumption so that the government's SI balance—the difference between saving and investment—can be tabulated directly as $S_G - I_G$. The government's saving, S_G, is the difference between T (government tax revenue less transfers) and C_G (government consumption). The government's SI balance is then plotted as the difference between government saving and investment: $(T - C_G) - I_G$. Since total government spending G is simply $C_G + I_G$, the SI balance of the government, as illustrated in figure 2.8b, is equivalent to its cash surplus:

$$T - G = S_G - I_G \tag{2.3}$$

Government spending for investment in Japan has been quite high, at 6 to 7 percent of GDP. Perhaps because it remained high, figure 2.8b also shows that the Japanese government often ran with significant cash deficits. Varying between 1 and 10 percent of GDP, Japanese government saving was much more volatile than investment. But overall government saving in Japan has been positive—partly because structural saving is higher, but also because government deficits have not been as great in cyclical downturns as in the United States. This positive government saving in combination with the very high private gross saving rate (now about 26 percent of GDP, as shown in figure 2.8a), results in national saving of about 33 percent of Japanese GDP. Why Japanese saving rates remain so high, relative to those of other industrial countries in general and of the United States in particular, is not well explained by the standard theoretical models of saving behavior—such as the life-cycle model —used by economists.

The American government's contribution to national saving and investment is more obscure because (1) the U.S. national income accounts do not distinguish capital-account from current-account government expenditures; and (2) the United States is a federal system with fiscally independent state governments that effectively own the local governments —counties, municipalities, and so on. The great bulk of the U.S. federal government's expenditures is for current purposes, whereas the states and localities make relatively more capital expenditures for public works. In the absence of any good measure of overall government investment, American national income accounts are often presented as if all government

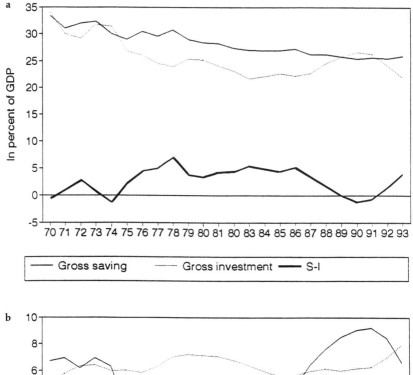

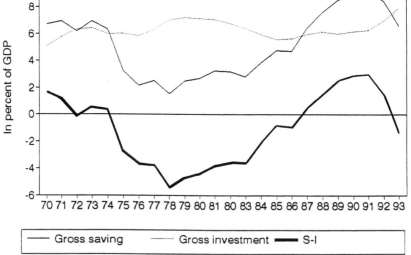

Figure 2.8
Saving and investment (*a*) Japanese private sector; (*b*) Japanese general government. *Source:*
Economic Planning Agency.

spending is for current consumption. Although that simplification fits the federal government better than it does the state or local governments, overall investment as a share of GDP tends to be understated in the U.S. national income accounts.[11] Thus, official U.S. data exist on gross private saving and investment (figure 2.9a) and on government cash surpluses (federal and local governments' $T - G$ in figure 2.9b), but not on government investment or saving. In effect, the levels of the variables on the left-hand side of equation 2.3 are known, but we do not have separate estimates for those on the right-hand side—although outside international agencies such as the OECD make rough guesses, as we shall see.

The United States as an Unusually Low Saver

Although cross-country comparisons of saving and investment are treacherous, among the industrial countries the United States seems to be an unusually low saver on both the government and private sides. In contrast to the states and localities, which have had mildly positive saving in the 1980s and 1990s, the federal government has had negative net saving of about 3 percent of GDP if we take $T - G$ as our measure of government saving (figure 2.9b)—albeit with some degree of downward bias. This government dissaving has a large endogenous component from the deficit spikes in business-cycle downturns in 1975, 1982–83, and 1991–92. But figure 2.9b also shows a clear structural deterioration beginning in the early 1980s when tax cuts accompanied the Reagan defense buildup.

On the private side, U.S. household (or personal) saving seems to be exceptionally low and perhaps falling relative to other major countries. Based on OECD data—using somewhat different definitions than the U.S. Department of Commerce in order to facilitate international comparison —the U.S. household saving rate of 4.2 percent in 1994 was by far the lowest of the G7 countries. The Japanese household saving rate of 14.9 percent was much higher but not unique among the G7 countries—Italy (15.0 percent) and France (13.5 percent) had similarly high rates. Why U.S. personal saving should be so low is not well understood. The most promising, though unproven, explanation is the advent of social security programs—retirement pensions, medicare, and the like—that make people feel more secure even if they do not save. Because these programs are underfunded in the United States (i.e., the existing assets of the social security system are not built up sufficiently to cover future liabilities), apparent government saving does not increase to offset low personal saving, for which tax incentives are inadequate.

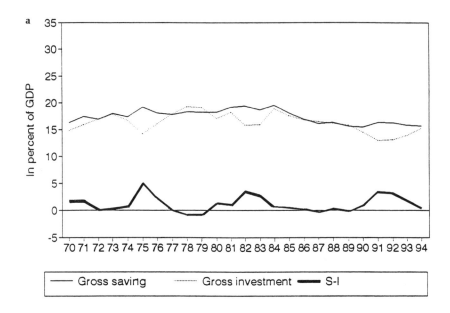

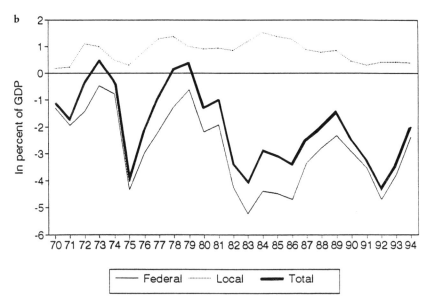

Figure 2.9
(*a*) Saving and investment, U.S. private sector; (*b*) Fiscal surpluses, U.S. government sector.
Source: U.S. Department of Commerce.

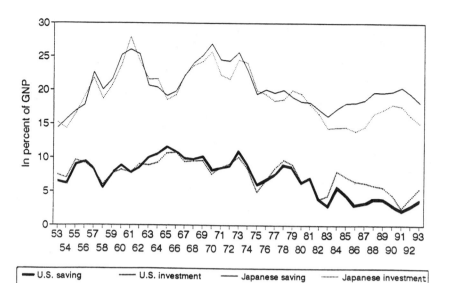

Figure 2.10
Net savings-investment balance in percent of GNP. *Sources:* OECD, *National Accounts: Main Aggregates,* vol. 1, 1960–91 and 1952–81. National data are used for 1992–93.

Because U.S. gross national saving is dominated by private saving in the business sector, and most of that saving is in the form of depreciation allowances (table 2.2), *net* national saving—excluding mere replacement of existing capital stock—is low. In Japan, with its much higher gross national saving rate, household saving is about as important as that in the business sector, so that net saving is proportionately much higher. Using OECD data that include some (probably inadequate) allowance for government investment and saving in the United States, figure 2.10 dramatically illustrates how much lower *net* saving and investment have been in the United States compared to Japan since 1953. In 1993, at 18.3 percent of GNP, Japanese net national saving was almost five times as high as that in the United States (3.8 percent).[12] Starting in the early 1980s, figure 2.10 also shows that Japanese saving has exceeded its investment and that U.S. saving has been less than its investment—with much of Japanese excess saving mobilized to finance American excess investment.

The lesson seems clear enough. The relative saving gap between the United States and Japan has been due mainly to the dissaving of the U.S. federal government on the one hand, and the very low personal saving of the American household sector on the other. (Although by 1996, the U.S. federal government's deficit had been sharply reduced toward just 1 percent of GDP, personal saving continued to drift downward so that the American current-account deficit remained large—more than 2 percent of GDP.) As a result of asymmetrical saving and investment patterns, particularly since the 1980s, the United States is now the world's largest borrower and debtor, while Japan has grown to be the largest lender as well as creditor.[13] In the short run, the United States has become surprisingly vulnerable to any sudden interruption in the availability of foreign capital, as we show more clearly in chapter 5, which discusses the credit crunch of 1991. To maintain U.S. gross investment at normal levels in the longer run, heavy reliance on foreign capital over the past decade and a half has been necessary—but even then, some slippage in the investment share of GDP has occurred.

It does not seem too far-fetched to add that American ambivalence and hostility toward Japan in recent years is, at least in part, that of a debtor toward its creditor. During the nineteenth century, a segment of popular opinion in the United States was hostile to Britain, the major international lender of that age.

The Current-Account Balance: Multilateral versus Bilateral

It is a country's multilateral (alternatively called *overall* or *global*) current-account balance—that is, the current-account balance against the rest of the world, not just against Japan or any other particular country—that reflects that country's domestic saving surplus or shortage. As figure 1.3 (chapter 1) shows, the United States has had a large multilateral current-account deficit and Japan has had an equally large multilateral current-account surplus, at least through 1994.

Capital is fungible, which means that the U.S. financing gap could also be filled by the excess saving of any foreign country other than Japan. Japanese saving is no different from other countries' saving, and its currently dominant role in financing the U.S. saving gap is merely accidental. To reiterate, the U.S. multilateral current-account balance is fundamentally a reflection of its domestic saving–investment imbalance and not the result of unfair trade practices on the part of individual trading partners. As long as the U.S. saving-investment gap remains as wide as it is today, a significant decline in the Japanese multilateral current-account surplus would require the United States to draw on savings from other countries. (And this seems to be happening in 1996 as Japan's current-account surplus falls even as that of the United States increases.)

It is possible that the world economy may face such a situation if the fiscal deterioration in Japan proceeds as projected in the years to come. By

1995, industrial depression from the bursting of the asset bubble, the overvalued yen, and the foreign (mainly American) pressure to stimulate domestic demand had prompted the Japanese government to launch a vigorous fiscal expansion program. The fiscal deficit of general government (central and local governments combined) was already 7.7 percent of GDP in 1995; it was partially offset by the social security surplus of 3.5 percent of GDP (OECD 1995). The central government budget for fiscal year 1996, agreed upon by the Japanese cabinet in December 1995, envisages a deficit equivalent to 4.5 percent of GDP and includes the largest-ever planned issue of deficit-financing bonds, amounting to more than 12 trillion yen.

The last time Japan turned to a major deficit-financed fiscal package was 1975–78 at the time of the first oil-shock recession. Subsequently, it took the Ministry of Finance more than a decade to return the general government budget to surplus (figure 2.8). If the fiscal expansion drive initiated in 1995 is as serious as that of the 1970s, it will produce an equally large fiscal deterioration.

Aggressive fiscal expansion would certainly reduce Japan's overall excess saving available to the rest of the world, unless there were an automatic offsetting increase in its private-sector saving (i.e., if the Ricardian equivalence held; in the late 1970s, there was no such offset). In other words, Japan's current-account surplus is likely to shrink—and that should please trade negotiators on the both sides of the Pacific.

Whatever its short-run political merits, such a sharp increase in the fiscal deficit may turn out to be highly undesirable in the long run. For Japan, the aging population will greatly increase the government's welfare-related spending and strain its budget in the early twenty-first century. A significant increase in its structural fiscal balance now will only worsen the fiscal crisis that is certain to come. In addition, the world economy—and especially the United States—will lose the most important source of foreign saving, with the likely result that real interest rates will rise everywhere, and global investment will be impeded.

Appendix: Divergent Trends in Productivity in Japan and the United States

To illustrate the divergent trends in relative industrial prices due to ongoing technical change, a model based on a cost function defined over input prices is presented. The model also allows the possibility of profit-margin adjustments in response to exchange-rate fluctuations.[14]

Consider a Japanese industry, denoted i, producing a tradable commodity under constant returns to scale. Inputs are labor (nontradable) and materials (tradable). The unit cost function in terms of yen is specified as Cobb-Douglas with technical change:

$$\dot{c}_i = \alpha_i \dot{w} + (1 - \alpha_i)\dot{q} - \phi_i, \tag{2.4}$$

where w is wage and q is materials price. α_i is the share of labor in total cost and also measures the tradability of input,[15] and ϕ_i is the rate of technical change. The cost function is defined in terms of rate of change, which the dot signifies.[16] Similarly, the cost function for the U.S. industry in terms of dollars is

$$\dot{c}_i^* = \alpha_i^* \dot{w}^* + (1 - \alpha_i^*)\dot{q}^* - \phi_i^* \tag{2.5}$$

Note that the cost of capital is not explicitly incorporated into this model; this may be considered its weakness. On the other hand, the formulation allows direct expression of bilateral international competitiveness.

Next, the output price is determined by a markup over unit cost. The markup is not constant but may vary as the exchange rate fluctuates. For example, when the yen is overvalued against the dollar (i.e., when Japanese unit cost is higher than U.S. unit cost) Japanese manufacturers may squeeze profit margins to stay competitive in overseas markets. The markup equation is generally accepted as an appropriate specification for estimating exchange-rate pass-through and pricing-to-market behavior (Mann 1986; Krugman 1987; Ohno 1989b; Marston 1991). Thus the output equation is given by

$$\dot{p}_i = \theta_i \dot{s}_i + \dot{c}_i + \eta_i, \tag{2.6}$$

where η_i is an error term representing all factors other than the exchange rate affecting the firm's markup: business cycles, sectoral demand shifts, changing market structure, and so on. Because the formulation is in change form, markup drops off from equation 2.6 if it is constant. s_i is the real exchange rate, defined as the relative bilateral cost of production:

$$\dot{s}_i = (\dot{c}_i^* + \dot{e}) - \dot{c}_i, \tag{2.7}$$

where e is the nominal yen-dollar exchange rate. Thus, a rise in s_i signifies real depreciation for the home (Japanese) industry.

The parameter θ_i measures the pricing strategy of industry i. From equations 2.6 and 2.7, one obtains

$$\dot{p}_i = (1 - \theta_i)\dot{c}_i + \theta_i(\dot{c}_i^* + \dot{e}) + \eta_i. \tag{2.8}$$

The output price is a convex combination of domestic cost and foreign cost (measured in domestic currency), plus an error term. θ_i normally takes a value between 0 and 1, and indicates the extent to which profit margin responds to competitiveness as measured by the relative production cost. If $\theta_i = 0$, profit margin is insensitive to changes in foreign cost. If it is unity, domestic price will move proportionately with foreign cost regardless of domestic cost.

From equations 2.4 and 2.6, the output price equation can be rewritten:

$$\dot{p}_i = \theta_i \dot{s}_i + \alpha_i \dot{w} + (1 - \alpha_i)\dot{q} - \phi_i + \eta_i, \tag{2.9}$$

and similarly for the foreign country,

$$\dot{p}_i^* = \theta_i^* \dot{s}_i^* + \alpha_i^* \dot{w}^* + (1 - \alpha_i^*)\dot{q}^* - \phi_i^* + \eta_i^*. \tag{2.10}$$

Using two-digit-level Japanese and U.S. manufacturing data from 1954 to 1990, equations 2.9 and 2.10 are simultaneously estimated for each industry by the three-stage least squares (3SLS) method. The instruments used are once-lagged all-right-hand-side variables, plus population growth rates in Japan and the United States and the change in the oil price. In estimation, the cross-equation restriction that Japan and the United States have the same input composition (i.e., $\alpha_i = \alpha_i^*$) is imposed.[17] Table 2.3 reports the results.[18]

Parameter α_i, which measures the nontradable component of input, falls between 0 and 1 except for oil and gas. For oil and gas, the hypothesis that α is 0, and therefore cost is determined solely by materials price, cannot be rejected. The α_i coefficients for machinery industries (rows 11–14) are between 0.80 and 0.92, indicating that labor is a relatively important input. For all other industries that are more materials intensive, α_i ranges from 0.39 for paper to 0.80 for wood products—except nonferrous metals, for which estimated α_i is positive but insignificant.

The elasticity of markup with respect to competitiveness (θ_i) is insignificant or of the wrong sign, except for U.S. wood products. Overall, there is little markup adjustment to exchange-rate changes, and therefore price and cost do not diverge even in the short run. This is not necessarily inconsistent with the pricing-to-market behavior observed in many Japanese exports, because the weighted average of domestic and export prices is used in this estimation. Japanese manufacturers do not adjust *domestic* markups in response to over- or undervaluation, although they do adjust *export* markups.[19]

The most striking result is the presence of positive technical change (ϕ_j) in the large majority of Japanese industries and the general absence of

Table 2.3
Estimation of the output price equation

Industry	α	ϕ_J	ϕ_{US}	θ_J	θ_{US}		SE	DW
1	0.733*	0.0452*	0.0119*	−0.044	0.088	Japan:	0.047	1.38
Food and tobacco	(0.064)	(0.0084)	(0.0051)	(0.210)	(0.144)	U.S.:	0.027	1.65
2	0.759*	0.0678*	0.0230*	−0.580	0.050	Japan:	0.066	2.11
Textiles	(0.069)	(0.0116)	(0.0037)	(0.307)	(0.107)	U.S.:	0.020	2.22
3	0.803*	0.0352*	0.0147	−0.380	0.728*	Japan:	0.083	2.03
Wood products	(0.130)	(0.0155)	(0.0111)	(0.388)	(0.321)	U.S.:	0.065	2.10
4	0.388*	0.0315*	−0.0059	−0.438*	−0.424	Japan:	0.048	1.82
Paper	(0.088)	(0.0095)	(0.0081)	(0.200)	(0.212)	U.S.:	0.049	1.67
5	0.475*	0.0489*	0.0022	−0.298	0.002	Japan:	0.041	1.13
Chemicals	(0.075)	(0.0080)	(0.0108)	(0.174)	(0.011)	U.S.:	0.060	1.58
6	−0.100	−0.0110	−0.0244	−0.141	0.928	Japan:	0.075	2.14
Oil and gas	(0.148)	(0.0158)	(0.0178)	(0.349)	(0.490)	U.S.:	0.090	1.91
7	0.624*	0.0364*	0.0006	−0.050	−0.349	Japan:	0.045	1.46
Ceramics and stone	(0.083)	(0.0089)	(0.0067)	(0.203)	(0.186)	U.S.:	0.039	1.79
8	0.462*	0.0420*	−0.0065	−0.521	0.288	Japan:	0.070	1.27
Iron and steel	(0.119)	(0.0113)	(0.0083)	(0.318)	(0.236)	U.S.:	0.049	1.92
9	0.232	0.0291	−0.0022	−0.940*	0.320	Japan:	0.098	1.82
Nonferrous metals	(0.180)	(0.0193)	(0.0149)	(0.447)	(0.418)	U.S.:	0.084	2.14
10	0.538*	0.0350*	−0.0012	−0.418	−0.049	Japan:	0.056	1.11
Metal products	(0.099)	(0.0108)	(0.0073)	(0.249)	(0.204)	U.S.:	0.042	2.11
11	0.803*	0.0541*	0.0028	0.089	−0.248	Japan:	0.047	0.62
General machinery	(0.082)	(0.0092)	(0.0053)	(0.215)	(0.148)	U.S.:	0.028	1.70
12	0.843*	0.0830*	0.0120*	0.127	−0.187	Japan:	0.051	0.42
Electrical machinery	(0.086)	(0.0097)	(0.0054)	(0.221)	(0.146)	U.S.:	0.027	1.50
13	0.900*	0.0788*	0.0126*	0.162	−0.134	Japan:	0.047	0.44
Transport machinery	(0.073)	(0.0088)	(0.0041)	(0.197)	(0.109)	U.S.:	0.022	1.30
14	0.921*	0.0849*	−0.0016	0.069	−0.168	Japan:	0.042	0.57
Precision machinery	(0.064)	(0.0077)	(0.0040)	(0.189)	(0.113)	U.S.:	0.023	1.31
0	0.621*	0.0479*	0.0018*	−0.202	−0.308	Japan:	0.034	0.49
All manufacturing	(0.062)	(0.0067)	(0.0057)	(0.162)	(0.165)	U.S.:	0.033	1.85

Note: Standard errors in parentheses. Equations 2.9 and 2.10 are estimated by three-stage least squares for each industry. The sample period is 1954–90. A cross-equation restriction of $\alpha_J = \alpha_{US}$ is imposed. The asterisk shows significance at the 5 percent level. DW refers to the Durbin-Watson statistic.

technical change in the United States (ϕ_{US}). During the entire sample period of 1954–90, in Japan, all industries except oil and gas have annual technical change of 2.9 percent or higher. Technical change in electrical machinery is as high as 8.3 percent. In contrast, only four U.S. industries (food and tobacco, textiles, electrical machinery, and transport machinery) have statistically significant rates of technical change, and the highest among them is 2.3 percent for textiles.

Figures 2.1a and 2.1b report the value of ϕ_i for the two subperiods of 1954–73 and 1974–90. These estimates are obtained using the dummy variable technique.

Two observations are in order. First, both countries had a marked slowdown in the average rate of productivity growth. Japanese productivity growth in overall manufacturing declined substantially, from 6.3 percent during 1954–73 to 3.4 percent during 1974–90. In the United States, the average productivity growth fell from 1.1 percent to a dismal −0.7 percent. Although negative productivity growth does not necessarily mean technical regression (because of quality change and a shifting product mix), it cannot be denied that productivity growth in U.S. manufacturing was very low during the floating-rate period.[20]

Second, Japanese manufacturing industries have had not only high but *divergent* rates of productivity growth compared with the United States, especially for the high-growth period of 1954–73. During this earlier period, the standard deviation of productivity growth among fourteen industries was larger in Japan (2.77 percent) than in the United States (1.12 percent) by a factor of 2.5. During the floating-rate period, the standard deviation declined in Japan to 2.48 percent and rose in the United States to 1.40 percent, with the result that the ratio between them fell to 1.8.

3

Exchange-Rate
Fluctuations and Their
Consequences: Price
Diffusion and *Endaka*
Fukyo

A successful international monetary system must contain a mechanism to facilitate needed reallocation of resources without undue microeconomic distortion or macroeconomic instability. As chapter 2 demonstrated, the higher productivity growth in Japan in the postwar period, and the need to transfer saving to the United States in recent decades, presented—and still presents—a substantial adjustment problem.

Is the flexible exchange-rate system (albeit with the acknowledged shortcomings of instability and unpredictability) the only practical method of relative price adjustment among countries with open and diversified industrial bases? By and large, mainstream international economists, whether Keynesian or monetarist, answer affirmatively. In this and the following chapters we would like to present a dissenting view.

When evaluating relative price movements under alternative exchange-rate regimes, it is crucial to distinguish real economic signals from mere noise. Real, or warranted, signals arise from changes in technology, resources, and taste, and their aggregate movements tend to be gradual, although individual goods are subject to sudden supply and demand shocks. On the other hand, noise typically results from monetary and financial disturbances, which can be large and sudden even at the aggregate level. The predominance of real signals is conducive to the smooth operation of market economies, whereas a large amount of noise, that is, financial volatility, obscures real signals and undermines efficient resource allocation. Despite the initial high expectations of academic economists for floating exchange rates, the experience since 1971 has taught us that exchange flexibility does not necessarily improve—and in fact, often worsens—the working of the price mechanism, as demonstrated in the following section.

3.1   Typology of Exchange-Rate Instability

What kind of exchange-rate instability is harmful to the real economy? Before we discuss the various adverse effects of the unstable yen-dollar exchange rate, it is useful to distinguish three types of exchange-rate movement that would impact the real economy differently.

Volatility

The short-term volatility of floating exchange rates is highly visible and well documented. Under capital mobility, the exchange rate is essentially an asset price that equates the stock demand and stock supply of financial assets denominated in different currencies. Because the demand for these assets is essentially based on expectations, the exchange rate is highly sensitive to incoming news and to the shifting sentiments of the investing community. Nevertheless, as long as volatility remains a short-term, temporary phenomenon, a movement of the exchange rate away from the correct level for a day, a week, or even a month does not seriously impinge on international business and investment.[1] The ever-expanding menu of computerized financial derivatives (options, swaps, and others) would protect manufacturers and investors from such volatility.

Misalignment

However, if the daily movement of the exchange rate has a tendency to accumulate in one direction, medium-term misalignment will emerge. In such a situation the exchange rate is significantly overvalued or undervalued relative to the correct exchange rate for a few years or more. Such misalignment is extremely harmful to macroeconomic stability and microeconomic efficiency. It scrambles domestic price structure and causes imported inflation or deflation (as discussed later in this chapter). In Japan, the overvaluation of the yen has a visible impact on domestic production and spending (especially investment spending) in a situation popularly known as *endaka fukyo*, or high-yen-induced recession (discussed here and in chapter 5). *Endaka fukyo* and associated forced deflation in Japan in turn produce considerable instability in global capital flows. For many industrial countries, but especially for Japan, exchange misalignment has become a major external shock to the economy. However, if the Bank of Japan overreacts to *endaka fukyo* and expands domestic credit too much, the Japanese economy is further destabilized through resultant homemade inflation and asset bubbles (see chapter 5).

Long-Term Drift

Short-term volatility and medium-term misalignment of floating exchange rates are widely recognized, but another type of exchange instability between Japan and the United States is equally injurious to economic activity: the long-term drift of the nominal yen-dollar exchange rate. Temporary fluctuations aside, the yen tends to appreciate against the dollar over the long run (figure 1.1). This long-term trend has also been firmly incorporated into the expectation of the market participants. Even if the appreciation of the yen is temporarily interrupted or reversed, the investment community will continue to expect its appreciation in the long run because of the syndrome of the ever-higher yen (chapter 1).

Even though the real yen-dollar rate may remain constant in the long run (chapter 7), why should the *nominal* appreciation of the yen be damaging to the real economy? First, persistent yen appreciation imposes downward pressure on Japanese tradable prices relative to American. Chronic price deflation depresses industrial activity in Japan both directly and indirectly through what we call the virtual liquidity trap—the real interest rate cannot be lowered sufficiently because the nominal interest rate cannot fall below zero (chapter 5). Second, the falling tradables prices disturb the natural wage adjustment mechanism whereby countries with high labor productivity growth will have faster money wage increases than countries with lower labor productivity growth (chapters 4 and 9). Third, the unanchored exchange expectation imparts a considerable degree of uncertainty in other key variables (especially prices and interest rates) and increases the volatility of long-term interest rates relative to short-term interest rates, further discouraging long-term physical investment (chapter 8).

3.2 Correct Signals for Structural Change

In the static world of pure trade theory, prices of internationally tradable goods must be equal across countries or there can be no goods market equilibrium. In an actual, dynamic world economy, however, the law of one price for those goods that are—or can be—traded is rarely observed. Generally, international price gaps are neither temporary nor explainable solely by transportation costs and financial volatility. Price differentials exist even under a fixed exchange-rate system, and a floating exchange-rate system tends to further amplify price discrepancies. From the viewpoint of efficiency and growth, some of these price gaps are good and others are bad. Let us start with good ones.

Shifting competitiveness at the level of individual tradable firms and industries is the driving force of structural change. A firm enjoying rapid productivity growth will draw labor, capital, and other resources from the rest of the economy. It will also drive domestic and foreign rivals out of competition by continuous underpricing. Although the successful always appear predatory (Bhagwati 1991), this is precisely the process by which comparative advantages and trade patterns change over time. Industrial leaders are incessantly challenged by newcomers with lower prices or better products.[2]

The dynamism of the world economy cannot be captured adequately by static trade models such as those of Ricardo or Heckscher and Ohlin, and the new trade theory of monopolistic competition and increasing returns only begins to formalize the hitherto neglected Schumpeterian feature of international trade. The hallmark of dynamism that eludes attempts at modeling is change in the overall economic structure and the state of competition. Shifting industrial profitability and trade patterns are hard to predict and are partly the result of private competition and partly the result of government intervention (including monetary and exchange policies), deliberate or inadvertent.

Let us consider industrial economies with many tradable industries. Suppose these industries employ different proportions of two inputs—say labor and materials. Labor represents a single nontradable input whose market is assumed to be integrated nationally so that each economy has one prevailing wage (adjusted for skill levels). Materials are inputs with globally integrated markets. The two inputs represent the opposite ends of the tradability spectrum.[3]

The assumption of a uniform domestic wage is supported by data. Figure 3.1 shows how closely money wages of the six major Japanese manufacturing industries evolved over the past forty years. The sectoral wage structure changed very little. The *lowest* correlation coefficient of all possible pairs among thirteen industries that make up the manufacturing sector is found to be 0.996 for the wage level and 0.628 for its change. Similarly, principal component analysis shows that as much as 99.88 percent of total variance in money wages can be explained by a common (i.e., national rather than industry-specific) factor.[4] In view of this, the Hicksian

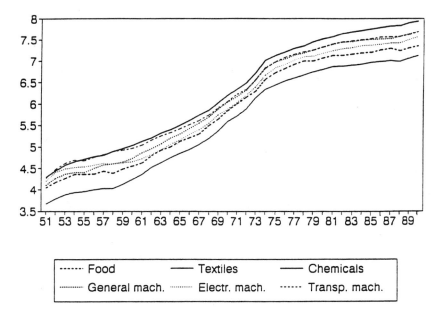

Figure 3.1
Sectoral hourly wages: Japan (semilog scale).

aggregation of wages across different manufacturing industries is fully justified.

Furthermore, the assumption of the globally integrated market for materials does not conflict with the data. Figure 3.2 shows changes in aggregated materials prices in Japan and in the United States expressed in a common currency (yen) for 1953–90. Despite the potential aggregation problem (the index contains a motley basket of energy, metals, and agricultural commodities), the two inflation rates moved in tandem with the correlation coefficient of 0.846. The only large discrepancies occurred in 1974 and 1980, when Japanese materials prices rose faster than those in the United States at the times of the oil shocks.

Even though wages are common in each country and materials prices are equalized internationally, output prices of various tradable industries will diverge over time (figure 3.3), leading to structural changes, as observed in chapter 2. The main reason for price divergence is the difference in production costs. These in turn depend on the input share and technical change (which are industry-specific) as well as national wage movements (which are country-specific). Short-term deviations could also occur through markup adjustments. However, adjustments in profit

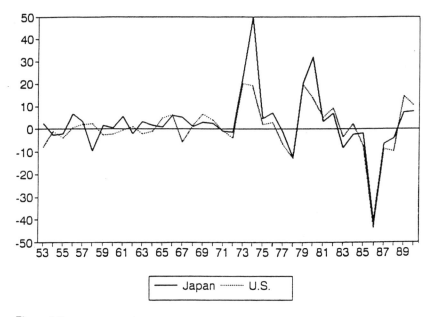

Figure 3.2
Raw materials price changes (percent per year, measured in yen).

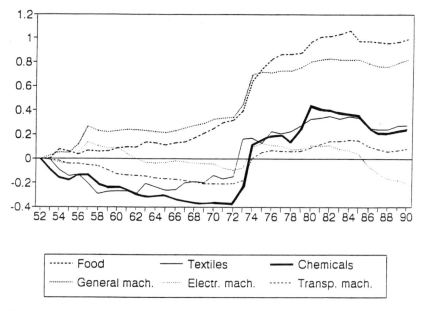

Figure 3.3
Output price developments: Japan (semilog scale; 1952 = base).

margins alone will not be able to offset permanent changes in cost competitiveness; in the long run, price must move in parallel with cost. The longer the time horizon, the more important is technical change as a determinant of the sectoral price structure (Marston 1987, 1991). As we saw in chapter 2, remarkable shifts in the relative productivity of Japanese and U.S. manufacturing industries occurred during the postwar period.

Relative price changes caused by technical innovations are real signals that warrant a response by firms and households. There is no economic reason to suppress them—in fact, doing so would cause the world economy to stagnate. The question we now ask is, What type of exchange-rate regime does the best job of enhancing real signals while silencing noise unrelated to underlying supply or demand conditions?

3.3 Nonneutrality of the Exchange Rate

A popular idea has it that a depreciation of the home currency is an efficient device for changing the relative price structure. The argument is based on the presumption that exchange adjustment can solve the coordination problem of having to adjust millions of prices better than resorting to general deflation or inflation. This presumption is often dubbed the "daylight saving time" argument for flexible exchange rates. As Friedman (1953) originally put it:

The argument for flexible exchange rates is, strange to say, very nearly identical with the argument for daylight saving time. Isn't it absurd to change the clock in summer when exactly the same result could be achieved by having each individual change his habits? All that is required is that everyone decide to come to his office an hour earlier, have lunch an hour earlier, etc. But obviously it is much simpler to change the clock that guides all than to have each individual separately change his pattern of reaction to the clock, even though all want to do so. The situation is exactly the same in the exchange market. It is far simpler to allow one price to change, namely, the price of foreign exchange, than to rely upon changes in the multitude of prices that together constitute the internal price structure. (P. 173)

And more recently, Krugman (1989b) reiterated the point:

What a currency depreciation does is solve the coordination problem. When the dollar falls against the yen and the ecu, all U.S. wages fall together and simultaneously, with no need for anyone to cut a nominal wage. Of course, if wages were indexed to the exchange rate, or to the general price level with a quick pass-through of exchange rates into prices, a dollar depreciation would immediately be reflected in massive inflation. However, though this may happen in near-hyperinflation economies, it just doesn't happen in advanced economies with moderate to low inflation. (P. 25)

However, the validity of this line of thought depends critically on peculiarly asymmetrical assumptions about the goods market. When the cost of inflation and deflation is examined, an economy with a multitude of goods is presupposed—how else could there be a coordination problem? —yet when it comes to defending the efficacy of exchange adjustment, the authors revert to an implicit assumption of a single-good economy, as if depreciation did not seriously upset internal relative prices. Inflation and depreciation are, respectively, declines in the internal and external values of the home currency. In either case, the effects on various prices are far from uniform. If these modes of adjustment are compared in a multi-good world with varying degrees of price stickiness and exchange pass-through, either inflation-deflation or exchange-rate changes will have disruptive consequences on resource allocation and income distribution. Thus, the clear advantage of exchange adjustment over general price change disappears. It is as if the clock were advanced by 60 minutes for some individuals, 40 minutes for others, and 25 minutes for yet others; the ensuing confusion would be no less than in the case of uneven inflation or deflation.

Each good differs in the degree of its exposure to foreign competition. Let us classify goods into three groups: *nontradables*, which are virtually insulated from foreign competition (most services and labor); *tradables I* (manufactured products), which compete with foreign goods but with less than perfect commodity arbitrage; and *tradables II* (oil, precious metals, and other primary commodities), for which the law of one price always holds in electronically linked global markets. This classification follows Harrod (1953) and McKinnon (1979).

Suppose the home currency appreciates suddenly and greatly at a time when domestic prices have been relatively stable. (Assume also, as is commonly the case, that this appreciation is the market's response to "news"—whether substantive or spurious—rather than a delayed adjustment to past changes in the fundamental variables.) The appreciation will typically induce a wrenching effect on the domestic price configuration. Prices of tradables II will fall immediately and almost proportionately with the exchange-rate change. Prices of tradables I will, probably with a lag, also fall to close the international price gap generated by the appreciation. In contrast, prices of nontradables will be affected little or not at all. Let us call the impact of exchange-rate movement on domestic prices *price pressure*, and the scrambling of the domestic price structure caused by price pressure *price diffusion*.

a

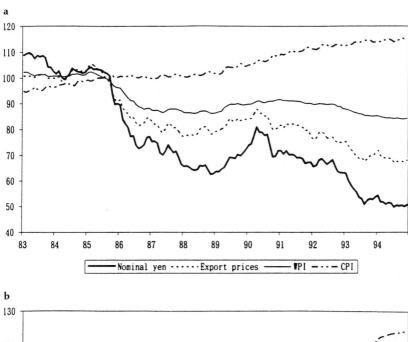

b

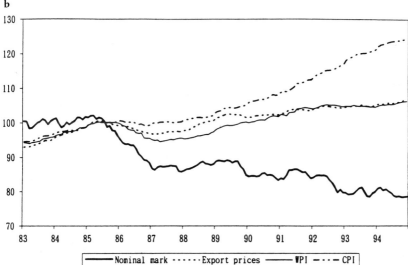

Figure 3.4
Exchange rate and prices (*a*) Japan, 1985 average = 100; (*b*) Germany, 1985 average = 100;
(*c*) United States, 1985 average = 100.

c

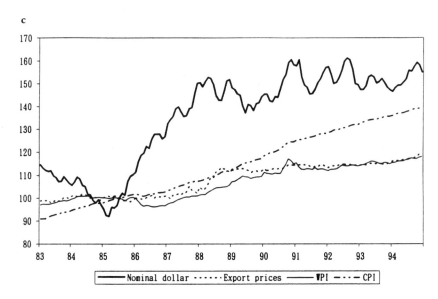

Figure 3.4 (cont.)

Price pressure and price diffusion are common in open industrial economies with floating exchange rates. Recall, for instance, the sharp appreciation of the Japanese and European currencies following the Plaza Agreement of 1985. For Japan and Germany, figures 3.4a and 3.4b plot the nominal effective exchange rate (with a fall indicating appreciation) and three price indices.[5] In Japan, the effective yen rate against hard-currency trading partners (as calculated by the IMF) appreciated 40 percent in nominal terms between February 1985 and February 1988. During the same three-year period, the export price index fell 31 percent, wholesale prices declined 17 percent, and consumer prices rose 2 percent. Thus the exchange appreciation caused an enormous reorganization of the domestic price structure. Similarly, but slightly less dramatically, the deutsche mark appreciated 17 percent in nominal effective terms against major trading partners during the same period. The declines in the export price and in wholesale prices were 8 percent and 4 percent, respectively, while consumer prices rose 1 percent.

A skeptic may ask, Were these price falls merely coincidental with global tradable deflation rather than caused by the appreciations? To see whether the exchange rate exerts price pressure independently of world-wide price trends, the regression of *relative* WPI of G7 countries, with the United States as the common comparator, is run on its own lags and

Table 3.1
Relative WPI inflation and the exchange rate (dependent variable is relative WPI)

	Own lags	Exchange-rate lags	$\bar{R}^2$	SE	DW
Japan 1975:Q2–90:Q4	0.040 (0.20)	0.178 (2.96)*	0.335	0.012	2.01
Germany 1975:Q2–90:Q4	0.563 (4.27)*	0.111 (3.55)*	0.420	0.008	2.19
France 1975:Q2–85:Q4	0.493 (3.14)*	0.179 (1.97)	0.541	0.013	1.93
U.K. 1975:Q2–90:Q4	0.601 (4.98)*	0.079 (2.07)*	0.433	0.010	2.28
Italy 1975:Q2–89:Q4	0.268 (1.60)	0.203 (3.11)*	0.416	0.014	1.95
Canada 1975:Q2–90:Q4	0.489 (2.68)*	0.178 (2.15)*	0.294	0.007	2.12

Source: IMF, *International Financial Statistics,* various issues.
Note: The quarterly rate of change in the relative WPI between the country and the United States is regressed on own lags (−1 to −3) and similar three lags of the change in the bilateral dollar exchange rate. The asterisk shows significance at the 5 percent level.

the lags of the nominal bilateral exchange rate (table 3.1).[6] All variables are expressed as logarithmic changes. Lagged exchange rates carry a small but significant positive sum of coefficients in all but one case, implying that price pressure does emanate from bilateral exchange-rate movement, independent of worldwide price trends.[7]

Changes in relative prices also occur at the level of individual goods and services. Profitability of each industry is differently affected by exchange fluctuations, depending on the tradability of inputs and outputs. When the yen appreciates, Japanese electric power companies with a highly tradable input (mainly oil) and a nontradable output (electricity) enjoy the benefit of reduced cost and improved profitability. By contrast, machinery industries are adversely affected as their export prices in yen have to be marked down to stay competitive abroad, with much smaller benefits of cheaper imported materials.

If one estimates PPP when price diffusion associated with currency appreciation is under way, a commodity basket composed of gold, oil, and other tradables II will indicate, not surprisingly, that the current exchange rate *is* the PPP, and there is no international price gap. Alternatively, if a basket of manufactured products with sticky prices is used, the estimated PPP will be higher in, say, yen per dollar than the actual exchange rate, and the basket appears more expensive at home than abroad. Finally, a basket of mostly nontradables will suggest an even higher PPP and a larger price differential. Thus, PPP and international price differentials estimated under a floating-rate regime depend on the content of the basket as well as on the actual exchange rate (chapter 9).

The related concept of *PPP drift* can now be introduced. As prices keep adjusting to the exchange rate, PPP, which is the relative price between two economies, also continues to drift until the law of one price is restored. When the yen remains overvalued, the yen-dollar PPP rate declines, as if to chase the actual exchange rate, and gradually offsets the initial deviation. To paraphrase, countries with overvalued currencies tend to have lower inflation in manufactured goods than countries with undervalued currencies do. Note that the main causality underlying the concept of PPP drift is the opposite of what Cassel (1922), the godfather of PPP, assumed. Here, it is relative prices that catch up with exchange rates, rather than exchange rates adjusting to differentials in national inflation rates as Cassel originally supposed.

PPP drift occurs continuously under floating rates because actual exchange rates do not coincide with tradable PPP except momentarily and by chance. For instance, by the PPP criterion the yen has been overvalued against the dollar since about 1986. As a consequence, the yen-dollar PPP rate, estimated by various authors and agencies and using different baskets, has shown a declining trend since then.[8] (The concept of PPP drift is treated more extensively in chapter 9—see figure 9.1.)

Thus, the argument that exchange-rate changes are just a veil over an unchanging domestic price structure is about as convincing as the view that money is a veil with no repercussions on the real economy. Not only do changes in the exchange rate have substantial real effects, but they also become a major source of instability in both the microeconomic and the macroeconomic sense. Rather than passively adjusting to align national prices, the exchange rate often acts as a forcing variable that pushes national price levels in one direction or another.

3.4   The U.S. Economy with Modest Exchange Pass-Through

Another feature of the U.S.–Japan economic relationship that should be underscored is the two countries' asymmetric sensitivity to the movement of the yen-dollar exchange rate: the U.S. economy is, at least in the short run, much more insulated from the effects of exchange-rate instability than is the Japanese economy. This asymmetry in pass-through (which refers to the degree to which the movement of the exchange rate affects domestic prices) can go a long way to explain the different monetary policy reactions to exchange fluctuations between the U.S. Fed and the BoJ (chapter 4).

To confirm the asymmetry (figure 3.4), compare the graph of price developments in the United States following the reversal of the huge dollar appreciation of the early 1980s (figure 3.4c) with the two similar graphs for Japan and Germany (figures 3.4a and 3.4b). As the dollar's nominal effective exchange rate against major trading partners greatly depreciated beginning in March 1985, there was no similar increase in the American general price level. (The slight fall in the American WPI in 1986 was due to the collapse in the global oil price and not directly related to the dollar's fall.) WPI and export prices moved in tandem, independently from the movement of the dollar. In the United States, CPI had a higher and smoother trend than WPI, but it does not seem to have been systematically influenced by the movement of the dollar, either.

The empirical literature of exchange pass-through provides more formal evidence about the U.S.–Japan price asymmetry. Since the 1980s, a number of researchers have identified a very slow response of U.S. prices to a large dollar movement (Dornbusch 1987a; Hooper and Mann 1987; Mann 1986; Woo 1984), as is seen in figure 3.4c. Other studies directly compared the sensitivity of American prices to the exchange rate with that of Japanese or German prices (Knetter 1989; Marston 1991; Ohno 1989a). The results of these studies vary, and a large part of that variation may reflect the difference in their data sets. Nevertheless, most empirical studies agree that, overall, the asymmetry in price response does exist between the United States and Japan.[9]

The relatively small response of U.S. prices to the exchange rate can be explained in various ways. In the past, the large size and closed nature of the U.S. economy compared with the Japanese were cited as the chief causes of the bilateral asymmetry. However, because of the persistent overvaluation of the yen and the increasingly important role of international trade for the United States, that characterization is no longer valid today. In 1994, the Japanese economy was 68 percent as large as the U.S. economy, and the United States was more open than Japan, as measured by the ratio of the sum of exports and imports to GDP. In 1994, this ratio was 0.228 for the United States and 0.168 for Japan.

However, other aspects of the bilateral economy are still unbalanced. Almost all of U.S. trade is invoiced in dollars, whereas the majority of Japan's trade is invoiced in foreign currencies (presumably most of it in dollars); as of the mid-1990s, only 40 percent of Japan's exports and 20 percent of its imports are invoiced in yen. This results in much higher *immediate* pass-through of the exchange rate in Japan than in the United States.

In addition, resource-poor Japan imports large amounts of food, energy, and industrial materials whose prices are set globally in terms of dollars and are thus more readily passed through to the domestic market. The share of Japan's total imports accounted for by these primary commodities has fallen significantly in recent years, from 77 percent in 1980 to 48 percent in 1993, due mainly to the collapse of the price of oil in the mid-1980s and the increased imports of manufactured goods from the rest of Asia. But even today, this percentage is much higher than the comparable ratio in the United States (26 percent).

The consequence of the asymmetric price responses is twofold. First, when the yen-dollar exchange rate moves away from its correct level, most of the price adjustment to offset the bilateral price gap takes place on the Japanese side. Second, American policy makers tend to pay less attention to the exchange rate than their Japanese counterparts do in formulating domestic monetary policy, because the impact of an unstable dollar is not immediately apparent. However, such inward orientation by the center country was very costly to the world economy in the 1970s and 1980s (McKinnon 1996). Moreover, it is central to the syndrome of the ever-higher yen (chapter 1) insofar as U.S. monetary policy is independently determined but Japan's is not.

3.5 Generalized Float and Growth Slowdown

The major puzzle of postwar economic history is the slowdown of the growth trends of major industrial countries in the early 1970s. The timing of the slowdown largely coincided with the introduction of generalized float among those countries. Might there be a causal link between the two events? Did weaker growth somehow necessitate an era of exchange fluctuations? Or can we say that the acquiescence to exchange instability led to the deterioration of real performance?

It would be brazen to assert that such causality, in either direction, can be proven to the satisfaction of the economics profession. Here, our goal is the more modest one of presenting a hypothesis—accompanied by some circumstantial evidence—consistent with our previous arguments that can explain the concurrence of floating exchange rates and impaired growth.

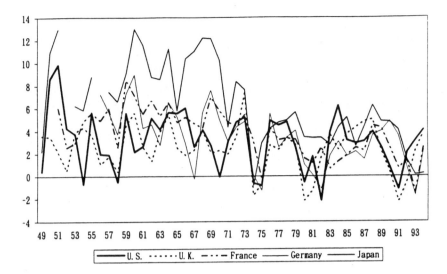

Figure 3.5
Real GDP, annual percent change.

Let us look at the facts. Comparing real growth in G5 countries (United States, Japan, Germany, France, and United Kingdom) during 1952–70 and 1971–92, the following features are noteworthy.[10] First, growth slowed in all these countries. In the cases of Japan and the United States, the average growth rate declined from 9.4 percent to 4.2 percent, and from 3.3 percent to 2.5 percent, respectively.[11] Second, variance in the growth rate did not show any systematic change between the two periods: it declined in Japan and Germany, rose in the United States and United Kingdom, and remained about the same in France. Third, as is evident from figure 3.5, a peculiar feature of the floating exchange-rate period is increased synchronization of business cycles; good years and bad years tend to roughly coincide across major industrial countries. Using principal component analysis, it can be confirmed that the contribution of the first component (i.e., global cycles) to the total variance increased from 49.9 percent to 66.3 percent after the breakdown of fixed parities in 1971—although this synchronization was more pronounced from 1975 to 1984 than after 1985 (McKinnon 1996).

The popular explanation for lower output growth and more synchronous business cycles in recent decades points to external causes (Bosworth and Lawrence 1982; Brown 1985; Bruno and Sachs 1985). The prime suspect is OPEC and the oil shocks it caused during the 1970s. Simply put, the steep rises in the oil price constituted supply shocks that shifted the aggregate supply curve upward, causing stagflation. In response, monetary authorities allowed (partial) monetary accommodation to lessen the negative effect on output. These supply shocks were common to all countries, because oil was an important traded commodity. This, coupled with downward wage rigidity, can explain the poorer real performance of the 1970s and thereafter. According to this view, the international monetary system and world business cycles are not causally related. But, by happy accident, the world economy had completed the transition to a floating exchange-rate system by the first oil shock, which absorbed its impact relatively smoothly.

The problem with the foregoing interpretation is that the collapse of oil prices after the mid-1980s did not revive high growth trends. By 1993 the real dollar price of crude oil (deflated by U.S. wholesale prices) was 19 percent lower than in 1974, the year immediately after the first oil shock. Furthermore, adjusting the oil price for Japanese WPI and the yen-dollar exchange rate reveals that the real yen price of crude oil declined as much as 42 percent during 1974–93. Today OPEC is much meeker and out of the news. In retrospect, the oil price was a *lagging* indicator of global inflationary and deflationary trends. The belligerency of OPEC during the 1970s looks more like a result of a global liquidity glut than an independent cause of macroeconomic disturbance.

Our alternative hypothesis is that the deterioration of global economic performance is of monetary and financial origin. We further suspect that exchange fluctuations have much to do with it. It is plausible that reduced productivity growth (figures 2.1a and 2.1b) and output (figure 3.5) since the 1970s has been, at least in part, the consequence of noisy price signals associated with inflation and deflation, exchange misalignments, and volatility in long-term interest rates. Dysfunctions of the price mechanism naturally reduce allocative efficiency, especially that of physical investment.

It is well known that the size and speed of exchange-rate fluctuations under the current system are much greater than those engendered by the adjustment efforts reasonably expected of a typical manufacturing firm. Miyashita (1994), financial director of Nissan, a major Japanese automaker, explains the arithmetic of exchange-rate noise as follows:

It is crucial to reduce cost further. However, in the case of auto industry, the situation is akin to wringing a bone-dry towel. We would be greatly pleased if the cost per vehicle could be cut by one or two thousand yen. Suppose the export price per vehicle is roughly $15,000. This means appreciation of one yen against the dollar takes away 15,000 yen. If it is ten yen, then a loss of 150,000 yen. In the factory we make desperate efforts to cut thousands, hundreds, and even tens of yen per vehicle while exchange fluctuations brutally tax us 100,000 yen. This has a very bad morale effect on the cost-cutting struggle on the factory floor. Management does take various measures including restructuring and plant closure. But plant closure would save only tens of thousand yen per vehicle which could be easily swamped by an appreciation of ten yen.

When financial noise is greater than "real" signals by a factor of 100 or so, as Miyashita implies, investments in human and physical capital that would otherwise be profitable may well fail because of an unfavorable exchange rate.

Additional and large uncertainty due to exchange fluctuations can be neither separated from other business uncertainties nor hedged by computerized financial arrangements. This is because precise production and delivery plans cannot be made in advance for industrial investments with long gestation periods. Thus, even if forward exchange markets were available into the indefinite future, an industrial firm would not know the proper amounts, currencies, and maturities for hedging contracts. Technically, this "Arrow-Debreu dilemma" reflects incompleteness of forward markets for goods and services due to the moral hazard problem associated with such contingent futures (McKinnon 1988 and 1996).

Currency dealers and portfolio managers often feel that today's manufacturers are sufficiently protected against foreign-exchange risk by the large and expanding menu of derivative instruments made possible by computer and communications technology. They think this because their financial business is itself not so burdened by unhedgeable future contingencies, and foreign-exchange risks can be fairly easily offset.

What these financial experts fail to understand is the two-step logic of the Arrow-Debreu dilemma faced by industrial enterprises. For hedging investments made today that produce output many months or years later, the first step is to secure contracts for future sales to domestic and foreign buyers at agreed-on prices, and the second is to hedge any foreign-exchange risk by selling the resulting foreign-exchange proceeds forward at different terms to maturity. Although a rich menu of futures and option contracts in foreign exchange now exists (step 2), any manufacturer producing specialized brand-name goods—tradables I as defined on page 58—is highly limited in how much of his own future output he can sell forward today (step 1). Organized futures, or forward markets in heterogeneous commodities, are very limited: the famous "missing markets" in

the Arrow-Debreu framework. Without a complete set of forward commodity contracts in hand (step 1), the manufacturer can only guess at
which foreign currencies, and how much of each, he wants to go short in
today for making delivery months or years hence (step 2). At the time the
industrialist must make his investment decision, any short position in a
foreign currency will necessarily be somewhat speculative because he
doesn't yet know with much accuracy what his future commodity sales
in the country in question will be. So the presence of a complete set of
foreign-currency futures can, at best, only partially offset exchange risk.
Thus manufacturers typically don't hedge much more than short-term
accounts receivable in foreign monies (McKinnon 1979).

But, in the medium term of, say, six months to five years, industrialists
with heavy fixed investments are vulnerable to exchange-rate misalignments (page 52). For example, the overvaluation of the dollar in the
early 1980s created an industrial "rust bowl" in the American Midwest.
More recently, episodes of a severely overvalued yen—in 1986–87 and
1993–95—greatly reduced the profitability of Japanese firms, caused a
sharp drop in private investment, and caused *endaka fukyo*.

This great volatility in exchange rates, and associated volatility in
interest rates (as shown in chapter 8), has led to the proliferation of complex financial derivatives for (partially) hedging financial risks and to an
explosion of foreign-exchange turnover relative to the underlying trade
flows. If exchange rates and exchange-rate expectations were better anchored in the medium and longer terms, there would be less need to rely
on complex computer programs in order to export, import, or invest
abroad. In a more stable financial environment, international investors
would better respond to price signals that reflect true comparative costs.
In chapter 10, we suggest how Japan and the United States could better
harmonize their monetary policies to create such an environment.

3.6   *Endaka Fukyo* or High-Yen-Induced Recession

Among the industrial countries, Japan is particularly vulnerable to fluctuations in its dollar exchange rate, because of (1) the dominance of the
dollar as an invoicing currency in Japan's exports and imports; (2) the
importance of the United States as a trading partner; (3) the absence of a
regional exchange arrangement such as the European Monetary System;
and (4) the co-movement of many Asian currencies with the dollar—
the Hong Kong dollar is formally pegged to the U.S. dollar, and the
currencies of other newly industrializing economies (NIEs) and ASEAN

countries also tend to follow the dollar's movement. If the yen appreciates against the dollar when the Japanese economy is in a downturn, the effect can be devastating.

During the last decade, Japan has been buffeted by two recessions: 1986–87 and 1991–95. The first was acute but relatively short, whereas the second, from which the economy is only slowly recovering, turned out to be much longer and more severe. These recessions are clearly reflected in the operating profits of Japanese manufacturing industries (figure 3.6a).[12]

Other business indicators also tell similar stories. Industrial production of mining and manufacturing, which rose 16 percent between 1983:Q1 and 1985:Q1, remained virtually flat in the subsequent two years. Then it climbed briskly, by 28 percent, during 1987:Q1–1991:Q1. Finally, it *fell* 12 percent in the following three years. Real investment in machinery and equipment tracks basically the same path, with stagnation in 1986 and a hard fall of 17 percent during 1991–93 extending through 1995.

Two monetary phenomena, the asset bubble and the fluctuations in the yen-dollar exchange rate, can go a long way to explain this macroeconomic roller coaster. The asset bubble, as measured by the Nikkei stock index (figure 3.6b), accelerated and peaked in the last quarter of 1989. An alternative index, land prices in six major cities, peaked about a year later, in the second half of 1990. Both indices subsequently fell. The asset effect of the speculative bubble, together with its fleeting optimism, supported vigorous private investment and consumption in the late 1980s, with an equally devastating effect once the tide turned.[13]

At the same time, the exchange rate exerted powerful price pressure on Japanese manufacturing. Figure 3.6c, which plots the percentage deviation of the yen-dollar exchange rate from the PPP exchange rate for manufactured products, illustrates its severity. In figure 3.6c, the absolute level of PPP is estimated by the price survey conducted by the Research Institute for International Price Mechanism (1993). (Other estimates of PPP for tradable goods yield similar results; see chapter 9.) A positive deviation implies inflationary pressure on the Japanese economy, and vice versa. A yen appreciation of 50 percentage points occurred in 1985–87. Dramatic price diffusion associated with this episode is presented in figure 3.4a. Roughly half of the appreciation was a correction to the previous undervaluation, but the rest of it was due to overshooting by the PPP criterion. Then, after returning almost to the PPP level in 1990, another appreciation started. Although smaller than the previous one, this appreciation was entirely a movement away from PPP.

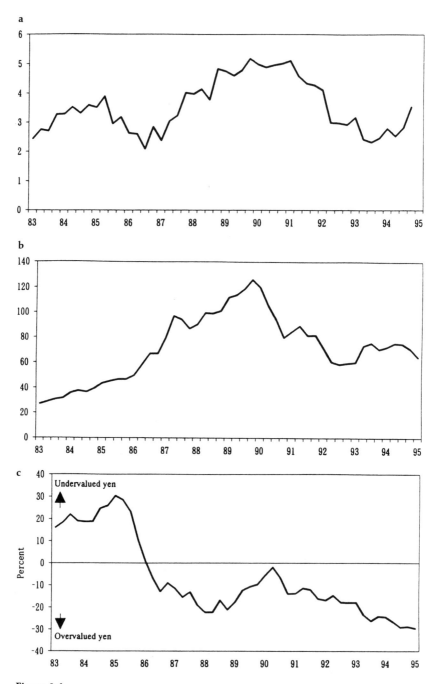

Figure 3.6
(a) Operating profits of manufacturing in trillions of yen; (b) Nikkei Stock Index, 1990 average = 100; (c) Price pressure, actual versus PPP yen-dollar rate.

The recession of 1986 to early 1987—we shall call *endaka fukyo I*—was caused by the enormous yen appreciation and the damage it did to the terms of trade of the manufacturing sector. It did not last very long, partly because of the stimulative effect of the ongoing asset inflation: the asset bubble offset the deflationary impact of exchange-rate overvaluation. However, in the recession of 1991–95, the second *endaka fukyo*, *endaka fukyo II*, coincided with the bursting of the asset bubble and thus was much worse than the first. This time, virtually all industries—including service industries—were adversely affected. The recovery process has been extremely slow and weak, and many firms and financial institutions are saddled with heavy capital losses and nonperforming loans.

Despite being overvalued in 1993, the yen continued to be talked up and finally broke the century mark against the dollar by mid-1994. Beginning in March 1995, another wave of precipitous yen appreciation, triggered by the Mexican financial crisis and the heated U.S.–Japan dispute over automobile components, took the rate momentarily below 80 on April 19, causing panic among otherwise healthy Japanese manufacturers and their workers. The high yen plunged the Japanese economy, which was then on a modest recovery path, into another stagnation. Feelings of despair and resignation began to spread: *endaka fukyo II* seemed far beyond what individual firms could cope with by intensive restructuring.[14]

Although Japan's macro economy, particularly the fragile banking system, did indeed seem on the verge of an almost irretrievable breakdown in the late spring of 1995, a remarkable change in American policy toward Japan in early summer 1995 prevented this greater calamity. As described in detail in chapter 11, American mercantile pressure that had been driving the yen upward was lifted, and joint intervention by the Fed and the BoJ to drive the yen down clearly signaled that the American authorities would tolerate a major devaluation of the yen. This permitted the BoJ to reexpand the Japanese economy as the yen depreciated from its April 1995 high of 80 to the dollar by almost 35 percent by late 1996. Thus was Japan rescued from *endaka fukyo II*.

Our main concern in this chapter, however, has been twofold: (1) to show the nonneutrality of exchange-rate changes in a general microeconomic sense—the extraordinary scrambling of relative prices that introduces noise and obscures relevant price signals on resource scarcity; and (2) to show the unfortunate macroeconomic repercussions on Japan of episodic yen appreciations, a subject to which we return in chapter 5. Although *endaka fukyo II* was highly traumatic, as long as the syndrome of the ever-higher yen is only in remission and not cured, *endaka fukyo III, IV, . . .* and so on, can't be ruled out in the future.

4 Balancing International Competitiveness in the Longer Run: Wage Adjustment versus Yen Appreciation

Although fluctuations in untethered exchange rates can be very harmful, isn't some degree of exchange-rate flexibility desirable to facilitate international adjustment? The common belief among influential economists—often those who write textbooks (see Krugman and Obstfeld 1994; Caves, Frankel, and Jones 1996)—is that *asymmetric real shocks*, those disturbances in aggregate demand or supply that affect one economy much more strongly than the others, can be better accommodated by flexible exchange rates. Because these economists also assume that money wages are fairly rigid (the so-called Keynesian case) when these asymmetric shocks occur, they argue that exchange-rate flexibility is necessary in order to "smoothly" readjust relative prices and wages—as per Milton Friedman's daylight saving time analogy (see chapter 3).

Unfortunately, this concern with asymmetric real shocks is misplaced. The shocks that appear in textbooks are not a good portrayal of the real adjustment problems between Japan and the United States over the last four and one-half decades, nor of those between most other highly diversified industrial economies over any sustained period of time. We do not deny that the textbook scenario could be valid in fairly special circumstances for particular kinds of countries. But, in the appendix to this chapter, we show in detail why the standard analysis is empirically irrelevant for the Japan–United States economic relationship.

What is the main problem with the textbook approach? The relevant time horizon over which asymmetric shocks have their impact is implicitly presumed to be quite short—more or less matching the horizon over which the level of money wages is very rigid. Yet the problem of balancing international competitiveness between Japan and the United States has persisted for decades. Chapter 2 showed that, since the early 1950s, manufacturing industries in Japan have had higher and more divergent productivity growth than those in the United States. This chapter focuses on mutual adjustment over this longer time horizon. We show that (annual) *rates of change* in money wages—which, within a country, tend to be remarkably uniform across industries (figure 3.1)—are sufficiently adaptable to offset international differences in long-term productivity growth.

But there is an important proviso. If the differential growth rate in money wages is to adjust smoothly and in a timely fashion, the two countries' monetary regimes must be generally stable so that their *nominal* exchange rate is fixed and expected to remain so. Conversely, when exchange rates are untethered and so move erratically (as under our syndrome of the ever-higher yen), this undermines the natural tendency for growth in money wages in each country to reflect growth in labor productivity. In this longer-run context, the standard textbook argument is turned on its head: exchange-rate flexibility can impede adjustment to asymmetric productivity shocks. Indeed, misplaced concern with asymmetric shocks has become a theoretical as well as a psychological barrier to constructive debate on a new, workable system for stabilizing exchange rates.

To offset the higher productivity growth of Japan relative to the United States in the postwar period, two alternative adjustment mechanisms have been in place: (1) From 1951 through 1971, the nominal exchange rate was fixed while expansionary monetary policy in Japan induced money wages to rise much faster than those in the United States; and (2) after 1971, the continual appreciation of the yen forced a relatively deflationary monetary policy on Japan. By the 1990s, this had slowed the naturally high growth in Japanese money wages down to rates more or less the same as those experienced by the United States.

The two adjustment mechanisms would hardly differ in a hypothetical world with no friction or uncertainty and where money was a veil. However, in reality, committing a volatile financial variable (i.e., a floating exchange rate) to the task of real adjustment inevitably leads to overshooting and misalignment because of the well-known self-fulfilling nature of the asset markets (chapter 3). Most important for our purposes in this chapter, the advent of floating—with an erratically appreciating yen—upset the natural tendency for money wages in Japan to grow in line with productivity in manufacturing. Instead, with long and variable lags, growth in Japanese money wages began to reflect the appreciating yen more than it reflected productivity growth in Japanese tradable goods industries.

Let us consider the two adjustment mechanisms in historical perspective.

4.1   Wage and Price Adjustment under the Fixed-Rate Dollar Standard, 1951–71

In retrospect, the years from 1951 to 1971 were the most harmonious in economic relationships between the U.S. and Japan. Under the fixed-rate international dollar standard, the Bank of Japan geared its domestic monetary policy to keeping the exchange rate at 360 yen per dollar, while the U.S. Federal Reserve anchored the common price level for tradable goods. Global inflation in wholesale prices was confined to about 1 percent per year—for the United States and Japan, as shown in figure 1.4, but also for hard-currency Europe (McKinnon 1996). This remarkable record of stability subsequently gave way to floating exchange rates and the inflations of the 1970s.

During the same twenty years, protectionist barriers came down, and trade between the two countries grew rapidly. Fiscal and current-account imbalances remained modest. Financial stability was instrumental in producing rapid economic growth throughout the industrial world. The economic growth of the United States, Japan, and other industrial countries was generally higher—with minimal inflation—than that seen before or since (Maddison 1989).

Then, more than now, the pace of growth varied across countries and industries. Starting from much lower absolute levels in 1951, Japanese industrial output and real GNP grew at an astonishing 13.1 and 9.4 percent, respectively, for twenty years—roughly three times faster than corresponding American rates of growth (table 4.1). With 1951 as 100, the extraordinary divergence in growth of industrial output and real GNP between the two countries is shown in figure 4.1. With the exchange rate fixed and exchange controls on Japanese capital flows,[1] how did bilateral competitiveness adjust?

In the tradable goods sector, secular adjustments in average money wages more or less accurately offset this differential growth in average productivity. On an annual basis, the IMF data in table 4.1 show that money wages in Japanese manufacturing grew faster by 6 percentage points than hourly wages in U.S. manufacturing—10.2 percent versus 4.2 percent. But inflation in tradable prices was virtually the same in both countries: the U.S. wholesale price index (WPI) increased annually by 1.1 percent and the Japanese by 0.7 percent in the same twenty-year period of unmatched worldwide growth. Balanced international competitiveness, in the sense of the alignment of average tradable price levels at the "factory gate," was fairly well maintained because Japanese money wages grew

Table 4.1
Key economic indicators: Japan and the United States, 1951–94 (average annual percent change)

	Wholesale prices		Money wages		Consumer prices		Industrial production	
	U.S.	Japan	U.S.	Japan	U.S.	Japan	U.S.	Japan
1951–71	1.1	0.7	4.2	10.2	2.2	4.4	4.1	13.1
1971–94	5.2	2.6	5.4	6.6	5.9	4.8	2.6	2.8
1972–83	8.9	7.0	7.9	10.4	8.2	8.0	2.0	3.2
1983–94	1.6	−1.7	2.9	2.8	3.7	1.6	3.1	2.4

	Real GDP		Nominal GDP		Narrow money		Labor productivity	
	U.S.	Japan[a]	U.S.	Japan	U.S.	Japan	U.S.	Japan
1951–71	3.3	9.4[b]	6.2[c]	14.5[c]	3.3[c]	15.9[c]	2.3	9.7[d]
1971–94	2.5	3.6	8.1	7.7	7.3	7.0	1.0	4.7
1972–83	2.1	3.8	9.9	10.7	6.8	8.0	0.8	5.8
1983–94	2.9	3.4	6.4	4.7	7.8	5.9	1.3	3.6

Source: IMF, International Financial Statistics, CD-ROM, June 1995, unless otherwise noted below. Japanese nominal wages including semiannual bonuses are obtained from the Ministry of Labor. For labor productivity, the U.S. index for the nonfarm business sector (Bureau of Labor Statistics) and the Japanese index for manufacturing (Japan Productivity Center) are used.
a. Real, GNP.
b. 1952–71.
c. 1953–71.
d. 1955–71.

much faster than their American counterparts. (After 1968, however, excessive upward drift in U.S. money wages nudged U.S. wholesale price inflation above that in Japan and some other industrial countries.)

Alternatively, more direct measures of labor productivity growth in the 1950s and 1960s might be compared with growth in money wages to determine whether or not relative wage adjustment was sufficient between the two countries. The Japan Productivity Center estimates that Japanese productivity in manufacturing grew 9.7 percent per year from 1955 to 1971 (table 4.1), albeit with enormous divergences from this average for individual industries.[2] Because money wages in manufacturing increased at 10.2 percent per year, this increase almost perfectly offset absolute productivity growth, leaving very little pressure on the Japanese WPI.

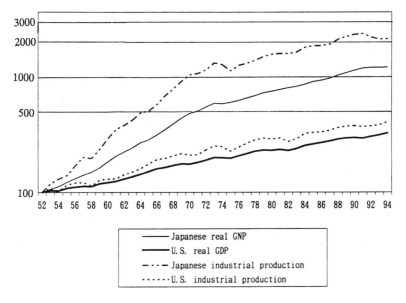

Figure 4.1
Real income and industrial production, semilog scale, 1952 = 100. *Source:* IMF, *International Financial Statistics*, CD-ROM, December 1995.

Starting from a much higher absolute level in 1951, American labor productivity in manufacturing grew 2.3 percent annually to 1971, 7.4 percentage points less than the corresponding figure for Japan. However, American hourly wages also grew slowly: 4.2 percent compared to 10.2 percent for Japan. This difference of 6.0 percentage points virtually offset the gap in productivity growth between the two countries. Figure 4.2 shows rather dramatically the greater buoyancy in Japanese money-wage growth compared to American over the two decades when the yen-dollar rate was fixed.

However, there is an important caveat. We said that the productivity gap was only *virtually* offset. Wage changes in the 1950s reflected Japanese productivity growth less systematically, compared to the relatively smooth adjustment of growth in money wages in the 1960s. Figure 4.2 shows an explosion in money wages in Japan in 1950–52; they increased almost 20 percent annually. The inflationary shock of the Korean War and the sharp rise in primary materials prices were coupled with domestic labor unrest. Coming out of the 1949 Dodge Plan for ending postwar inflation, the government's commitment to keep the yen-dollar rate fixed at 360 was still tenuous in the early 1950s. The main concern

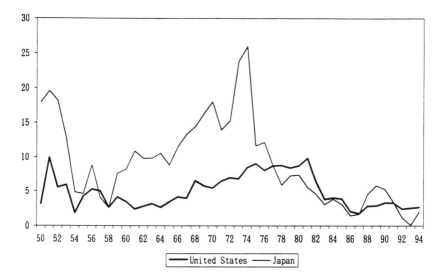

Figure 4.2
Nominal wage in manufacturing, annual change in percent. *Source:* IMF, *International Financial Statistics*, CD-ROM, December 1995.

was that, at this exchange rate, Japanese products were not competitively priced, and the need to cut costs was strongly felt. Domestic coal and steel, among other things, were deemed too expensive in world markets. So the exchange rate was suspect.

However, by the mid-1950s, the Japanese authorities resolved to disinflate and preserve the fixed exchange-rate regime. Thus, from 1954 to 1958, Japanese money wage growth fell sharply, to 5 percent per year, which was barely above that in the United States. This disinflationary episode eliminated the real overvaluation of the yen associated with the aftermath of exchange-rate-based Dodge stabilization and with the subsequent inflation from the Korean War.

By 1959–60, the exchange rate of 360 yen to the dollar finally seemed to be secure. Only then was Japanese monetary policy naturally loosened. Over the next dozen years, Japanese money wages grew much faster than those in the United States. Figure 4.2 shows this now steady and substantial gap in money-wage growth—averaging about 6 to 8 percentage points per year—between the two countries from 1959 to 1971.

Is there a lesson here? In a period of monetary turbulence when the exchange rate is insecure, establishing *steady* growth in money wages that accurately reflects growth in productivity in manufacturing (tradables) industries is difficult. Because of uncertainty about the future purchasing power of domestic money, workers (perhaps represented by trade unions) and managers cannot easily coalesce around a program for letting *money* wages increase in line with *real* productivity growth. Monetary policy is naturally more cyclical and punctuated with sharp disinflations in order to defend the (tenuous) exchange rate.

Once the monetary regime is solidly anchored, however, appropriate adjustment in money-wage growth over the longer term follows naturally. Indeed, this wage-setting process based on productivity growth in the tradables sector—manufacturing, in the Japanese case—is now standard in the context of the so-called Scandinavian model of inflation (Lindbeck 1979). It was applied to Norway, Denmark, and Sweden in their high-growth phase of the 1950s and 1960s.

Following the Scandinavian model, partition the economy into an open tradable T-sector, and a sheltered nontradable N-sector. Each sector produces one composite good. Let lowercase variables represent percentage rates of change, and uppercase represent absolute levels. In general,

$$p_T = p_W + e, \tag{4.1}$$

where the rate of price change in domestic tradables, p_T (as measured by the WPI), p_W, is equal to world inflation, plus the expected change in the exchange rate. In context of the Scandinavian model, authors such as Lindbeck then define the "room" for nominal wage increases (without making the tradables sector uncompetitive internationally) to be

$$w_T = p_T + q_T, \tag{4.2}$$

where q_T is the rate of productivity growth in the tradables sector, presuming constant factor shares in the underlying production function.

Based on the Japanese experience of the 1950s, however, we would amend the Scandinavian model. Unless the exchange rate is securely fixed so that $e = 0$, and the world price level is fairly well tied down, labor-market expectations will be too variable to secure a predictable result for wage increases in the short and intermediate terms, even if something like equation 4.2 still holds in the very long run.

However, when the nominal exchange rate is credibly fixed and (world) price inflation in tradable goods is fairly low, equation 4.2 then defines the maximum increases in money wages that producers of tradables—largely manufacturing industries, in the Japanese case—perceive they can afford and still stay competitive internationally. The stable monetary regime makes the limits on wage bargaining more transparent. Indeed, workers and unions can now link their increased money-wage claims to their own perceived productivity growth.

Once the room for wage increases in the open sectors is established, wage setting in the nontradable or sheltered sectors is endogenously determined by the principle of labor solidarity—according to the Scandinavian theory.

$$w_N = w_T. \tag{4.3}$$

The rate of change in nontradables prices then depends on this common rate of wage increase less productivity growth, q_N, peculiar to the nontradables sector (again assuming constant factor shares).

$$p_N = w_N - q_N. \tag{4.4}$$

Because productivity growth in the sheltered, largely service sector is lower than in the goods-producing tradables sector, the rate of inflation in nontradables exceeds that in tradables:

$$q_T > q_N \quad \text{and} \quad p_N > p_T. \tag{4.5}$$

Correspondingly, suppose we have a more general price index that includes both tradables (with weight α) and nontradables (with weight $1 - \alpha$) that could be either the consumer price index (CPI) or the GNP deflator. That is,

$$P = \alpha P_T + (1 - \alpha)P_N. \tag{4.6}$$

Then, by simple substitution of equations 4.2, 4.3, and 4.4 into 4.6, we get the standard Scandinavian result that

$$p = p_T + (1 - \alpha)(q_T - q_N). \tag{4.7}$$

The rate of change in the CPI will exceed that of the tradable price index (WPI) by the difference in productivity growth in the two sectors, weighted by the importance of the nontradables sector in the economy. And this difference in productivity growth is nothing more than the well-known Balassa-Samuelson effect discussed in chapter 2—whether applied in Japan, Scandinavia, or elsewhere.

However, the scope of the sheltered sector in Japan went well beyond any natural definition of nontradable services. It also included agriculture and a number of other, potentially tradable, protected industries—what we shall call pseudo-nontradables. The government actively protected these initially less favored sectors by assuring them the domestic Japanese market for their particular outputs. (See the discussion of Japanese developmental authoritarianism in chapter 2.) This form of protectionism made the weight $(1 - \alpha)$ for the sheltered sector—both genuine and pseudo-nontradables—very large relative to its weight in other industrial countries, most particularly compared to the United States. But rapidly growing wages in the favored internationally competitive sectors, which were Japan's major exporters, were still the benchmark for wage increases in the sheltered sector. This is an important reason why the increase in the Japanese CPI relative to its WPI was greater than what the standard Balassa-Samuelson effect would predict.

But not the only reason. Sheltered sectors such as retailing or construction had substantial restraint of trade among domestic competitors, as well as limits on direct investment by potential foreign entrants. This overregulation likely slowed their productivity growth (i.e., q_N) below comparable rates in other industrialized economies. But Japanese exporters in the open sectors were world beaters in competitiveness—q_T was high by international standards. Thus, the factor $(q_T - q_N)$ in the right-hand term of equation 4.7 was also unnaturally large.

The upshot of these two effects was the rapid increase in the Japanese CPI relative to its American counterpart since the mid-1950s, as shown in figure 2.4 (chapter 2). And most revealingly, figure 2.6 shows how much the Japanese price level as of 1994 exceeded that of other OECD countries with comparable real incomes per capita. Mainly because of Japan's developmentalism, the internal price level in 1994 was 60 percent *above* its norm (for that per capita income), while the price level of the United States was almost 30 percent *below* its norm. But part of this gap was due to the overvaluation of the yen, and undervaluation of the dollar, against other OECD countries in 1994. (How to measure purchasing power parity correctly will be taken up in chapter 9.)

4.2   Expansive Monetary Policy in Japan in the 1950s and 1960s

In the 1950s and 1960s, Japanese monetary policy had to be expansionary to support the very high growth in money wages and in consumer prices. From 1951 to 1971, Japan's CPI increased by 4.4 percent annually, whereas the American CPI increased by only 2.2 percent (table 4.1). If the Japanese monetary authorities had focused on stabilizing the CPI rather than on the dollar exchange rate and the WPI, growth in Japanese money wages would have had to be much slower. Then, in order to keep tradable goods prices approximately aligned between the two countries, the yen would have had to continually appreciate against the dollar. (For the future, we stress in chapter 10 the importance of anchoring a common WPI for the two countries.)

Money growth in Japan in the 1950s and 1960s was indeed very high. Table 4.1 compares rates of growth in narrow money[3] in each country to rates of growth in their nominal GDPs from 1956 to the present. Changes in the velocity of money are notoriously difficult to interpret—although were perhaps less so in the 1950s and 1960s when inflationary expectations (in goods prices) were minimal. Nevertheless, from 1953 to 1971 the growth in the stock of narrow money in yen outstripped the rapid growth in Japanese nominal GDP—the respective figures were 15.9 percent versus 14.5 percent on an annual basis. In the more mature American economy, where the U.S. Federal Reserve System effectively anchored the common price level in both countries (McKinnon 1993), the opposite was true. From 1953 to 1971, narrow money grew much more slowly than nominal GDP: 3.3 percent versus 6.2 percent.

By both measures—higher internal (CPI) price inflation and higher money growth relative to nominal GDP—Japanese monetary policy was indeed expansionary compared to that pursued by the United States during the era of fixed exchange rates and very high real growth. However, figure 4.3 shows that Japanese money growth through the mid-1950s, when the exchange rate was still insecure, was much more erratic.

Japan's relatively expansionary monetary policy arose naturally out of its obligation to fix the yen within a narrow 2 percent band against the dollar. In a vigorous export-driven economy with a fixed exchange rate, the central bank is virtually forced to allow the money supply to grow rapidly enough to maintain import demand so that the exchange rate does not appreciate. (This effect is even stronger if controls on capital outflows are in place.) Thus, the Japanese authorities did not base their monetary policy mainly on immediate domestic considerations. Rather, they focused on the international balance of payments, which, because of capital controls, in practice meant the current account. If a current-account surplus appeared, the Bank of Japan (BoJ) permitted a domestic credit expansion—and vice versa for a deficit.

Unlike Germany in the same period, Japan did not use purchases of foreign exchange as the principal technique for increasing its domestic monetary base. Rather, the BoJ preferred to keep foreign-exchange reserves fairly small by increasing domestic credit availability to offset (incipient) changes in the balance of payments, at least until 1968 (McKinnon 1993).

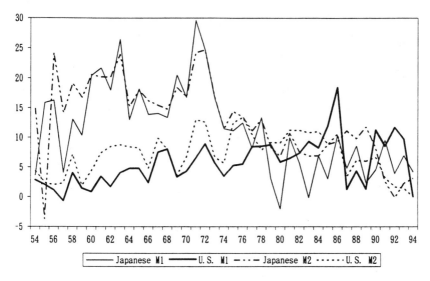

Figure 4.3
Money growth, percent. *Source:* IMF, *International Financial Statistics*, CD-ROM, December
1995. The U.S. M1 and M2 data for 1953–59 are obtained from Michael R. Darby and James
R. Lothian, *The International Transmission of Inflation* (Chicago: University of Chicago Press,
1983).

Even so, the BoJ still needed the U.S. Federal Reserve System, which
could formulate its own monetary policy to anchor the common price
level for tradable goods.

In summary, the 1950s and 1960s did see adjustment problems. Because the pace of productivity growth across individual Japanese industries was uneven, some U.S. industries lost worldwide market share to
Japanese competitors uncomfortably quickly. But overall macroeconomic
adjustment, where differential growth rates in average productivity between the United States and Japan were offset by higher money-wage
growth in Japan, worked fairly smoothly. Current-account imbalances and
price-level misalignments, which loomed so large in the years after the par
value system for exchange rates broke down, were comparatively minor.

4.3   Dollar Devaluations and Forced Relative Deflation in Japan:
The Breakdown of Wage Adjustment after 1971

Beginning in 1968, U.S. prices and wages began to increase a bit too fast
for the American WPI to remain stable, and for the gap in productivity

growth between the United States and Japan and other industrial countries to be offset. In contrast to the 1 percent annual growth observed from 1951 to 1967, American wholesale prices began rising about 3.5 percent per year from 1968 to 1971 (figure 1.4). The American nominal anchor, and the economic rationale, for the fixed-rate dollar standard began to slip. Economists in the United States, Europe, and Japan began to advocate more flexibility in exchange rates. And, on the American side, exchange-rate flexibility meant dollar devaluation.

When President Nixon shut the gold window in August 1971 and imposed a temporary import surcharge to enforce his demand that the dollar be officially devalued against the yen and other important currencies (as it was by the following December), he was following conventional economic wisdom. Most of his economic advisers, whether monetarist or Keynesian, applauded the transformation of the heretofore rigid exchange rate into an "adjusting" variable. According to the textbooks of the time, wages were determined autonomously within each country, and were too rigid to adjust to changing conditions of international competitiveness. Beginning with the dollar devaluation, the move to floating exchange rates was widely applauded for introducing additional flexibility to facilitate aligning the costs of production—largely wages—internationally.

The problem is, of course, that growth in money wages is not determined autonomously. We shall argue that American pressure on Japan to appreciate the yen undermined the wage-adjustment mechanism that had prevailed during the 1950s and 1960s.

Because of two kinds of monetary confusion, relative growth in money wages no longer reflected differences in productivity growth across the two countries. First was the worldwide inflationary explosion associated with the breakdown of the old system of fixed dollar parities. Under the short-lived but highly insecure Smithsonian Agreement, from December 1971 to February 1973, Japan and other countries attempted to repeg their currencies (at appreciated levels) against the dollar. Because the new pegs were not credible, there was a massive flight from dollars into yen, marks, sterling, and so on. Faced with an incredible upsurge in its foreign reserve position, the BoJ could not prevent a huge increase in the Japanese monetary base and internal bank lending. The resulting internal inflationary explosion was manifested in massive wage settlements of more than 20 percent in 1973–74 (figure 4.2), as well as in a spike of inflation in the WPI (figure 1.4) from the first oil shock. (Chapter 10 suggests a better way of dealing with parity commitments that are subject to speculative attack.)

Second, even in the absence of this initial inflationary explosion, there would be lags in the adjustment of expectations to the new, relatively deflationary regime associated with an appreciating yen. Even so, the gap by which wage growth in Japan exceeded that in the United States shrank from 6 percentage points over 1951–71 to 1.2 percentage points from 1972–94. From 1983–94, the pace of wage growth was about the same, averaging 2.8 to 2.9 percent per year in each country (table 4.1). Most recently, from 1993 to 1995, Japanese money wage growth has been a percentage point or so less than its American counterpart—although the numbers are erratic.

Of course, this slowdown in relative wage growth is part of the relative fall in the Japanese price level (figure 1.4). From 1983 to 1994, the American WPI (PPI) rose by 1.6 percent per year and the Japanese WPI *fell* by 1.7 percent per year (table 4.1). On a twelve-month basis, the absolute fall in the Japanese WPI was greatest (10.9 percent) from September 1985 to September 1986, followed by another significant decline (5 percent) from August 1992 to August 1993. These declines coincided with the periods of rapid yen appreciation (see chapter 3).

Granted, in the face of monetary and exchange-rate shocks, long and variable lags exist in the wage-setting process. But can we roughly identify the time when expectations changed and Japanese firms and workers came to believe that the yen would go indefinitely higher, so that growth of money wages in Japan began to decline relative to those in the United States? As figure 4.2 indicates, that expectation certainly didn't exist in August 1971, when President Nixon's closure of the gold window forced the first great yen appreciation. However, figure 4.2 also suggests that by 1977–78, growth in Japanese money wages had fallen dramatically relative to American—substantially narrowing the gap that existed in the 1960s. So, by the Carter period, with the second great postwar run on the dollar in 1977–78, expectations in the Japanese labor market of future price inflation had dramatically shifted downward. And money-wage growth in both countries has, on net balance, been drifting slowly downward ever since.

That the run on the dollar in 1977–78 was a major turning point for expectations of an ever-higher yen in the longer term is fully consistent with the behavior of both countries' long-term interest rates, as analyzed in chapters 1 and 5. Figure 1.5 shows that Japanese long-term nominal interest rates fell below their American counterparts for the first time in 1977, and have stayed persistently lower ever since. The effects of long-run exchange-rate expectations on Japanese interest rates and on money-wage growth had become broadly consistent with one another: by the late 1970s, the syndrome of the ever-higher yen had become fully embedded in both labor and capital markets. Although the process by which the yen ratcheted up in the foreign exchanges was extremely uneven and disruptive in the short and medium terms, Japanese enterprises, workers, and financiers came to expect that the yen, on average, would increase by 3 to 4 percentage points per year against the dollar in the longer term. (And this expectation of an even higher yen persisted through 1996, even after the yen had fallen from 80 to the dollar in April 1995 to 120 by the end of 1996.)

4.4 Idealized Wage Adjustment: A Concluding Note

Let us conclude our historical overview of mutual wage and price adjustment with a counterfactual simulation. Suppose that the American authorities had properly interpreted the rules of the game of the fixed-rate dollar standard—as laid out in some detail in McKinnon (1996)—so that the old regime did not break down—and that the U.S. government continued its low-inflation policies of the 1950s through the mid-1960s indefinitely. Then, it is not far-fetched to presume that the Bank of Japan would have continued pegging to the dollar, which would still be worth 360 yen. In effect, the American WPI and the world price level for tradables— including the Japanese WPI—would have remained securely anchored through the 1970s and until the present time.

If productivity growth in the two countries had remained unchanged under this hypothetical scenario of the yen-dollar rate remaining at 360 with stable WPIs, what then would have been the pattern of adjustment in money wages and consumer price indexes in the two economies? Figure 4.4 simulates what happens when growth in each country's WPI is 0; each WPI is represented by the horizontal line level at 100. Each country's actual time series for money wages and CPI is divided by its actual WPI, and then plotted for the period from 1960 to 1994. For the last decade of deflation, simulated Japanese money wages increase much more than they actually did. For the whole period since 1960, simulated money wages in Japan rise by 550 percent while U.S. money wages rise less than 50 percent. Figure 4.4 also shows that the simulated Japanese CPI more than doubles, while that of the United States increases very modestly—on the order of 20 or 30 percent.

This simulation implicitly presumes that productivity growth in the two countries was the same as it actually was during the monetary chaos

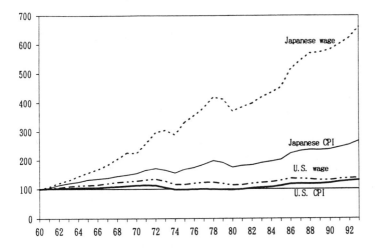

Figure 4.4
Counterfactual simulation with stable tradable prices and exchange rate (1960 = 100). *Note:*
Both U.S. and Japanese WPIs are assumed to be stable at 100 throughout.

of the period from the 1970s into the 1990s. If a more stable monetary
regime (like that of the Bretton Woods period) had begotten higher
productivity growth, then of course the plots of money wages in both
countries in figure 4.4 would be substantially higher. In the long run,
money-wage growth would adjust smoothly once the exchange rate and
common price level were securely anchored.

Appendix: A Polemic on Textbook Shocks and the Need for
Exchange-Rate Flexibility

What are the principal counterarguments? Tethering the yen-dollar
exchange rate indefinitely conflicts with textbook wisdom on why nominal exchange rates should remain flexible. The prevailing view is that all
countries are subject to unpredictable and asymmetric shocks in goods,
labor, and financial markets. Thus the exchange rate should be left free
to adjust. Even if stable exchange rates and stable exchange-rate expectations are preferred ex ante, policy authorities should—in this view—
still leave exchange rates untethered. Otherwise, once unexpected shocks
occur, the option of adjusting the exchange rate ex post to better maintain the economy's macroeconomic equilibrium will be foreclosed.

The view just described has an important corollary about market
expectations. Once an asymmetric macroeconomic shock occurs, market

makers will understand that the authorities may want to change an otherwise pegged exchange rate. Because the government cannot credibly commit not to change the rate, it cannot prevent speculative attacks in anticipation of some future macroeconomic shock. Consequently, it is better not to try to fix the exchange rate to begin with.

The literature on fixed versus floating exchange rates and the extent of the optimal currency area for countries in differing circumstances is analyzed in the companion volume to this text (McKinnon 1996). Without addressing this broader debate here, we consider the textbook approach narrowly in the context of the particular characteristics of the Japanese and American economies and the interaction between them.

First is the question of whether, over the past twenty-five years, the untethered yen-dollar exchange rate has been a passively *adjusting* variable ex post, or a *forcing* one ex ante. Chapter 1 showed that the ratcheting up of the yen was a response to episodic mercantile pressure from the United States to reduce the competitiveness of Japanese goods in world markets in the short run. Although this method of "adjustment" failed in its broader objective of correcting the U.S.–Japan trade imbalance (see chapters 6 and 7), the incidental effect was to impose relative deflation on Japan. Rather than passively adjusting to independently chosen monetary policies in the two countries as textbooks would have it, continual yen appreciation has forced a change in the long-run monetary stance of the BoJ (see chapters 1 and 9).

Second, is the need to adjust exchange rates ex post facto to *asymmetric shocks in goods markets* empirically relevant? In the textbook model, countries are presumed to produce only one commodity—or at most a small number of them, as in Milton Friedman's daylight saving time analogy discussed in chapter 3. Because of this simplifying assumption, countries seem more vulnerable to sudden shifts in the demand for their national products than they really are. Correspondingly, their market-clearing terms of trade appear unnaturally volatile if, for purposes of two-dimensional geometric analysis, each country is assumed to produce just one good.

In his chapter entitled "The Costs of a Common Currency," Paul De Grauwe (1994, p. 6) nicely reviews this standard textbook argument. "Let us suppose for some reason that [European] consumers shift their preference away from French-made to German-made products." Then, if market-clearing equilibrium is to be maintained, the prices of French-made goods must fall suddenly relative to those of the German ones. But this can't happen without unemployment in France, or inflation in Germany, unless real wages fall in France relative to those in Germany. Because money wages are sticky in both countries in the very short run, what better way to resolve the dilemma than by having the franc depreciate against the mark?

However, assuming that each economy produces a single composite good seriously misrepresents large, diversified economies. Japan and the United States each produce tens of thousands different commodities, with overlapping product categories. Aggregate private-sector demand doesn't suddenly shift from American goods collectively to Japanese goods collectively. Rather, firms in either country often introduce new products, for which initial demand might be intense but that remain a small part of total trade, and fickle consumers show cycles in their demand for, say, automobiles—affecting both countries. Thus, necessary price changes are product- (not country-) specific, as emphasized in chapter 2, and relative price variance among commodities will be substantial in any progressive market system. At a microeconomic level, a stable monetary cum exchange-rate regime will clarify these relative price signals and minimize noise as demand (or supply) shifts from product to product (chapter 3). But authorities on the same monetary regime need not worry that *aggregate* private demand will suddenly shift from one industrially diversified country's goods to another's and so necessitate some major change in the aggregate terms of trade and the exchange rate.

Over a long period the demand for one country's goods could change in favor of another's—as exemplified during Japan's recovery from the war. As new and better products were introduced, with rapid technical progress in the production of old goods, international demand shifted toward Japanese goods in an important sense.[4] It is precisely over this long horizon, however, that growth in relative money wages is the appropriate smoothly adjusting variable—as seen for Japan from the late 1950s through 1971 (figure 4.2), when the yen-dollar rate was credibly fixed.

Third, textbooks focus on *international differences in labor-market institutions* (De Grauwe 1994, pp. 18–24). If one country's wage-setting mechanism is more rigid than another's, there could be an adjustment problem to a common supply-side shock. Faced with, say, a sharp increase in the price of oil, one country's labor force might resist the necessary cut in real wages more than the other's. Alternatively, one country's whole wage structure might be more volatile—with a tendency to "blow up" more for political than for economic reasons—as seen in the postwar history of France. Either situation might warrant a discrete devaluation of the impacted country's currency. Such differences in labor-market flexibility between European countries pose substantial problems for the European Monetary Union.

However, both Japan's and America's labor markets are very flexible by European standards. Both countries have highly decentralized wage bargaining; unions are relatively weak and have become much more so since the 1950s and 1960s. Labor markets function well, so that wage setting (in any given skill category) is remarkably uniform across all industries (see chapter 3 for the case of Japan). If the common price level and exchange rate seem secure, both countries' labor-market institutions are flexible enough to promote mutual wage adjustment through time. In this important labor-market dimension, Japan and the United States seem better placed to stabilize the yen-dollar exchange rate than the more closely integrated (in commodity trade) European countries are able to secure exchange stability among themselves.

Fourth is the problem of *asymmetrical policy shocks*. Because the two countries have different political regimes, could a shock from a sudden shift in one government's macroeconomic policies warrant changing the exchange rate? Asymmetric shifts in national monetary policies certainly can be troublesome, and can lead to rather violent changes in exchange rates, which then seriously impact private investment. Or, as we argue in this book, the causality can go in the other direction. But this asymmetry is precisely what monetary cooperation to fix the yen-dollar exchange rate would be designed to avoid (chapter 10). In this sense, a Japan–U.S. monetary cum exchange-rate pact is necessary to prevent undesirable monetary shocks—particularly in Japan—that unhinge private investment (see chapter 5).

Even if successfully concluded, however, such a monetary pact would leave each country's fiscal policy to be a "free" variable. Can fiscal changes constitute a policy shock sufficiently great to warrant a discrete adjustment in the yen-dollar exchange rate?

If national monetary policies, and hence also international monetary cooperation, were undermined by either fiscal authority's resorting directly to excess money issue and the inflation tax to cover fiscal deficits, then exchange-rate stability would certainly be an important casualty. However, both Japan and the United States are hard-currency countries with enormous (although not infinite) capabilities for issuing nonmonetary debt to cover current fiscal deficits. Both have independent central banks. So the question then becomes whether asymmetric fiscal shocks, associated with deficits and nonmonetary debt issues, could warrant changes in the exchange rate.

Chapter 2 described how changes in fiscal deficits in Japan or the United States have a first-order impact on aggregate national saving and, possibly, on current-account imbalances. Figures 2.8b (for Japan) and 2.9b (for the United States) show that both countries have had substantial shifts, amounting to as much as 3 to 4 percent of GNP, in the size of their structural fiscal deficits. Nevertheless, these shifts don't occur overnight. They typically take some years to develop, and then to be corrected. To take an admittedly extreme example, in the 1995–96 budgetary dispute in the United States, the U.S. Congress wanted to eliminate the U.S. budget deficit—then about 2 percent of GNP—over seven years, while President Clinton wanted to stretch the process out over ten years!

Planned or projected budget changes in Japan seem similarly slow-paced. When the Japanese government lost control of its budget so that its deficit reached about 4 percent of GNP in the late 1970s, almost a decade elapsed before the Japanese government could recover the situation and return to budget balance (figure 2.8b).

When the economy starts at full employment, however, a sudden planned or structural increase in a country's fiscal deficit could warrant an offsetting appreciation of the currency. In the textbook solution, an appreciation could facilitate the generation of a current-account deficit that matches the inflow of foreign capital necessary to cover the fiscal deficit without igniting inflation. Yet, for the Japanese and U.S. economies, the point is largely moot. In practice, structural changes in these governments' fiscal positions are spread out over so many quarters or years that any sudden change in the exchange rate would be inappropriate—and likely futile, as we show more precisely in chapters 6 and 7.

The foregoing analysis does not deny that there could be some sudden and extreme fiscal change in a large, diversified industrial economy that warrants some discrete change in the exchange rate to help balance-of-payments adjustment. A good example was the massive increase in government expenditures in Germany in 1990 and 1991 because of the costs of reunification, with a correspondingly sudden deterioration in the German current account, from a large surplus to a large deficit over one year (see chapter 5). Adjustment could have been made with less inflationary pressure in Germany if the mark had appreciated in an orderly fashion in 1991. Instead, by provoking speculative runs on the currencies of Germany's trading partners, the Bundesbank's tight monetary policy for combating inflation eventually did force an appreciation of the mark in 1992 and 1993. But our main point is that this was a rare event, and anything comparable in the United States or Japan seems very unlikely.

Textbooks aside, monetary cooperation to tether the yen-dollar exchange rate, and to escape from the disruptiveness of unpredictable exchange-rate volatility, would seem to have very little opportunity cost. The balance of payments of either Japan or the United States could still adjust smoothly to plausibly specified macroeconomic disturbances— even if they are asymmetric. Indeed, the 1993–96 deterioration of the public finances in Japan was a direct result of yen overvaluation and trying to combat *endaka fukyo*. Under a more stable exchange-rate regime, the government's net budgetary position would be much less subject to such stressful changes, which threaten to become unsustainable.

5

The Transfer Problem
and Macroeconomic
Fluctuations: *Endaka*
Fukyo, Bubbles, and
Credit Crunches

By the mid-1980s Japan emerged, with saving surpluses, as the biggest lending country in the world; and the United States emerged as the biggest borrower, with negative government saving and low private saving (see chapter 2). In this chapter, we briefly describe the financial mechanisms that brought about this great transfer of capital, beginning with the domestic and international liberalization of Japan's financial markets in the early 1980s. But our main concern is to show how the syndrome of the ever-higher yen generated instability in the transfer mechanism itself and, after 1985, aggravated business cycles in both Japan and the United States.[1]

For Japan, sharp yen appreciations are linked to deflation and business-cycle downturns in 1985–86 and 1993–95, for which the Japanese have coined the term *endaka fukyo* to connote high-yen recessions. Less well known, the asset bubble in Japanese stock and land prices beginning in 1986–87 can also be associated with the syndrome of the ever-higher yen. Low nominal interest rates created an incipient liquidity trap for Japanese monetary policy that could be sprung only by begetting the unsustainable bubble economy. Although the yen remained high after the *endaka fukyo* of 1985–86, wealth effects from the rising asset values stimulated domestic consumption and investment sufficiently to allow the economy to recover in the late 1980s.

The collapse of the bubble in 1990–91 not only depressed the Japanese economy but disrupted the normal flow of long-term finance to the United States. We associate the so-called credit crunch and cyclical downturn of 1991–92 in the American economy with the collapse of the Japanese asset bubble—and with a reduction of capital inflows from Europe due to German reunification. We ascribe the subsequent Clinton-era boom, in 1993–97, in part to the resumption of "normal" Japanese lending to the United States.

The predicament of the Japanese monetary authorities in dealing with the *endaka fukyo* of 1993–95 was more acute. In 1993 and again early in 1995, sharp run-ups of the yen far above purchasing power parity made private investment in Japan very unprofitable—and it slumped over the whole period 1993–95. At the same time, expectations of an ever-rising yen in the future drove nominal interest rates toward zero: a liquidity trap that inhibited the Bank of Japan (BoJ) from restimulating the economy in the face of an overvalued yen. But, unlike the 1986 *endaka*, the 1995 situation was complicated by the impairment of the capital positions of major Japanese lending institutions such as banks by the previous fall in stock market and real estate values, and because the BoJ itself was worried about too-loose monetary policy restarting a bubble.

Finally, we return to the transfer problem. Because of macroeconomic instability over the past 10 years, inhibitions on the normal outflow of long-term capital from Japan have reinforced the syndrome of the ever-higher yen. The liquidity trap in Japanese financial markets, and severe post-bubble capital constraints on Japanese banks and other financial institutions, have inhibited private capital outflows. This has uncovered Japan's naturally large current-account surplus, and so helped drive the yen higher still from 1992 to early 1995—until its engineered fall after mid-1995 (described in chapter 11).

5.1 Financing the Transfer: The Opening of the Japanese Capital Market

Before 1981, Japan's current-account surpluses were generally small and not persistent. Indeed, current-account deficits were interspersed with surpluses. This could reflect the fact that long-term Japanese capital markets were not open to foreigners throughout the 1960s and 1970s, and indeed were hardly liberalized for domestic transacting. In any event, adjustments in short-term trade credits—largely denominated in dollars—and in official exchange reserves were more or less sufficient to finance the small swings in the current account.

The Japanese authorities "were concerned that extensive foreign holdings of their currency would reduce their degree of control over the money supply, and would increase the variability of their exchange rate" (Frankel 1984, pp. 33–34). The authorities were also concerned that substantial swings in international capital flows could interfere with domestic stabilization. According to Tavlas and Ozeki (1992, p. 10), before 1981

The Japanese financial system was tightly regulated via controls on the quantity and distribution of credit and on interest rates, which were generally kept below market clearing levels. In particular the financial system was rigidly segmented and designed to enhance personal savings so that the investment needs of private industry and the rebuilding of public infrastructure could be met (financed) at low interest rates. In addition, controls on capital flows insulated the financial market from foreign influences. The guiding principle underlying foreign influences was to forbid virtually all capital transactions, except by prior approval. (P. 10)

However, maintaining such insular and tightly regulated domestic financial markets was inconsistent with Japan's emergence as a major international creditor in the 1980s, let alone with its becoming the dominant international creditor in the early 1990s. Tavlas and Ozeki nicely summarize the major liberalizing measures that eventually opened Japan's capital markets to the rest of the world. These measures facilitated private finance for her subsequent large current-account surpluses.

For freeing domestic financial markets, the first significant measure was to authorize the resale of government bonds by syndicated banks, thereby creating a secondary market for the rapidly accumulating government debt in the late 1970s. (Before that time, the banks had been captive buyers.) Both primary and secondary bond markets then expanded rapidly, and yields on primary issues rose toward those on secondary markets. Similarly, at short term, the Gensaki market (based on repurchase agreements for government bonds) expanded rapidly—along with the free determination of interest rates on large-denomination certificates of deposit. Not until the late 1980s, however, could nonfinancial firms issue commercial bills, and the government itself issue Treasury bills, to compete directly with bank deposits.

The Foreign Exchange and Trade Control Law of 1980 established that international capital flows should be free unless specifically restricted —although explicit prior approval requirements remained on yen-denominated bonds issued by nonresidents, issues of Euro-yen bonds and certificates of deposit, and interest paid on nonresidents' yen-denominated deposits. But these restrictions were gradually relaxed for various classes of bond issuers throughout the 1980s. In fact, the regulations were sufficiently loosened to allow the development in 1986 of the Tokyo Offshore Market. Banks could accept deposits from nonresident institutions (not individuals) without meeting the reserve requirements and other restrictions applicable to deposits received from Japanese residents in the domestic market. Courtesy of Tavlas and Ozeki, table 5.1 shows the remarkable growth in the Tokyo Offshore Market from 1986 to 1990,

Table 5.1
Development of the Tokyo offshore market, 1986–90 (in billions of U.S. dollars)

Item	1986	1987	1988	1989	1990
Positions vis-à-vis nonresidents	88.7 (100.0)	191.9 (100.0)	331.0 (100.0)	429.0 (100.0)	495.0 (100.0)
Yen	19.2 (21.6)	69.0 (36.0)	131.0 (39.6)	183.0 (42.7)	215.0 (43.4)
Foreign currencies	69.5 (78.4)	122.9 (64.0)	200.0 (60.4)	246.0 (57.3)	280.0 (56.6)
Positions vis-à-vis residents	5.0 (100.0)	46.9 (100.0)	97.0 (100.0)	— (100.0)	— —
Foreign currencies	5.0 —	15.6 (33.3)	41.0 (42.3)	67.0 —	92.0 —
Total foreign currencies	— —	138.5 (58.0)	241.0 (56.3)	313.0 —	372.0 —

Source: Tavlas and Ozeki 1992, p. 20.

which was just one facet of Japan's growing financial interaction with the outside world.

By the mid-1980s, then, the private financial markets in Japan were effectively open—if not fully free of official intervention—for arbitrage with the outside world. Even as early as 1981, the evidence suggests that the covered interest differential between short-term interest rates in yen in the Japanese financial markets and those in the dollar-based world markets had largely disappeared. What were the consequences of this opening for (1) the overall behavior of interest rates—nominal and real— in Japan and the United States, and (2) the quantitative nature of the capital flows themselves?

Interest-Rate Behavior in Japan and the United States

Figures 5.1 and 5.2 show the behavior of nominal long- and short-term interest rates in the United States and Japan, respectively. After the great inflationary turmoil of the 1970s through 1982, short rates in Japan tended to track long rates relatively closely. In the United States, on the other hand, long rates generally remained significantly above short rates—as if there were a significant liquidity premium in the term structure of interest rates. This gap between federal funds and ten-year bond rates was particularly marked in 1991–92, about 2 or 3 percentage points, at the time of the credit crunch and cyclical downturn in the American economy—to which we shall return.

Figure 1.5 (chapter 1) compares long-term nominal bond yields of Japan and the United States. In the mid-1970s and earlier, long-term interest rates were generally higher in Japan than in the United States—although figure 1.5 understates the difference because long-term rates in Japan were somewhat repressed by official policy. Until 1967, no series on Japanese long rates is even available. However, in the 1950s and 1960s, various short-term rates in the Japanese money markets that were fairly free— including prime and actual lending rates of banks—were typically 2 to 3 percentage points higher than their American counterparts (Horiuchi 1984) as shown in figure 5.3. By the early 1980s, however, expectations of the ever-higher yen took hold, and Japanese nominal bond rates became substantially lower—often 4 percentage points less than their American counterparts. (The one brief exception was the crisis in late 1990, with the deliberate attempt by the Bank of Japan to use tight monetary policy to burst the asset bubble.)

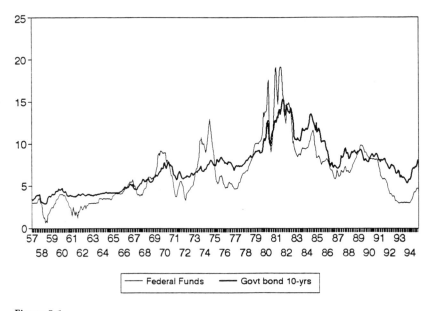

Figure 5.1
U.S. interest rates, percent. *Source:* IMF, *International Financial Statistics*, CD-ROM, March 1995.

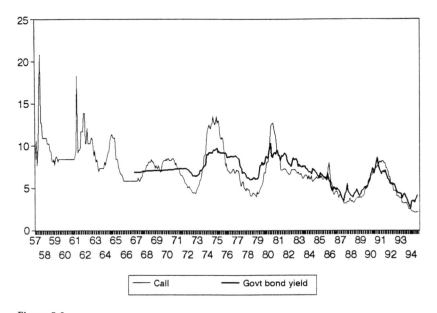

Figure 5.2
Japanese interest rates, percent. *Source:* IMF, *International Financial Statistics*, CD-ROM, March 1995.

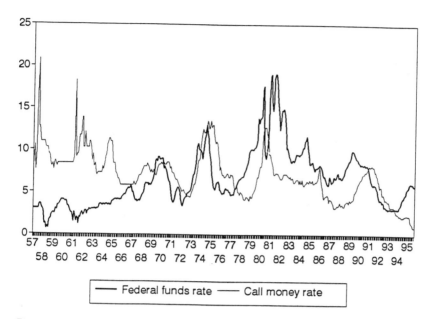

Figure 5.3
Short-term interest rates, percent Japan and U.S. *Source:* IMF, *International Financial Statistics,*
CD-Rom, March 1995.

Although the syndrome of the ever-higher yen has driven down nominal interest rates in Japan, the rate of wholesale price inflation in Japan has
also been much less than in the United States. (Figure 1.4 shows the
remarkable divergence of Japanese and American price levels after 1971.)
Thus, real interest rates in Japan have not necessarily been lower. Of
course, precise expectations of yen appreciation, or of future deflation in
Japan and inflation in the United States, are unknown. But if we choose
the wholesale price index (WPI) to measure the Fisher effect from domestic price-level movements, and then deflate nominal long-term interest
rates by a five-year moving average of past wholesale price inflation, figure 5.4 shows a remarkably good alignment of real returns on long-term
yen and dollar bonds since the late 1970s. Because the Japanese WPI fell
relative to the American, there was no persistent tendency for real returns
in dollars on dollar bonds to differ from those in yen on yen bonds. (The
variability of real yields in both countries has been high, but the origins of
this interest-rate volatility are taken up in chapter 8.)

Although figure 5.4 shows the domestic real cost of bond finance[2]
within each country, it says very little about the yen returns to Japanese

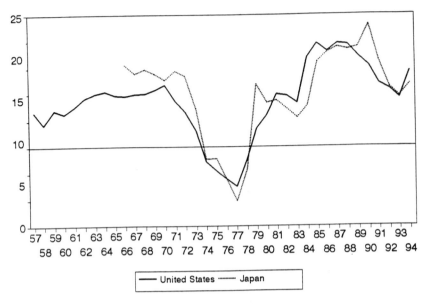

Figure 5.4
Real long-term interest rates, deflated by five-year moving average WPI. *Source:* IMF, *International Financial Statistics*, CD-ROM, March 1995.

investors investing in dollar securities. Over substantial periods of time, exchange-rate movements need not line up exactly with movements in relative wholesale prices. Although the yen-dollar exchange rate is the forcing variable for relative deflation in Japan (see chapter 4, and a more rigorous proof in chapter 9), trends in price movements adjust slowly to sharp movements in exchange rates, as in the past decade. From early 1985, at 260 to the dollar, the yen began to rise unexpectedly rapidly until April 1995, when it touched 80 to the dollar. The average annual rate of appreciation was about 11 percent, whereas the nominal interest rate on dollar bonds exceeded that on yen bonds by only about 4 percentage points per year. Relative to holding yen securities, any Japanese investor who bought a ten-year dollar bond in early 1985 and held it to maturity took a beating. (But, of course, if he rolled over his position until the yen began to fall sharply after mid-1995, he might have recouped some of his losses.)

The rather dramatic risks involved in investing across currencies when exchange rates fluctuate are illustrated more comprehensively by figure 5.5.[3] The upper panel shows the cumulative gains in yen of buying in January 1985 a ten-year U.S. Treasury bond, with the then-rich coupon

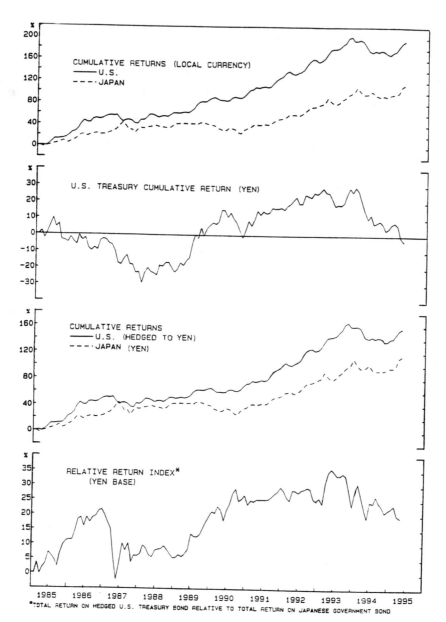

Figure 5.5

Relative performance of U.S. and Japanese government bonds. *Source:* The BCA "Interest Rate Forecast," May 1995, vol. 17, no. 5, p. 26.

yield of 11 percent, unhedged through various holding periods that cul-
minate in the bond's maturity in January 1995. The cumulative gains from
changes in market interest rates and exchange rates vary greatly. Figure
5.5 shows that they became strongly negative as of 1987 (if the bond
was sold then), to weakly positive in 1992, to zero at the closeout in
January 1995. Even starting with a remarkably high coupon rate on the
dollar bond, the investor would have been much better off holding yen
securities.

The third panel in figure 5.5 shows the cumulative yield on dollar
bonds that are (imperfectly) hedged with rolling one-year currency for-
wards for the ten-year bonds. These hedged bonds do better—in part
because they capture some of the gains from the rising yen, but also
because they benefit from a narrowing of the forward discount on the
dollar as the very high U.S. nominal interest rates (at the beginning of
1985) come down a bit relative to those on yen bonds. Without this latter
effect, holding yen bonds may still have been preferred.

In conclusion, even if real returns on bonds denominated in each
currency—with nominal interest rates deflated by domestic price (WPI)
inflation—are similar, Japanese investors holding dollar-denominated securities face enormous risks. Other, anecdotal evidence also suggests that
Japanese financial and nonfinancial corporations have been badly burned
on their overseas investments in the past decade—although they would
have done rather well before the yen's most precipitous ten-year increase
began, in 1985.

Japan as a Dollar-Based International Creditor

The risks facing Japan as the world's largest international creditor are
inherently greater than those faced by the United States in the 1950s and
1960s or by Britain during the thirty years before 1914, when each ran
large current-account surpluses that dominated international lending. Both
the United States, under the dollar standard, and Britain, under the international gold standard, lent in terms of their domestic currencies. (Because
Britain was fully committed to the gold standard, domestic lenders could
treat gold-denominated bonds as equivalent to sterling bonds.) Thus domestic lenders—institutions or individuals—avoided any direct exchange
risk. Because the system of fixed exchange rates was fairly secure (until
the end of each regime), the United States and Britain also largely avoided
indirect exchange risk, whereby an unanticipated devaluation in a debtor
country undermines the ability of borrowers in that country to repay.

Japan is in the historically unusual situation of being a dominant creditor country whose currency is still surprisingly little used to denominate either current-account or capital-account transactions, as nicely summarized in Tavlas and Ozeki (1992). As of 1990, less than 40 percent of Japan's exports and less than 15 percent of its imports were invoiced in yen. On capital account, the use of the yen seems even less robust given Japan's huge net creditor status, perhaps because of protracted delays in liberalizing the domestic financial system. From their comprehensive study ending about 1990, these authors conclude that

Japan's emergence as both an important international financial intermediary and as the world's largest net creditor nation has not been accompanied by Japan's emergence as a world banker. Japanese banks and nonbank financial institutions have lent overseas in securities denominated in currencies other than yen because of high yields available overseas and the relaxation of restrictions on capital flows. Owing to such factors as prudential regulations, the banks have hedged (long-term) foreign lending with (short-term) foreign currency borrowing. Consequently, Japan's international financial intermediation has not, to any substantial extent, ... facilitated the use of the yen as an international currency. (P. 41)

On the other side of the coin, the United States has largely maintained its role as international banker, despite slipping from being a net creditor to being a net debtor. Thus the dollar is still widely used in invoicing trade in primary commodities and in those industrial goods either exported from or imported into the United States or the "dollar area" of North and South America (McKinnon 1979). Having U.S. trade in "sticky-price" industrial goods invoiced in dollars when so much of it is with Japan implies that the American price level is not so immediately sensitive to fluctuations in the yen-dollar exchange rate as is the Japanese. (In chapter 3, we noted the extraordinary and diffuse responsiveness of internal Japanese prices to the great yen appreciation of 1985–86.)

On capital account, Japan's lending to the rest of the world is denominated largely in dollars—almost exclusively so for lending to the United States, which still provides the most important vehicle currency for spot and forward foreign-exchange markets. Only Japanese lending to developing countries on concessional terms is denominated in yen. Thus, Japanese lenders have direct exposure to foreign-exchange risk for most of their hard lending. But they may also face indirect currency risk on soft lending. The sharp run-up of the yen from early 1993 to early 1995 induced China and Indonesia, which have significant borrowings in yen, to appeal for relief on their yen debts.

Table 5.2
Summary of Japan's capital account (in billions of U.S. dollars)

	1980	1981	1982	1983	1984	1985	1986	1987	1988	1989	1990	1991	1992	1993	1994
Current-account balance	-10.7	4.8	6.8	20.8	35.0	49.2	85.8	87.0	79.6	57.2	35.8	72.9	117.6	131.4	129.1
Net long-term capital	2.3	-9.7	-15.0	-17.7	-49.7	-64.5	-131.5	-136.5	-130.9	-89.2	-43.6	-37.1	-28.5	-78.3	-82.0
By type of capital															
Net direct investment	-2.1	-4.7	-4.1	-3.2	-6.0	-5.8	-14.3	-18.4	-34.7	-45.1	-46.3	-29.4	-14.5	-13.6	-17.0
Net securities	9.4	4.4	2.1	-1.9	-23.6	-43.0	-101.4	-93.8	-66.7	-28.0	-5.0	41.0	-26.2	-62.7	-48.9
Bonds	—	—	-1.0	-10.1	-23.3	-49.0	-95.1	-66.2	-107.4	-91.7	-12.0	-47.0	-43.8	-30.1	-83.9
Equities and other	—	—	3.2	8.3	-0.3	5.9	-6.3	-27.6	40.8	63.6	6.9	87.9	17.6	-32.6	34.9
Net loans	-2.8	-5.3	-8.1	-8.5	-12.0	-10.5	-9.3	-16.3	-15.3	-4.7	16.9	25.0	8.3	-3.8	-17.4
Other	-2.1	-4.1	-4.9	-4.2	-8.1	-5.2	-6.5	-8.0	-14.3	11.3	-9.2	0.4	3.9	1.9	1.3
By asset or liability															
Assets	-10.8	-22.8	-27.4	-32.5	-56.8	-81.8	-132.1	-132.8	-149.9	-192.1	-120.8	-121.4	-58.0	-73.6	-110.2
Direct investment	-2.4	-4.9	-4.5	-3.6	-6.0	-6.5	-14.5	-19.5	-34.2	-44.1	-48.0	-30.7	-17.2	-13.7	17.9
Securities	-3.8	-8.8	-9.7	-16.0	-30.8	-59.8	-102.0	-87.8	-86.9	-113.2	-39.7	-74.3	-34.4	-51.7	-83.6
Bonds	—	—	-6.1	-12.5	-26.8	-53.5	-93.0	-72.9	-85.8	-94.1	-29.0	-68.2	-35.6	-29.9	-64.1
Equities and other	—	—	-3.7	-3.5	-4.0	-6.3	-9.0	-14.9	-1.1	-19.1	-10.7	-6.1	1.3	-21.8	-5.4
Loans	-2.6	-5.1	-7.9	-8.4	-11.9	-10.4	-9.3	-16.2	-15.2	-22.5	-22.2	-13.1	-7.6	-8.2	-14.1
Other	-2.1	-4.1	-5.2	-4.4	-8.1	-5.2	-6.4	-9.4	-13.5	-12.3	-10.9	-3.3	1.2	-0.1	-7.7
Liabilities	13.1	13.1	12.4	14.8	7.1	17.3	0.6	-3.7	19.0	102.9	77.2	158.5	29.5	-4.7	-0.9
Direct investment	0.3	0.2	0.4	0.4	—	0.6	0.2	1.2	-0.5	-1.1	1.8	1.4	2.7	0.1	28.2
Securities	13.1	13.2	11.9	14.1	7.2	16.7	0.5	-6.1	20.3	85.1	34.7	115.3	8.2	-11.1	0.9
Bonds	—	—	5.0	2.4	3.5	4.5	-2.1	6.7	-21.6	2.4	17.0	21.2	-8.2	-0.2	0.5
Equities and other	—	—	6.8	11.8	3.7	12.2	2.7	-12.8	41.9	82.7	17.7	94.0	16.4	-10.9	49.0
Loans	-0.2	-0.2	-0.2	—	-0.1	-0.1	—	-0.1	-0.1	17.8	39.1	38.1	15.9	4.3	-9.6
Others	—	0.1	0.3	0.2	—	—	-0.1	1.3	-0.8	1.0	1.7	3.7	2.7	1.9	2.3

Errors and omissions	-3.1	0.5	4.7	2.1	3.7	4.0	2.5	-3.9	2.8	-22.0	20.9	-7.8	-10.5	-0.3	-17.8
Basic balance[a]	-11.5	-4.4	-3.4	5.2	-10.9	-11.4	-43.2	-53.4	-48.5	-54.1	-28.7	102.1	78.6	52.9	29.3
Short-term capital	-1.9	-1.3	-6.6	-3.5	13.3	9.9	56.9	95.7	64.0	29.4	7.8	-119.2	-80.0	-29.4	-32.6
Bank	-5.0	-3.6	-5.0	-3.6	17.6	10.8	58.5	71.8	44.5	8.6	-13.6	-93.5	-73.0	-15.0	-22.7
Nonbank	3.1	2.3	-1.6	0.0	-4.3	-0.9	-1.6	23.9	19.5	20.8	21.5	-25.8	-7.0	-14.4	-8.9
Overall balance	-13.4	-5.7	-10.0	1.6	2.4	-1.5	13.7	42.3	15.5	-24.7	-20.9	-17.1	-1.4	23.5	-2.3
Increase in reserves	4.9	3.2	-5.1	1.2	1.8	0.2	15.7	39.2	16.2	-12.8	-7.8	-8.1	-0.3	26.9	27.3
Other[b]	-18.3	-8.9	-4.9	0.4	0.5	-1.7	-2.0	3.0	-0.7	-11.9	-13.0	-9.0	-1.1	-3.5	-29.5

Source: Baumgartner and Meredith 1995.
a. Including errors and omissions.
b. Including yen-denominated holdings of foreign monetary authorities (with sign reversed).

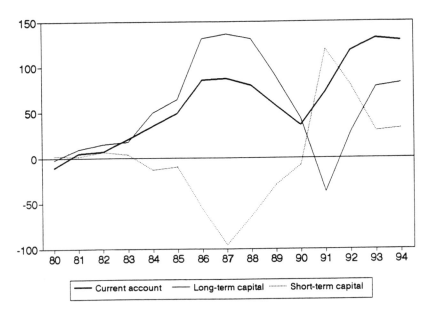

Figure 5.6
Current-account and capital outflows in billions of U.S. dollars. *Source:* Bank of Japan.

With this currency composition and associated risk in mind, consider the ebb and flow of long- and short-term capital to and from Japan in the 1980s and 1990s. Courtesy of the International Monetary Fund (Baumgartner and Meredith 1995, p. 16), table 5.2 gives a detailed accounting breakdown of Japanese capital flows financing the current-account surplus, which is shown in the top row. Strikingly, from 1981 to 1990, the cumulative outflow of *long-term* capital more than matched Japan's large current-account surpluses. The resulting deficit in the basic balance was covered by large inflows of short-term capital—mainly a buildup of foreign (dollar) deposits in Japanese banks—which accumulated particularly rapidly during the bubble period from 1986 to 1989. Figure 5.6 also shows this inverse relationship between short- and long-term capital flows.

It was this willingness to borrow short in order to lend long (in excess of the current-account surplus) that prompted Tavlas and Ozeki (1992) to liken the Japanese financial system in 1990 to a giant "international financial intermediary" (p. 21) in the mode of the United States in the 1950s and 1960s and of Britain before 1914, albeit one that denominated its assets and liabilities in foreign monies rather than its own. But on the downside of the bubble, from 1991 through 1994 this model fell apart. Japan stopped behaving as an international financial intermediary. Indeed, in 1991 it actually *repatriated* long-term capital so as to create a huge surplus in its basic balance, which remained positive into 1995. The slack was taken up by net short-term lending abroad, which reached a massive $119 billion in 1991; and, although long-term capital outflows recovered somewhat from 1992 to 1994, short-term capital outflows have continued to be an important financing mechanism for the current-account surplus. Much of this outflow of short-term capital in the early 1990s took the form of running off the Euro-dollar deposits that the Japanese banks had acquired in the bubble years of the late 1980s. In effect, there was disintermediation.

In conclusion, not only have the Japanese taken huge losses on their largely unhedged net holdings of foreign assets over the past ten years, but the mechanism for financing Japan's current-account surplus is distressingly volatile. If foreigners are not eager to borrow at long term in yen securities, nor willing to hold deposits in Japanese banks in yen because of their usefulness as money in the world economy at large, the model of Japan as an international financial intermediary is not robust.

Could Japan realistically opt to become a world banker in order to mitigate this exchange risk? When price levels are fairly stable in the other industrial economies, as in the late 1980s and early 1990s, the syndrome of the ever-higher yen, coupled with domestic deflation, militated against Japan's becoming a (or the) world banker such that it could lend and borrow with yen-denominated assets and liabilities. Apart from lingering problems with the overregulation of particular financial instruments, the yen appreciated too erratically and was too volatile to be attractive as international money. Nor would the precipitous fall in the yen, more than 35 percent from mid-1995 to late-1996, enhance its attractiveness— however useful the fall has been in promoting recovery from *endaka fukyo II* (see chapter 11).

Because of this volatility, the world-banker route for absolving Japan's lending institutions from exchange risk seems out of the question in the near future. However, if the yen is properly stabilized in the foreign-exchange markets (as we discuss in chapters 10 and 11), Japan's becoming more of a world banker in the more distant future is a distinct possibility.

We now analyze how domestic macroeconomic instability in both countries impinged on, and was influenced by, the syndrome of the ever-higher yen and these vagaries of the transfer mechanism.

5.2 *Endaka Fukyo*, Liquidity Traps for Interest Rates, and (Potential) Asset Bubbles in Japan

How was the task of macroeconomic management in Japan complicated by the syndrome of the ever-higher yen? Chapter 3 covered two facets of the syndrome: the scrambling of relative prices, and the depression in domestic investment when the yen rose discretely above its purchasing power parity. Indeed, figure 3.6c shows the yen rising sharply—that is, the yen-dollar rate falling—above PPP from 1986 through 1989, and then rising above PPP from 1991 through 1995.

Endaka fukyo I, when the yen rose from 260 to the dollar at the beginning of 1985 to about 150 to the dollar throughout 1987, caused a sharp fall in output growth for just one year. In fiscal year 1986 (April 1986 through March 1987), the growth in national output was almost halved. From the previous trend rate of 5 percent per year, GNP growth declined to 2.7 percent in fiscal 1986 before recovering to 5 percent or so in fiscal years 1987–89. This sharp recovery was driven exclusively by a remarkable increase in domestic demand: "The contribution of domestic demand to the real growth rate in fiscal 1987 was 6.7 percent; that of external demand was minus 1.4 percent" (Suzuki 1989, p. 63). That the Japanese economy could recover so rapidly from the blow of a sudden appreciation of more than 40 percent surprised almost all observers: "The Japanese economy confounded the majority of forecasters and conquered the high yen recession ... unexpectedly and quickly" (Suzuki 1989, p. 66).

But *endaka fukyo II* was a different story. As illustrated in chapter 3, at 145 to the dollar, the yen was close to PPP at the end of 1990. It then rose slightly above PPP to average about 125 to the dollar over 1991 and 1992. Then the roof fell in. By the end of 1993 it had risen to 112 to the dollar, by the end of 1994 to 99, and by the end of June 1995, a dollar would buy only 85 yen. The cumulative appreciation was again more than 40 percent. From 1992 through early 1995, real GNP growth was less than 1 percent per year, with negative growth in several quarters.

Not only does a sharp increase in the value of any country's currency above purchasing power parity make production for export less attractive, but both national and multinational corporations see that country as a high-cost place in which to invest. Even if expectations of the future exchange rate are static—that is, without the syndrome of the ever-higher yen—one expects some slump in private investment (McKinnon 1980; also see chapter 6) as companies decide to invest overseas where costs are lower. In the high-dollar era of 1981–84, American firms rushed to invest

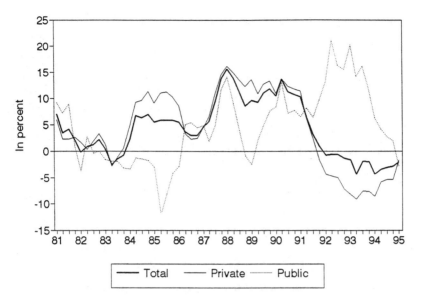

Figure 5.7
Japan: investment in fixed capital, change over four quarters. *Source:* Economic Planning Agency.

overseas, and investment slumped at home. In the late 1980s to the present, this hollowing-out process affected high-cost Japan, as Japanese firms invested throughout Asia, but also in North America, rather than at home.

Figure 5.7 shows that, in *endaka fukyo I,* growth in the huge flow of private investment in Japan fell from about 10 percent per year to just 3 percent in calendar year 1986 before quickly recovering to very high levels. But in *endaka fukyo II,* growth in private investment became sharply negative from 1992 through 1995. Even highly expansionary public investment was insufficient to prevent total investment from falling—which was an important reason for the sustained recession.

As suggested in chapter 3, the economy's different responses to the two high-yen episodes was conditioned by whether or not there was a bubble in asset values. Figure 5.8 shows that stock and land values began to increase rather sharply in 1986, and then began to fall even more sharply in 1990–91. Land prices continued to fall through 1995. The initial wealth effects—increasing both consumption and investment (more on this below)—allowed the Japanese economy to escape with only a mild growth slowdown in 1986. That is, the bubble in asset values was the mechanism by which the Japanese economy escaped from a more serious economic downturn in fiscal 1986 and afterward. But, of course,

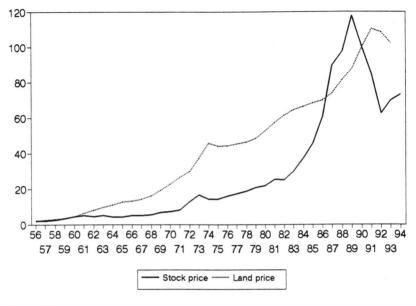

Figure 5.8
Asset prices: Japan, 1990 = 100. *Note:* The stock price index is annual average. The land price index is end-March. *Sources:* IMF, *International Financial Statistics*, CD-ROM, March 1995 (stock price) and Japan Real Estate Institute (land price).

this is hardly a satisfactory countercyclical policy. The inevitable collapse in asset values aggravated *endaka fukyo II* in 1992–95.

The Virtual Liquidity Trap

How might the syndrome of the ever-higher yen create a Keynesian-like liquidity trap on the one hand, while making an asset bubble more likely on the other?

The tendency for nominal interest rates to become very low (within a percentage point or two of zero) while real interest rates remain substantial and investment is depressed is what we mean by a "liquidity trap." For Japan, it is related to the syndrome of the ever-higher yen in two important respects. First the periodic tendency for the yen to increase sharply above purchasing power parity—as in 1986–87 and again in 1993–95—depresses investment and the demand for bank credit. Second is the expectation that the yen is likely to be yet higher in the distant future. There is no regressivity in exchange-rate expectations. Even if the yen has just risen sharply, it is expected to continue appreciating at its longer-term average—say, 4 percent per year. Because expectations of future increases in the yen are inelastic with respect to current changes in the yen-dollar exchange rate, international investors continue to demand a higher nominal yield on dollar bonds relative to yen bonds to offset expected dollar depreciation (chapter 1). The upshot is that in the 1980s and 1990s nominal interest rates on yen assets averaged about 4 percentage points less than their American counterparts (figures 1.5 and 5.3).

As long as American nominal interest rates remained high—say 9 percent or more—and the yen was not greatly overvalued in the near term as in the decade before 1985, the Bank of Japan had room to maneuver. By targeting growth in M2 plus CDs at some modest level, or through countercyclical movements in its discount rate, the BoJ kept the economy on a fairly even keel by influencing real interest rates in the short term (although, in the longer term, Japan's wholesale price index still drifted downward relative to that in the United States).

However, when American nominal interest rates fall to 7 percent or less, and when the yen is sharply appreciated above PPP, the BoJ *may not* be able to get domestic real interest rates low enough to prevent a serious downturn in the economy. Although normally about 4 percentage points, this interest differential between yen and dollar assets is squeezed when nominal yields on yen assets become bounded from below by zero. By mid-1995 (May), Japanese interest rates had been fallen to remarkably low levels. Table 5.3 shows that the discount rate was 1 percent, overnight call money 1.26 percent, prime loan rate 3.6 percent, three-month Gensaki 1.4 percent, and the 10-year government bond rate was 2.73 percent. Table 5.3 also shows that American interest rates were 4 to 5 percentage points higher at all terms to maturity as of mid-1995, although they had been both lower and higher in the previous two years.

Because of the depressed demand for bank credit during an *endaka fukyo* (without an asset bubble) *and* because of the expectations of an ever-higher yen, this liquidity trap may be more virtual than actual. In the textbook model of a Keynesian liquidity trap,[4] the image is one of the central bank vigorously expanding the domestic money supply through bond purchases, thus driving interest rates down to the horizontal segment of the demand-for-money (liquidity preference) function. We would then expect to see monetary aggregates growing vigorously as people built up their cash balances by disgorging bonds to the central bank at an unchanging low rate of interest. However, within our syndrome of the

Table 5.3
Japan: indicators of monetary conditions

	1991	1992	1993	1994	1993	1994				1995	1995				
					IV	I	II	III	IV	I	Jan.	Feb.	Mar.	Apr.	May
Money and credit aggregates															
Reserve money: ¥ trillion	47.2	45.4	48.1	49.4	48.1	43.3	44.5	43.3	49.4	45.7	44.4	44.3	45.7	—	—
% change over last year	−1.4	−2.8	5.9	2.8	5.9	4.6	4.9	6.0	2.8	5.6	3.8	2.1	5.6	—	—
M1: ¥ trillion	117.1	122.4	126.0	132.8	127.8	130.0	132.2	134.4	134.8	136.5	136.6	136.8	136.2	139.0	—
% change over last year	5.2	4.5	3.0	5.4	3.5	4.7	5.2	6.2	5.5	5.0	5.5	4.9	4.5	5.9	—
M2 + CD: ¥ trillion	500.7	503.6	509.0	519.4	510.7	533.1	518.9	521.4	524.6	531.1	528.9	532.0	532.5	534.6	—
% change over last year	3.6	0.6	1.11	2.1	1.6	1.7	1.8	2.1	2.7	3.5	3.2	3.7	3.6	3.1	—
M3: ¥ trillion[a]	838.1	866.2	900.0	936.3	885.4	896.7	903.7	913.8	921.8	933.9	927.4	928.5	933.2	—	—
% change over last year	5.3	3.4	3.0	4.0	3.9	3.6	3.3	3.6	4.0	4.2	4.4	4.4	4.2	—	—
Domestic credit: ¥ trillion[a]	626.0	644.3	649.3	646.8	649.3	637.1	636.3	636.1	646.8	639.3	639.1	638.5	639.3	—	—
% change over last year	2.9	2.9	0.8	−0.4	0.8	−0.9	0.2	−0.2	−0.4	0.4	0.5	0.6	0.4	—	—
Bank lending: ¥ trillion	460.5	471.8	477.6	478.3	477.6	474.8	466.8	472.3	478.3	475.9	472.6	472.9	475.9	472.5	—
% change over last year	4.4	2.5	1.2	0.1	1.2	0.5	0.3	0.3	0.3	0.2	0.3	0.3	0.2	0.6	—
Interest rates															
Overnight call money rate	7.4	4.56	2.99	2.13	2.42	2.20	2.05	2.37	2.20	2.15	2.19	2.15	2.12	1.47	1.26
Long-term prime lending rate	7.50	5.96	4.86	4.43	4.03	3.80	4.40	4.60	4.90	4.80	4.90	4.90	4.63	3.93	3.60
Average short-term loan rate	7.81	5.80	4.49	3.55	4.03	3.71	3.58	3.54	3.39	3.47	3.49	3.48	3.46	3.34	—
3-month Gensaki rate	7.01	4.12	2.66	1.89	1.99	1.77	1.85	1.90	2.04	1.94	2.05	2.05	1.74	1.39	—
10-year government bond rate	6.29	5.08	3.97	4.24	3.30	3.68	4.03	4.59	4.65	4.21	4.69	4.35	3.60	3.40	2.73

U.S. federal funds rate	5.70	3.52	3.02	4.20	2.90	3.21	3.94	4.49	5.17	5.81	5.53	5.92	5.98	6.05	—
U.S. prime rate	8.46	6.25	6.00	7.14	6.00	6.02	6.90	7.50	8.13	8.83	8.50	9.00	9.00	9.00	—
U.S. long-term goverment bond yield	7.86	7.01	5.82	7.11	5.61	6.07	7.08	7.33	7.95	7.48	7.78	7.47	7.20	7.05	—
Exchange rates															
Yen per dollar	134.7	126.7	111.2	102.2	108.3	107.0	103.3	99.1	98.8	96.3	99.7	98.2	90.8	83.7	85.1
Yen per deutschemark	81.4	81.2	67.3	63.0	64.3	62.4	62.2	63.4	64.1	65.0	65.1	65.4	64.5	60.6	60.5
Index of monetary conditions[b]	99.6	77.7	87.5	89.9	86.0	84.1	90.6	89.0	966.1	99.9	98.2	99.5	101.9	105.5	—

a. End-of-period data.
b. A weighted sum of the real short-term interest rate and the real effective exchange rate (1985 = 300); a rise indicates tighter monetary conditions.

ever-higher yen and moderately low interest rates in the United States, it is quite possible for Japanese nominal interest rates to approach zero with little or no unusual monetary expansion by the BoJ: a *virtual* liquidity trap.

The *endaka fukyo* of 1993–95 seems more like a virtual liquidity trap than the textbook Keynesian one. Table 5.3 also shows Japanese money growth rates from 1991 through mid-1995. In the slumping Japanese economy from 1993 to 1995, narrow monetary aggregates (reserve money and M1) show normal growth of 4 to 5 percent, whereas the broader monetary aggregate M2 plus CDs grew more slowly at the rate of 1 to 3 percent—probably reflecting low demand for bank credit in the depressed economy. (Growth in real money is somewhat higher because of the falling price level, with the WPI decreasing by about 2 percent per year.) This is hardly the robust money growth that one would associate with an actual—or, more accurately, a textbook—liquidity trap.

Whether virtual or actual, however, a trap is a trap. Suppose the BoJ tries to become more expansionary by, say, a domestic open-market operation in which it offers to buy domestic bonds in return for base money. In the absence of an asset bubble, the BoJ can't drive domestic nominal interest rates down enough to make a significant difference to private investment decisions.

A more subtle question is whether the BoJ could enter the foreign-exchange market and drive the yen down toward PPP by massive direct dollar purchases in order to stimulate exports and domestic investment. If unsterilized, this dollar intervention certainly would increase the monetary base in yen. If the economy is not in a liquidity trap, it could also drive down Japanese short-term interest rates and thus promote private capital outflows that weaken the yen in the foreign exchanges. However, if expectations of the ever-higher yen are firmly held, and Japanese interest rates can't be pushed lower, then unilateral intervention by the BoJ could fail. Indeed, from mid-1994 to mid-1995, Japanese official exchange reserves rose by 50 percent, to more than $150 billion, as the yen continued to increase. Unable to drive down either interest rates or the exchange rate, the BoJ on its own was unable to restimulate the economy.

(However, if there is a remission in the syndrome because American policy toward Japan changes, then the economy can recover. Chapter 11 discusses in detail how the relaxation of American mercantile pressure in mid-1995 permitted yen depreciation and at least partial recovery of the Japanese economy in 1996.)

The Bubble Escape Hatch

Another odd aspect of the literature on Keynesian liquidity traps is the absence of any mention of bubbles in longer-term asset values, and the associated wealth effects. Keynes (1936) couched his argument in term of British consols. When long-term interest rates became unusually low, he specified that people would become nervous about interest rates increasing in the future and the capital losses they might suffer if they bought consols today. The "speculative demand" for money would become enormous at very low interest rates as people sought to unload consols and hold ready cash. If, to stimulate investment, the monetary authority tried to push the interest rate down further by buying consols, it would fail as people dishoarded consols at a virtually unchanged (low) rate of interest.

But, depending on expected future earnings streams, asset values for equities and land can become very high if interest rates plunge toward zero. The standard asset valuation formula for determining the current price of an asset is

$$P = DIV/(i - g + \sigma), \tag{5.1}$$

where DIV is current dividends on common stock (or the coupon rate on a consol, or the rental rate on real property net of taxes and other costs), g is the expected rate of growth in dividends, i is nominal return on a "risk-free" asset, and σ is the risk premium. In effect, the capitalization rate, r, for the future flow of dividends is the sum of the risk-free interest rate and the risk premium. So we could rewrite equation 5.1 as

$$P = DIV/(r - g). \tag{5.2}$$

To make economic sense out of this method of describing asset-price valuations, we always assume that r exceeds g. In situations where r falls relative to g (in the limit, $r - g$ could approach 0), large increases in asset values would occur, and vice versa.

Note that a pure or neutral Fisher effect associated with an upward revision in the anticipated rate of yen appreciation from, say, 2 percent to 4 percent over the long run, and a corresponding greater expected fall in the WPI from 2 percent to 4 percent, need have no sustained effect on asset valuations. Both i and g would fall by 2 percentage points, and, assuming no change in the risk premium, P would be unchanged. The fall in expected growth in nominal dividends just matches the fall in the nominal interest rate.

So, to start an asset bubble—as Japan began to experience in the 1980s —r must fall relative to g. Authors have used many institutional explanations, including both tax issues and restrictions on land use (Kähkönen 1995; Taniguchi 1993), to explain why the great increase in land and stock market values perpetuated itself before the crash in 1990–91. However, no argument on how the bubble got started seems convincing. Indeed, there is no consensus on how to date the starting point of the bubble. Figure 5.8 shows that stock prices had already begun to increase sharply as early as 1983–84.

Here we lean toward the more general explanation that the risk premium, σ, in the Japanese capital market fell substantially from 1980 to 1985 because of the widespread liberalizations in domestic financial markets, the (gradual) dismantling of controls on capital account in the foreign exchanges, and the apparent success of the Japanese in keeping their price level stable from the late 1970s through 1985, in comparison to the more volatile price-level experience in the United States. In the 1960s, the risk premium in Japan was relatively high, and even the semicontrolled interest rates were higher than in the United States (figures 1.5 and 5.3) in the presence of a fixed yen-dollar exchange rate. By the 1980s, however, international investors became more confident about taking positions in yen assets without being constrained by arbitrary official regulations. And this increasing confidence in the Japanese financial system was bolstered by the widely touted industrial "miracle" based on Japanese manufacturing companies' making huge, successful investments on the frontiers of modern technology—which promised to increase dividend growth in the future.

But a substantial fall in σ (see equation 5.1) need not constitute a "bubble." A onetime upward valuation of existing assets from 1982 to 1985 would have been warranted by the new information pointing to a lower risk premium. In the *endaka fukyo* of 1986–87, however, authorities in the Ministry of Finance and the BoJ had to confront the problem of stimulating the Japanese economy. Facing a dramatically overvalued yen and a growth slowdown, they had already cut interest rates to very low levels by the historical standards up to that point (figure 5.2)—with the official discount rate down (to 2.5 percent in February 1987; its lowest level ever), and with the money supply growing rapidly. Yet, the remarkable fall of 10 percent in the domestic wholesale price index in 1986 alone (chapter 3) suggested that real interest rates remained quite high. The authorities felt that further easy money itself would not do the trick, and the government had just managed to reconsolidate the fiscal budget after the major deficits of the late 1970s and early 1980s (see chapter 2), so that the Ministry of Finance did not want a Keynesian-style fiscal expansion.

The perpetuation of the ongoing rise in asset values—particularly in land and real estate—seemed like a way out. As one anonymous high-ranking BoJ official stated in early 1988, "We intended first to boost both the stock and property markets. Supported by this safety net—rising markets—export-oriented industries were supposed to reshape themselves so they could adapt to a domestic-led economy. This step was supposed to bring about enormous growth of assets over every economic sector. The wealth effect would in turn touch off personal consumption and residential investment, followed by an increase in plant and equipment. In the end, loosened monetary policy would boost real economic growth" (quoted in Taniguchi 1993).

Taniguchi goes on to show how financial deregulation in the early 1980s squeezed the profit position of the banks by increasing interbank competition and by making it easier for the large blue-chip industrial corporations to finance themselves. The banks then turned to financing smaller enterprises and real-estate ventures—encouraged by enormous tax incentives to organize speculative deals with property companies. Bank loans secured by inflated property were used largely for the purchase of other land or stocks. The rise in the stock market further eased the capital constraints on bank lending at home and abroad because, in Japan, banks are major owners of common stock, whose market value can, in part, be treated as "own" capital. Throughout this great rise in asset values into 1989, the Ministry of Finance acted as a cheerleader—even taking steps to halt normal downward corrections in the upward spiral of stock prices—by calling on financial institutions to buy collectively when a downturn threatened. The Tokyo Nikkei stock market index reached its zenith of 39,000 yen in December 1989, then fell to a six-year low of 16,000 yen by June 1992, and has seesawed above and below that level since then. Land prices began falling in 1992 (figure 5.8) and were still coming down into 1996.

Although the asset bubble did provide an escape hatch from *endaka fukyo I*, the inevitable crash has had very unfortunate consequences for Japan in the 1990s. The proximate cause was very tight money policy by the BoJ in late 1989 to early 1990 (see the upward spike in interest rates at that time, shown in figure 5.2). And of course, in 1993–95, the bubble escape hatch was not available for overcoming *endaka fukyo II*. Memories of the earlier debacle are still so fresh, and the capital position of the Japanese banking system and many other financial institutions is so severely impaired, that another bubble would be difficult to generate even if the authorities wanted it. But, alarmed by the possibility of restarting a bubble, the BoJ may have been tighter than it should have been at some stages in *endaka fukyo II*—as the modest rate of Japanese monetary aggregates from 1991–95 (table 5.3) attests. So the change in American mercantile policy, permitting yen depreciation from April 1995 through 1996, was the only effective escape hatch from *endaka fukyo II*.

Not all the negative effects of the collapse of the asset bubble in 1991–92 were confined to Japan. Because of its status as the world's dominant creditor country, serious echo effects impacted the world's largest borrower, as we shall see.

5.3   The U.S. Credit Crunch of 1991

In chapter 2, we established that the United States had, since the early 1980s, become highly dependent on foreign saving to maintain a normal level of gross investment at about 16 percent of GNP. When the U.S. current-account deficit narrowed sharply in 1990–92 (figure 5.9) but the fiscal deficit stayed high, a domestic credit crunch ensued with a slump in

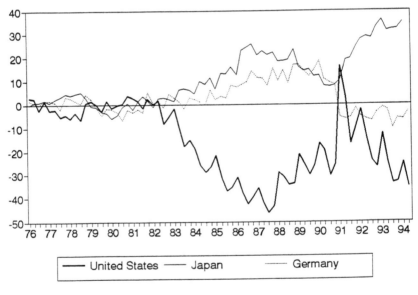

Figure 5.9
Quarterly current accounts, in billions of dollars. *Source:* IMF, *International Financial Statistics,* CD-ROM, December 1994.

U.S. investment, which bottomed out at 12.7 percent of GNP in 1991 (table 2.2, chapter 2). The resulting fall in real U.S. GDP in 1991 (figure 5.10) was sufficient to unelect a surprised President Bush! But what was cause and what was effect? Did investment and output fall first, reducing imports, the current-account deficit, and capital inflows—or did the reverse occur?

We claim that this credit crunch of 1990–92 was caused by a sharp slowdown in net capital inflows into the United States. But this is not the conventional wisdom. The usual explanation is that overzealous regulators placed excessive restraint on lending by American commercial banks. Because of the newly signed Basle Accord raising bank capital requirements, and because the American bank regulators themselves had been burned by the failure of so many commercial banks and savings institutions in the 1980s, it was commonly alleged that bank regulation became overly restrictive in the early 1990s. That explanation was sufficiently potent politically to cause the Bush administration to lean heavily on bank inspectors to ease up on their prudential regulations governing loan quality.

But this domestic regulatory explanation seems out of keeping with the sharpness and magnitude of the 1991 downturn, and it conflicts with the

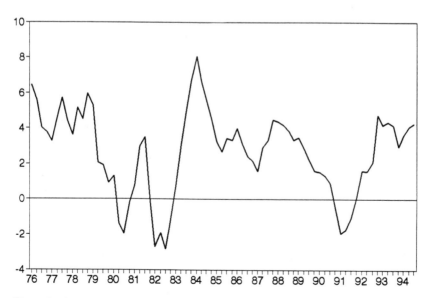

Figure 5.10
U.S. Real GDP, percent change over four quarters. *Source:* IMF, *International Financial Statistics*, CD-ROM, March 1995.

strange behavior of the term structure of interest rates. Suppose that the domestic regulatory "disturbance" had indeed predominated. Then the sudden preference of American banks for longer-term securities—requiring less bank capital (zero in the case of government bonds) under the Basle Accord—over normal shorter-term commercial lending with high capital requirements, should have driven long-term interest rates *down* relative to short rates. But figure 5.1 shows that just the opposite happened: U.S. short rates fell relative to long rates. Indeed, more detailed analysis of the term structure of U.S. interest rates in the 1991–92 period shows that long-term Treasury bonds were about 3 percentage points higher than three-month Treasury bills—an unusual spread in the yield curve.

We identify the initial cause of the downturn in 1991 to be sudden external restraint on the U.S. economy's access to foreign capital. In making this identification, we cite two factors exogenous to the American economy that suddenly reduced capital inflows.

First, the fiscal costs of reunification changed Germany almost over-night from being a big net international lender up to 1990 to being a net borrower in 1991. Figure 5.9 shows the remarkably sharp fall in Germany's current-account surplus from about $50 billion per year before 1991 to a *deficit* of about $20 billion in 1991 and subsequently. This sudden shock to the international financial mechanism contributed to America's short-term credit crunch in 1991.

Second, as discussed earlier in this chapter, the bursting of the Japanese bubble economy in 1990–91 and into 1992 suddenly reduced long-term capital outflows[5] from Japan, including those to the United States. The crash in the Japanese stock and property markets so impaired the capital positions of important Japanese financial institutions—banks, insurance companies, trust funds, and so on—that they shifted out of long-term international lending. As shown in figure 5.6, long-term capital was actually repatriated to Japan in 1991, before a very modest recovery in 1992. Consequently, foreign financial capability for buying Japanese goods was reduced so as to narrow Japan's current-account surplus in those two years, as also shown in figure 5.9.

To complete our picture of international disintermediation in the external balance sheet of the Japanese financial system, about $117 billion of short-term capital flowed out of Japan in 1991 (figure 5.2)—largely by Japanese banks' running off much of their eurodollar liabilities—as the counterpart of the inflow of long-term capital coupled with a current-account surplus. Not only was the total amount of foreign capital available to the American economy suddenly reduced because of the Japanese financial crash, but the form of finance shifted dramatically from long-term to short-term.

Nevertheless, the undiminished U.S. fiscal deficit—resulting in bond issues of about $270 billion per year in 1991—somehow had to be financed. In 1991, the U.S. yield curve began to steepen sharply. Long-term interest rates rose from a level about 1 percentage point higher than short rates at the beginning of the year to a level more than 3 percentage points higher at the end (figure 5.1). In the absence of foreign buying of U.S. Treasury bonds and other long-term securities, the bond-market yield curve had to steepen sufficiently to make bonds attractive to American domestic financial institutions and individuals.

By mid-1991, normal lending by commercial banks began to fall sharply despite the Fed's easy-money policy that reduced average U.S. interest rates. Instead of meeting the working capital needs of American business, commercial banks bought Treasury bonds and other securities (figure 5.11) in order to play the yield curve to increase their profitability. In addition, domestic banking disintermediation occurred within the United

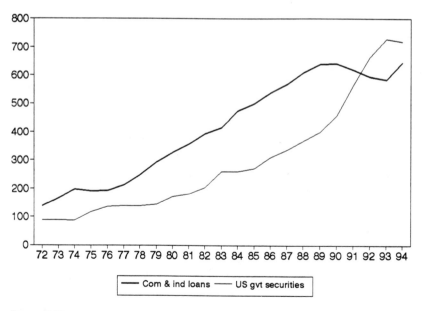

Figure 5.11
Credits of U.S. commercial banks, in billions of dollars. *Source:* Board of Governors of the Federal Reserve System.

States: people who normally held short-term bank deposits (M2) switched to longer-term, higher-yield bonds. The resulting sharp fall in normal bank lending for commercial and industrial loans in 1991 created what was then called "the credit crunch."[6] It induced the American cyclical downturn in 1991, and led to sluggish growth in 1992.

The subsequent Clinton boom in 1993–96 was in part associated with a mild resurgence in Japanese long-term lending (table 5.2) as its current-account surplus widened. Correspondingly, after narrowing in 1991, the American current-account deficit widened once more (figure 5.9). This renewed ability to borrow from the rest of the world—mainly, but not exclusively, from Japan—fueled the U.S. economic recovery from the credit crunch. By 1994, domestic gross investment in the United States had recovered to 15.3 percent of GNP (table 2.3) and had returned to a "normal" 16 percent of GNP in 1995 and 1996.

A fuller statistical analysis of the 1991 credit crunch is beyond the scope of this book. Here, we simply note the very different character of the 1981–83 cyclical downturn in the United States (figure 5.10) compared to the one in 1990–92. The former was "homegrown" by the need to disinflate from the inflationary excesses of the 1970s, whereas the latter was imposed from without by a sudden, dramatic change in the amount and term to maturity of foreign finance available to the American economy. Future disruptions in the availability of foreign capital to the American economy could work themselves out somewhat differently. However, the 1991 credit crunch illustrates how dependent the American economy has become on foreign capital.

5.4   Concluding Notes on the Transfer Problem

Exchange-rate stability, particularly in the long-run sense of investors' not expecting one currency to appreciate continually and unpredictably, would seem to be a necessary condition for reducing intermediate-term cyclical fluctuations in both Japan and the United States. In chapter 8 we make the related argument that the unusually high volatility in long-term interest rates in the world arises naturally out of a regime of untethered exchange rates wherein rates of inflation in national price levels can diverge in the long run.

But reducing exchange risk is also particularly important for an international lender, a natural surplus saver—that is lending net in foreign monies rather than its own. Its financial institutions become vulnerable to direct losses on foreign-exchange-denominated assets—as well as indirectly through macroeconomic turbulence that is foreign-exchange related. Once these lending institutions become seriously capital-impaired, as Japanese banks now are, their reluctance to lend further to finance the natural saving surplus of the country in question will create more turmoil in the foreign exchanges. In the case of Japan, private reluctance to lend on capital account to cover the trade surplus aggravated the syndrome of the ever-higher yen until its (temporary?) remission in mid-1995.

6

The Exchange Rate and the Trade Balance in Theory: Insular versus Open Economies

It is not very difficult to convince most people that exchange fluctuations since 1973 have had disruptive effects on prices, resource allocation, and business cycles in major industrial countries. But many people remain reluctant to endorse the stability of nominal exchange rates as a policy goal. What holds them back is the notion that, despite the known demerits of exchange flexibility, it still serves the useful purpose of adjusting trade flows.[1] Devaluation is considered to be an effective tool for reducing a trade deficit. Some believe that devaluation alone is sufficiently potent to correct the trade imbalance, while others want to combine it with fiscal, monetary, or structural measures. In either case, to give up an extra degree of policy freedom by deliberately fixing nominal exchange rates is deemed unwise. Why tie our hands when we need as many policy instruments as possible?

Those who think this way are correct only if what they have in mind are industrial countries in the 1930s to the early 1950s. In those days, industrial economies were sufficiently insular in the sense that international trade was small relative to the domestic economy, and cross-border capital flows were not very mobile. But their argument is less valid today, when industrial countries are more open to foreign goods, services, and especially capital. As interdependence grows, changes in nominal exchange rates begin to affect domestic economies through multiple channels, and the presumption that devaluation improves the trade balance becomes tenuous. (This is not to deny that soft-currency inflationary economies must devalue continually.)

True, devaluation immediately makes domestic products cheaper than foreign products. This *relative price effect* certainly works to improve the trade balance as long as the Marshall-Lerner elasticities condition holds. (We assume throughout this book that that condition is satisfied.) But in a highly open industrial economy, several other effects may partially or completely offset the favorable relative price effect.

The first is the reverse absorption effect: devaluation tends to stimulate part of domestic spending—particularly investment by tradable industries—and worsens the trade balance. Conversely, appreciation dampens domestic investment, causes recession, and perpetuates a trade surplus; this is the phenomenon known as *endaka fukyo* in Japan (see chapter 3). As Kawai (1994) shows, when the adverse effect of exchange movement on macroeconomic activity is present, the impact of real devaluation on the trade balance cannot be theoretically ascertained. In their empirical work, Miyagawa and Tokui (1994) estimate that a 1 percent real effective appreciation of the yen reduces domestic investment by the amount equivalent to 0.7–0.9 percent of total capital stock—although a reduction of imported material prices partially offsets it.

Second, there is the pass-through effect. If the home currency is kept substantially undervalued (overvalued) in view of the law of one price, imported inflation (deflation) will arise through commodity arbitrage, which dilutes and eventually eliminates the initial international price gap. In the long run, the price advantage of domestic industries will disappear, and the *real* exchange rate will be unaffected by manipulation of the *nominal* exchange rate.

Third, inflation will also result from expansionary domestic monetary policy. To engineer and sustain devaluation over many years, it is necessary to maintain an expansionary monetary policy relative to major trading partners. With such policy bias, sooner or later absorption will be stimulated, and domestic prices will edge up—and consequently the trade deficit will increase.

Fourth, the J-curve effect is known to increase the trade gap at least temporarily, until the quantities of exports and imports have had time to respond to the change in the relative price. The adverse effect lasts still longer if the country starts with the position of a substantial trade gap. In the very long run, Kawai (1994) suggests that the trade balance would return to the original level so that the curve is an elongated S rather than a J.

Fifth, a continued overvaluation of the yen prompts an exodus of Japanese manufacturing bases to China and Southeast Asia (i.e., the hollowing-out phenomenon). The immediate impact is to increase Japanese exports of capital and intermediate goods in order to build and operate new factories in these countries. Over time, the country origins of "Japanese" brand products will shift from Japan to the rest of Asia, a shift that will probably have only a minor impact on the global trade balance of the United States.

In this chapter, we present a pair of macroeconomic models highlighting insularity and openness, respectively, that capture the first three of these adverse effects. If the relative price effect of devaluation no longer dominates because of these other effects, the overall effect of devaluation on the trade balance becomes uncertain. Another way to put this is that, under free private lending and borrowing, a low-saving country lacking financial discipline can easily avail itself of foreign saving by running trade deficits whatever the exchange-rate regime. And devaluation alone is not likely to alter significantly the national propensities to overspend and to dissave.[2]

Our models will be simple. Physical and financial accumulations are ignored, and we will make simplifying assumptions about floating exchange rates under capital mobility. Furthermore, we will accept the one-good economy assumption of Krugman (1989b), and we will not rely on the multiplicity of goods as the reason for the ambiguity of devaluation impact.[3] Even so, these models are capable of showing when devaluing the currency in order to improve the trade balance is futile.

6.1   Two Views of the "Right" Exchange Rate

The insular notion that devaluation will surely improve a country's trade balance survives even today, when international penetration of goods and capital is greater than ever. The major blame for the continuation of no-longer-effective devaluation policy must fall not on high officials, bureaucrats, or journalists but mainly on the economics profession, which supplies models and theories. Economists' ideas simply have not caught up with reality, which has changed dramatically since the 1950s and 1960s.

Even if national monetary authorities are at times willing to stabilize exchange rates through policy coordination, economists cannot agree on target exchange rates in the first place. Diversity of opinion over what constitutes correct exchange rates at any point is a major—if not the only—reason why the cooperative spirit of G7 is always short-lived.[4] The disagreement over correct rates does not stem from mere differences on technical points. It is rooted in two distinct doctrines of what the exchange rate is expected to accomplish—purchasing power parity (PPP) or trade flow adjustment (TFA).

According to the PPP criterion, official exchange-rate targets should be set to align national price levels so that the real purchasing power of money, say one dollar, is roughly the same in terms of internationally tradable goods in each country. Monetary policies should be coordinated so that this common price level is stable and so that significant inflation or deflation is not imposed on any one of the trading partners. The PPP criterion looks at the exchange rate simply as an extension of domestic monetary policy to achieve a more uniform standard of value for international investment and resource allocation. The primary duty of the central bank is to stabilize the domestic *and* external purchasing power of the home currency by avoiding exchange instability and domestic inflation and deflation.

On the other hand, the TFA criterion regards the exchange rate as one of the commercial policy instruments. It argues that the exchange rate should be set to roughly balance the flows of imports and exports of any one country over a business cycle, allowing for the need to make interest payments and their debt-service requirements, and for relatively small net capital flows. Trade flows are assumed to be dominated by relative prices at home and abroad as determined by the exchange rate. Because demand and supply conditions in international commodity markets change frequently, the TFA criterion has it that continuous exchange flexibility—whether through free float or variable target zones—is necessary for external equilibrium. As long as a country has a large trade deficit, exchange rates should be adjusted to give that country a price advantage. Thus, according to this view, violation of the law of one price is not a problem but part of a cure—and the exchange rate is a potent policy instrument that can systematically affect international trade flows.

The difference between these two criteria is fundamental. During the last decade, with the persistent American trade deficit and Japanese trade surplus, the "correct" yen-dollar exchange rate according to the TFA criterion has always been much lower than that prescribed by the PPP criterion. Often, the actual dollar is judged grossly overvalued by the former and seriously undervalued by the latter. For instance, in late 1994, Bergsten estimated the correct dollar rate to be about 100 yen, whereas our and other PPP estimates using tradable baskets indicated it to be around 130–140.

What is needed is an analytical framework for clarifying *when* exchange-rate changes could serve as a useful control mechanism for the balance of payments. Let us confine the analysis to hard-currency countries: those that need not rely on ongoing price inflation as a fiscal necessity. We develop two alternative models.

The first model is that of an *insular* economy, where the TFA approach is valid. In such an economy, controlled manipulation of the exchange rate can influence the trade balance in a predictable way, that is, a devaluation can improve the trade balance. In the course of trying to talk the dollar down, many (if not most) economists, such as Bergsten (1994), Cline (1995), Dornbusch (1987b), Feldstein (1987a, 1987b), and Summers (1987) had some such insular model in mind as they pursued the TFA approach.

The second model is that of an *open* economy, where exchange-rate changes are endogenous and have no predictable effect on the trade balance. In such open economies, however, major exchange-rate changes still impair the efficiency of price signals in goods and labor markets (chapters 3 and 4)—sometimes with unfortunate consequences for macroeconomic stability (chapter 5). Then the PPP approach to exchange-rate determination is preferred.

Let us develop the algebra of each model in turn.

6.2   The Insular Economy

Major industrial countries in the 1930s into the 1950s were open in only a limited sense. The private international capital market was virtually moribund, and restrictions on commodity trade proliferated. Let us call this particular stage of international economic integration the "insular" economy (McKinnon 1981). Today, a large number of less developed countries exhibit similar insularity.[5]

In an insular economy, foreign trade is only a fringe activity, and exchange-rate changes do not have a significant direct impact on the overall domestic price level—although they do affect exports and imports. Financial transactions with the rest of the world are tightly regulated, and residents are effectively barred from acquiring or issuing assets in foreign currencies for purely financial reasons (i.e., reasons not related to trade, tourism, or direct investment). Consequently, the rate of interest is domestically determined, independently of the cost of capital in other countries.

Many macroeconomic models of both Keynesian and monetarist types are, even today, built with the implicit assumption of insularity in the sense just described. Modifying a model used by Marston (1985), let us present a simple analytical framework to illustrate how, in an insular economy, the exchange rate does indeed affect trade in a predictable fashion: devaluation improves the net trade balance.

Consider the following set of equations:

$Y = A + B$ Domestic output   (6.1)

$A = C(\underset{+}{Y}) + I(\underset{-}{i - \dot{p}}) + G$ Domestic absorption   (6.2)

$B = B(\underset{-}{A}, \underset{+}{e - p})$ Trade balance   (6.3)

$m - p = L(\underset{+}{Y}, \underset{-}{i}, \underset{-}{\dot{p}})$ Money market   (6.4)

$\dot{p} = \alpha(Y - \bar{Y}), \quad (\alpha > 0)$ Price equation   (6.5)

$p = \bar{p}$ Alternative price equation   (6.5′)

Exogenous variables:

G   Government expenditures

e   Exchange rate (domestic currency/foreign currency)

$\bar{Y}$ Full-employment output

m   Nominal stock of money

Endogenous variables:

Y   Real GDP

i   Domestic nominal interest rate

A   Domestic absorption

p   Domestic price level

$\dot{p}$ Actual (and expected) rate of price increase

B   Net trade balance

Note that, except for the interest rate i, lowercase letters denote the log of these variables. A rise in e signifies depreciation of the home currency.

The real exchange rate, $e - p$, is defined on the simplifying assumption that the foreign price level is fixed ($e + p^* - p$ where $p^* = 0$). Thus, $e - p$ is also the reciprocal of the economy's international terms of trade between exports and imports. In the pegged exchange-rate regime considered first, e is exogenously set by the monetary authority through sterilized intervention, which is feasible because our economy is financially insulated, with no private capital flows from the outside world.

Alternative equations determining the domestic price level suitable for an insular economy are offered. Equation 6.5 suggests that the rate of price increase depends on deviations from sustainable full-employment output Y. In the older Keynesian tradition, equation 6.5′ takes domestic prices to be fixed. Neither specification allows for any direct impact of the exchange rate on the overall level of domestic prices. In addition to price insularity, our economy is also insular in that the domestic interest rate is determined independently of those prevailing abroad, and in that absorption (especially investment) is not influenced directly by $e - p$.

However, the trade balance is influenced by the real exchange rate. Let us suppose that the Marshall-Lerner elasticities conditions are satisfied such that

$$\frac{\partial B}{\partial (e - p)} > 0, \tag{6.6}$$

that is, when absorption is constant. After a devaluation—an increase in e—equation 6.6 says that exports expand and imports contract so that the trade balance improves before any repercussions on domestic income and absorption are taken into account.

However, any such devaluation will eventually increase domestic output and then the price level, which will increase imports, but not to the extent of reversing the initial favorable effect. In final long-run equilibrium when $\dot{p}$ is again 0, from equations 6.1 through 6.5 we see that

$$\frac{dY}{de} = 0, \qquad \frac{di}{de} > 0, \qquad \frac{dB}{de} > 0. \tag{6.7}$$

This improvement in the trade balance implies that A has fallen relative to Y. The increased price level reduces the real stock of money, raises i, and thus crowds out domestic investment even though Y remains unchanged in long-run equilibrium under equation 6.5. Hence, in an insular economy, devaluation improves the trade balance after all macroeconomic repercussions work themselves out.

The upper panel of table 6.1 gives all the repercussions for a change in the exchange-rate peg for both the "short" and "long" runs.[6] The short-run solutions are instantaneous changes at time t_0, with predetermined p but with expected inflation possibly different from 0, while the long-run solutions are new steady-state solutions reached after $\dot{p} = 0$. (In this model we ignore physical and financial asset accumulations through I and B.)

Alternatively, if the domestic price level in our insular economy remains constant as per equation 6.5', income will increase with the devaluation, that is, $dY/de > 0$. This is likely to happen in a recession, when resources are underutilized. Because the domestic propensity to spend out of income is less than unity (otherwise the model becomes unstable) and investment

Table 6.1
Insular economy with a pegged but adjustable exchange rate: $e = \bar{e}$ (solutions to equations 6.1, 6.2, 6.3, 6.4, and 6.5)

Exogenous	m	G	e	m	G	e
Endogenous		Short-run			Long-run	
$\dot{p}$	+	+	+	0	0	0
p	0	0	0	+	+	+
Y	+	+	+	0	0	0
A	+	+	?	+	+	−
B	−	−	+	−	−	+
i	−	+	+	−	+	+

With a passively floating exchange rate: $B = 0$ (solutions to equations 6.1, 6.2, 6.3′, 6.4, and 6.5)

Exogenous	m	G	m	G
Endogenous		Short-run		Long-run
$\dot{p}$	+	+	0	0
p	0	0	+	+
$Y = A$	+	+	0	0
e	+	+	+	+
i	−	+	0	+

is again crowded out as i increases, absorption will still fall relative to income so that $dB/de > 0$ in response to a controlled rise in e.

What about the case where the exchange rate floats rather than being pegged by the government? Because there are no free capital flows, e must vary so as to balance imports and exports. Exporters and importers are the only participants in the foreign-exchange market because under a pure float the central bank stays out. And, in an insular economy, private capital flows are minimal. Such pure floating can be represented by allowing e to be endogenous such that exports equal imports:

$$B(\underset{-}{A}, \underset{+}{e} - p) = 0. \tag{6.3′}$$

This presumption that the net trade balance could be kept close to 0 by a variable exchange rate underlies the earlier advocacy of floating (Friedman 1953; Meade 1955). This earlier literature projected that *current* trade flows, aided by stabilizing speculators who need take only transitory positions in foreign exchange, would dominate exchange-rate determination. A floating exchange rate satisfying equation 6.3′ has the additional advantage that, given the absence of international capital mobility, domestic income and price level are determined independently of any disturbances in the market for internationally tradable goods—as represented by the B function satisfying the Marshall-Lerner condition. In an insular economy with a floating exchange rate, macroeconomic equilibrium is determined as if the economy were closed.[7]

Algebraically, one can see this immediately: when $B = 0$, one gets $Y = A$, and equations 6.1 and 6.2 reduce to $Y = C + I + G$, a standard domestic IS curve from which e is absent. Similarly, e is absent from the LM curve (equation 6.4) and from the price equation (6.5). Thus, the IS and LM curves and the domestic price equation determine Y, p, and i independently of any foreign disturbance (see the lower panel of table 6.1).

However, the trade flow adjustment (TFA) criterion is not innocuous. In the context of an insular economy, TFA implies that the "right" exchange rate must change continually in response to international and domestic disturbances. For example, a fall in the price of crude oil would benefit the Japanese trade balance much more than it would the American. This would prompt some analysts to lower their estimates of the desired yen-dollar exchange rate (whereas, under the PPP criterion, the exchange rate should be invariant to uniform worldwide changes in the price of oil or any other commodity).

In the early 1980s, the huge U.S. budget deficit raised interest rates and attracted capital from abroad, causing exchange appreciation and a correspondingly large American trade deficit. Of course, this capital inflow violated the strict assumptions of our model of the insular economy. For many (Feldstein 1986a; Branson 1985), this exchange appreciation was seen as necessary to generate the trade deficit (apart from its desirability). Only then, such observers believed, could foreign saving be transferred in real terms to help finance the U.S. fiscal deficit—another illustration of the supposed advantages of exchange flexibility.

Conversely, when the U.S. trade deficit became so large in the late 1980s, many economists, including Bergsten (1986), wanted the dollar devalued in order to improve the net trade balance, even though, realistically, the fiscal deficit remained as large as ever—or larger. Is it plausible that an engineered dollar devaluation, such as occurred in 1985–86 and 1992–93, would itself substantially diminish or eliminate the U.S. trade deficit? Only if the American economy was otherwise insular.

To see this important point, let us perform a simple thought experiment. Take equations 6.1, 6.2, 6.3', 6.4, and 6.5' (prices are fixed) describing an insular economy with a floating exchange rate such that $B = 0$.

Then shock the system by raising G (debt-financed government expenditures). Solving the system, we get, in equilibrium (in this case the short run and the long run are identical):

$$\frac{dY}{dG} > 0, \qquad \frac{di}{dG} > 0, \qquad \frac{de}{dG} > 0. \tag{6.8}$$

A depreciated currency and balanced trade are indeed consistent with debt-financed government expenditures in an insular economy. Instead of attracting capital from abroad, the rise in G stimulates domestic absorption and income, leading to an incipient trade deficit that depreciates the domestic currency: e rises and trade remains balanced.

True, the domestic interest rate rises—possibly very sharply—to crowd out domestic investment and thus make financial room for the increased G. Nevertheless, if one accepts this crowding-out of investment as an inevitable consequence of reducing the trade deficit, currency depreciation does have a predictable effect of preventing any substantial trade deficit from developing.

To people who are very worried about the current U.S. trade deficit and the protectionist pressure it generates, exchange depreciation seems like a plausible way of reducing the trade imbalance even if the American fiscal problem is not resolved. But people who argue this way clearly have something like our insular economy in mind—if only implicitly. If, instead, the American economy is truly open, the U.S. trade deficit will not necessarily improve because of devaluation per se, as we shall see.

6.3   The Open Economy

In a so-called open economy, international trade has substantial impacts on domestic economic activity, and capital movement is virtually free across countries. This description, better than that of insularity, suits the reality of major industrial countries of the 1990s.

Financial openness introduces two important changes in macroeconomic modeling. First, expected rates of return on comparable assets in different currency denominations tend to converge, and thus the rate of interest is determined internationally.[8] Second, because of free international lending and borrowing, a nation need not equate its income with its expenditure period by period. That is, $Y \neq A$ and $B \neq 0$ *even under free float*.[9] As long as a structural saving gap (say, due to a fiscal deficit and low private saving) exists, the exchange rate itself need not adjust in any significant way to eliminate the trade imbalance. In an open economy, there is no predictable or exploitable relationship between the exchange rate and the aggregate savings-investment balance.

To bring this important analytical point into sharp relief, the following set of five equations present a fairly extreme, but not empirically unreasonable, model of an open economy.

$$Y = A + B \qquad \text{Domestic output} \qquad (6.9)$$

$$A = C(\underset{+}{Y}) + I(\underset{-}{i} - \dot{p}, \underset{+}{e} - p) + G \qquad \text{Domestic absorption} \qquad (6.10)$$

$$B = B(\underset{-}{A}, \underset{+}{e} - p) \qquad \text{Trade balance} \qquad (6.11)$$

$$m - p = L(\underset{+}{Y}, \underset{-}{i}, \underset{-}{\dot{p}}) \qquad \text{Money market} \qquad (6.12)$$

$$\dot{p} = \beta(e - p), \quad (\beta > 0) \qquad \text{Price expectations} \qquad (6.13)$$

The endogenous variables are Y, A, B, p (or $\dot{p}$), and m. The exogenous variables are e, i, and G.

Consider first the financial side of the model if e floats. In keeping with the now widely accepted asset approach to exchange-rate determination (Frenkel and Mussa 1980, 1985), we assume that the exchange rate is a forward-looking variable—and even a "forcing" one. In open economies, international investors choose between domestic and foreign-exchange assets today on the basis of how they think the exchange rate is going to move in the future.

Furthermore, consider only those countries that exhibit no extreme price inflation—such as Germany, Japan, and the United States. Then the available empirical evidence indicates that exchange rates behave almost like random walks: they are unpredictable (out of sample) on the basis of any past information about relative money growth rates, interest rates, trade deficits, and so on; see Meese and Rogoff (1983) for the classical discussion on this point. More recent empirical studies have detected only small deviations from the random walk hypothesis, if any; see Takagi (1991) for a survey.

Under this hypothesis, today's spot exchange rate is the best guess of tomorrow's, so that

$$e_{t+1} = e_t + u_{t+1}, \qquad (6.14)$$

where $E_t(e_{t+1}) = e_t$. In an efficient market, the floating exchange rate moves only in response to new information, as represented by u_{t+1}. In equation 6.14, news occurs between time t and time $t + 1$. Thus, we treat the exchange rate, e, as an *exogenous* or leading variable in our model of the open economy.

To be sure, this convenient assumption of stationary expectations (i.e., people do not expect any long-term drift in the nominal exchange rate) is at odds with the syndrome of the ever-higher yen highlighted in the rest of the book. However, the inconsistency is more apparent than real. We ignore the long-term drift here because it simplifies the algebra without affecting reactions to short- and medium-term exchange-rate fluctuations, which are our concern in this chapter. Nothing significant would change in these results if the fact that the yen was expected to appreciate at, say, 3 percent per year in the long run was formally built into our algebra. Then the adverse long-term effects discussed in other chapters (unstable capital flows, virtual liquidity trap in Japan, unanchored long-term interest rates, etc.) could be superimposed on these short- and medium-term effects of exchange-rate fluctuations.

To further simplify, we focus exclusively on the arrival of news about what future price inflation and commensurate money growth will be in the domestic economy. (Monetary conditions in the rest of the world are taken as given.) If depreciation—a rise in e—is to be analyzed within the context of the asset approach, the model should incorporate explicit assumptions about a change in future expectations that the increase in e represents.

For an increase in e to be sustained, people might, for example, expect that the authority will (gradually) increase the money supply relative to its demand, and that price inflation will continue until purchasing power parity is restored—as described by equation 6.13—at the newly depreciated exchange rate.[10] This increase in e could arise from a conscious, but unexpected, international agreement such as the Plaza Agreement of September 1985. Alternatively, the election of a new populist government committed to monetary expansion may cause the exchange rate to jump. Other plausible expectational shifts to explain a jump in e are not explored in this chapter.

In interpreting equation 6.13, the key point is that the exchange rate leads (or causes in a Granger sense) domestic prices—unlike in our previous model of the insular economy. This is partly because of the pass-through effect of imported goods, but mainly—and more importantly—because the foreign-exchange market anticipates or even *forces* an expansionary domestic monetary policy. As Kawai (1994) notes, the possibility of self-fulfilling expectations is real: "An expectation of a future expansion of money supply will depreciate the exchange rate, and the depreciation will lead to domestic inflation. To this, the monetary authority may well respond by accommodation policy whereby the required money supply is actually supplied. If expectations about the future force the hand of policy makers, policy becomes indeterminate and the economy will be left without an anchor" (p. 124n). In that case, the inflationary impact of a rise in e raises the overall domestic price level, and not just that of tradables.

The second characteristic of our open economy is that

$$i = i^*. \tag{6.15}$$

Financial arbitrage is such that the domestic nominal rate of interest equals the foreign rate even when the exchange rate is floating. This again is carrying openness to an extreme, but it is consistent with the random walk hypothesis embodied in equation 6.14; today's exchange rate is the best guess of the future, so that expected exchange-rate movements need not appear in equation 6.15. One could include a variable risk premium in equation 6.15, but at this level of abstraction, we are going to ignore it.

Third, note that, in equation 6.10, domestic absorption is also impacted directly by the real exchange rate in an open economy (McKinnon 1981) in contrast to an insular one. That is,

$$\frac{\partial I}{\partial (e - p)} > 0. \tag{6.16}$$

Real depreciation—albeit temporary—in an integrated world makes the domestic economy look like a cheap place in which to invest, and so I (domestic investment) increases. The expected inflation and lowered real interest rate associated with depreciation will also increase I. Conversely, with a real appreciation, domestic investment is impeded and is partially replaced by an exodus of production capacity abroad.

We can now solve our model of the open economy represented by equations 6.9–6.13, presuming that e changes exogenously in the above sense. Following an arrival of news about the future stance of monetary policy, the exchange rate depreciates at time t_0 because people suddenly expect gradual monetary expansion and eventual inflation. Table 6.2 and figure 6.1 show the impact of e on the endogenous variables p, $\dot{p}$, Y, A, B, and m in both the short and long runs.

In the short run, when p is predetermined and $\dot{p}$ is variable, this unexpected depreciation at t_0 causes a proportional deviation from PPP (i.e., $e - p > 0$) and sets off domestic inflation by the mechanism of equation 6.13. An undervalued currency and inflation jointly stimulate domestic

Table 6.2
Open Economy with a forward-looking floating exchange rate (solutions to equations 6.9–6.14)

Exogenous		*e*	
Endogenous	Short-run	Long-run	G
$\dot{p}$	+	0	0
p	0	+	0
Y	+	0	+
A	+	0	+
B	?	0	−
m	? (*)	+ (*)	+ (**)

Note: (*) indicates changes in m necessary to support the inflationary expectations that depreciate (raise) e. (**) indicates a change in m necessary to accommodate an increase in G with e unchanged.

investment and increase both A and Y. However, *the net trade balance may improve or worsen because the increases in absorption and real depreciation have offsetting effects on it* (see equation 6.11). In table 6.2, these short-run changes are summarized as follows:

$$\frac{d\dot{p}}{de} > 0, \qquad \frac{dY}{de} > 0, \qquad \frac{dA}{de} > 0, \qquad \frac{dB}{de} \gtrless 0?$$

With solutions for these variables, equation 6.12 endogenously generates a path for money supply that supports the initial inflationary expectations. When the exchange rate floats, it is unusual to treat future money growth as endogenous. But to do so is consistent with the idea that the exchange rate signals the private sector's expectation about the future changes in public policy; the trajectory of monetary policy that would not upset the current private expectation is already circumscribed. Our model suggests that the initial change in m needed to support a depreciation is small, and that even its sign is ambiguous. However, as the economy advances toward a new steady state, m must definitely increase in strict proportion to e (and to p). Otherwise, the entire model becomes inconsistent, people's expectations collapse, and e must fall back to the original level.

Suppose that the monetary authority does (is obliged to) provide m as required over time, so that inflationary expectations are fulfilled. In the long run, nothing real changes—Y, A, and B return to their initial levels —and m and p increase with e to reestablish their proportionality and

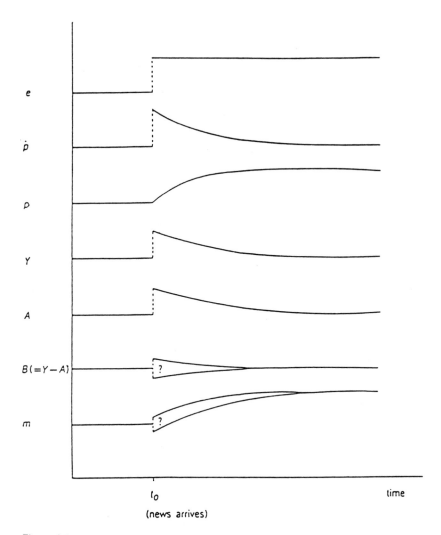

Figure 6.1
Responses to an "exogenous" rise in e in anticipation of future monetary expansion in an open economy.

PPP:

$$\frac{dY}{de} = \frac{dA}{de} = \frac{dB}{de} = 0, \qquad \frac{dp}{de} = \frac{dm}{de} = 1.$$

Thus, our open economy model has shown that the effect of a depreciation on the balance of trade is ambiguous in the short run and nil in the long run. These results are obtained by considering the various effects of e on the open economy while explicitly defining B to be the difference between Y and A. We have assumed an exchange-rate change to be exogenous, but it must be supported by particular subsequent paths of m and p.

Consider again the debate between the PPP and trade flow adjustment (TFA) criteria for setting the correct domestic exchange rate. In an open economy, represented by equations 6.9–6.13, the PPP is the only criterion that can avoid inflations and deflations (relative to p^*), where e is set equal to p (i.e., equal to $p - p^*$, because we have assumed $p^* = 0$). This conclusion is further reinforced if p^* (world price level) remains stable in the long run. Then, the PPP criterion approximates having a single international standard of value. Of course, this leaves open how to anchor the international price level p^*—a question taken up in chapters 9 and 10.

However, our PPP criterion says nothing about the state of the net trade balance. When purchasing power parity is satisfied, it could be positive or negative. And we have shown that, in an open economy, the TFA criterion for targeting the exchange rate is invalid because (1) balanced or near-balanced trade is not necessarily desirable; (2) continual changes in e in pursuit of some trade balance objective no longer have predictable effects on B; and (3) such changes in e now have adverse effects on domestic price stability and on the efficient allocation of investment.

How, then, is the net trade balance determined in an open economy? The best way to think about it is in terms of the gap between domestic saving and investment.[11] For instance, if G, measuring government dissaving, increases exogenously in an open economy, the net trade balance should deteriorate as the economy absorbs net capital from abroad, for any reasonably stable exchange-rate cum monetary policy that the government subsequently employs.

The right-hand column of table 6.2 shows the effect of increasing G on the presumption that the government follows a fixed exchange-rate (constant price level) rule by simply increasing money supply in response to the downward pressure on e (a tendency to appreciate). The new issue of government debt would put an incipient upward pressure on domestic interest rates, attract capital from abroad, and thus require the monetary authority to expand. The result is[12]

$$\frac{dA}{dG} > \frac{dY}{dG} > 0, \qquad \text{such that} - 1 < \frac{dB}{dG} < 0.$$

What is perhaps an inadequacy in our open economy model is the absence of explicit supply constraints on Y. If Y were constrained to be close to some natural level of full-employment output, say, $\bar{Y}$, then domestic private saving would not rise with G. Then the trade deficit would fully reflect the increase in government expenditures, that is, $dB/dG = -1$, with a fixed exchange rate. The same long-run result would hold if the exchange rate were floating and appreciated in response to the increase in G.

Notice the important difference from the insular case: there is no crowding out of domestic investment following an increase in G, and an increased absorption relative to income is automatically financed by borrowing abroad (i.e., a current-account deficit). This conclusion depends on our assumption of the exogeneity of i, and the result must be modified to the extent that i can deviate from i^* in case of nonzero exchange expectations or a risk premium.

However, our model does capture one important observed fact of the 1980s and 1990s, namely, that the U.S. Treasury appears to be able to finance its huge deficit without much increasing domestic interest rates, simply by borrowing from foreigners. Dollar appreciation was neither necessary nor helpful for the corresponding deficit in the current account to develop. Nor will dollar depreciation succeed in reducing that deficit. Only a change in the American saving-investment balance will reduce the current-account deficit. And, for this, no departure from a PPP exchange-rate rule would be necessary (see the appendix to chapter 4).

7

The Exchange Rate and
The Japan–United States
Trade Balance in Practice:
A Critique of the Modern
Elasticities Approach

In the ongoing debate over monetary and exchange-rate policies of open industrial economies, the so-called elasticities approach to the trade balance is frequently invoked. Correctly interpreted, it is a statement of an empirically valid relationship when the exchange rate is exogenous. If the economy is open rather than insular, however, the elasticities approach may also be misrepresented as a theoretical foundation for trade adjustment through intentional exchange-rate manipulation (chapter 6).

The purpose of this chapter is to critically review empirical studies based on the elasticities approach. Why have several econometric models been interpreted to support the notion that dollar devaluation will reduce the American trade deficit—or that yen appreciation will reduce the Japanese surplus?

7.1 The Elasticities Approach and Exchange-Rate Policy

The elasticities approach says that the quantities of exports and imports are each determined by the level of economic activity and relative prices. Typically, import volume (Q_m) is positively related to domestic income and negatively related to the relative price of foreign to domestic products (also known as the real exchange rate).[1] The export volume (Q_x) is similarly dependent on foreign income and relative price (with a reversed sign). Thus, for imports,

$$Q_m = Q_m(\underset{+}{y}, \underset{-}{ep^*/p}), \tag{7.1}$$

and for exports,

$$Q_x = Q_x(\underset{+}{y^*}, \underset{+}{ep^*/p}), \tag{7.2}$$

where y, y^*, p, p^*, and e are domestic and foreign income, domestic and foreign price, and the exchange rate, respectively. In what follows, Japan is the home country and the United States (with *) is the foreign country. Provided that quantity responses are fairly large, the trade balance (T) is also a function of activity and relative price:[2]

$$T = pQ_x - ep^*Q_m = F(\underset{-}{y}, \underset{+}{y^*}, \underset{+}{ep^*/p}).$$ (7.3)

The traditional elasticities model is often extended to include lags, dummies, commodity disaggregation, variables other than activity and relative price, and so on, but its basic property is invariant to these adaptations.

There is nothing to quarrel with in this trade-flow function if it is regarded simply as an empirical relationship among endogenous variables within a larger model. However, taken by itself and without due attention to interdependence among variables, it could also be misused as a proposition that currency depreciation, somehow engineered, can improve the trade balance—that is, the trade flow adjustment (TFA) criterion of exchange management (chapter 6). The distinction between the interpretations is crucial.

The latter (false) interpretation would assume a predictable causality from the real exchange rate to the trade balance. It would assert that a 1 percent real (and nominal, if prices are sticky) depreciation would reduce the trade deficit by, say, x percent, and that the equilibrium exchange rate consistent with a given trade balance target would be z yen per dollar. Because other factors—business cycles, oil prices, structural breaks, and so on—also affect the trade balance, a more sophisticated account would define the correct yen-dollar rate under normal business conditions and prescribed paths of commodity prices.

Warnings about the policy applicability of the elasticities approach have been many. They are mainly directed at its partial-equilibrium nature insofar as studies of the import and export markets in isolation do not take into consideration the full impact of exchange adjustment on the macroeconomy. Despite this objection, in practice, the policy proposition that a real depreciation improves the trade balance is widely accepted. Numerous empirical studies show that estimated elasticities in the export and import functions are statistically significant and have the expected signs. This evidence is often misrepresented as a proof that the commercial use of exchange policy is effective.

But even though export and import functions can be successfully estimated, such relationships cannot be usefully exploited by policy authorities. For open industrial economies of the 1990s, exchange rates are not directly controllable, and an attempt to influence them indirectly will inevitably upset other important macro variables in a complex way—ceteris paribus does not hold. As we have shown in chapter 6, depreciation will induce several repercussions whose total impact on the trade balance is ambiguous.

7.2   Today's Elasticities Approach

Let us sample recent trade and foreign-exchange discussions that are couched in the elasticities framework. To be fair, none of the works reviewed here claims that the exchange rate can be directly *manipulated*. Yet, these authors also suggest, to varying degrees, that the real exchange rate can be managed *indirectly* through the use of monetary and fiscal policies to influence the trade balance in a predictable way.

Two IMF economists, Meredith (1993) and Golub (1994), have reviewed the empirical applications of the modern elasticities approach to Japan's trade flows. Meredith conveniently summarizes past estimates by several authors of price and income elasticities of Japanese exports and imports; these include his own, which are reproduced in table 7.1. All estimates carry the expected signs. The price elasticity averaged over these estimates is −1.01 for exports and −0.61 for imports. The lower import elasticity is reasonable because Japan's imports have traditionally consisted of raw materials and energy, which are highly price inelastic.

Both Meredith and Golub successfully refute the prevalent view that Japan's closed markets are preventing the needed trade adjustment. On the contrary, they find that Japan's trade balance clearly responds to the traditional factors of income and relative price movements. The importance of exchange-rate changes, which affect the trade balance after about a two-year lag, is underlined. As for the long run, the authors assert that shifts in the structural savings-and-investment balance (which is the ultimate determinant of net trade flows) must be manifested in the current account *primarily through changes in the real exchange rate*. However, this is a highly controversial claim and an issue we will take up later.

Krugman (1991) presents a similar observation with respect to American trade flows. In his "Mass. Ave." model representing theoretical and empirical conventional wisdom in the Washington, D.C., and greater Boston areas, net exports are "assumed at minimum to depend on domestic income, foreign income, and the real exchange rate" (p. 6), although additional arguments could easily be added. Krugman also cautions that the

Table 7.1
Japan: Estimates of long-run elasticities of merchandise trade flows

	Exports		Imports	
Author(s) and sample period	Relative price	Activity level	Relative price	Activity level
1. Corker (1989) 1975:Q1–87:Q4	−1.10	2.00	−0.55	1.38
2. Corker (1990) 1975:Q1–85:Q4	−0.67	1.03	−0.48	0.96
3. EPA (1986) 1971:Q1–81:Q4	−1.18	1.50	−0.85	1.10
4. EPA (1989) 1980:Q1–88:Q4	−0.68	1.52	−0.60	1.28
5. Ueda (1988) 1970–87	−1.19	1.87	−0.41	1.04
6. Goldstein and Khan (1985) (survey)	−1.40	2.60	−1.00	1.20
7. Bank of Japan (1989) 1975:Q3–85:Q3	−0.76	1.03	−0.21	0.64
8. Krugman (1989) 1971–86	−0.85	1.65	−0.42	0.80
9. Chouraqui et al. (1988) (survey)	−1.37	2.20	−0.93	1.31
10. Meredith (1993) 1975–85	−0.92	1.72	−0.61	0.91
Unweighted average	−1.01	1.71	−0.61	1.06

Source: Meredith 1993, tables 1 and 2.
Note: For original citations and explanations of each estimate, see Meredith 1993. "EPA" stands for the Economic Planning Agency of Japan.

real exchange rate works with substantial lags. For the U.S. economy, median estimates of long-run price elasticities are −1.1 for imports and −0.8 for exports.

The external adjustment with growth (EAG) model proposed by Cline (1993a, 1993b) reveals the structure of the modern elasticities approach even more clearly. The EAG model predicts bilateral trade flows among seventeen major countries or regions on the basis of coefficient estimates obtained from quarterly data over the period 1973–87. For each pair, the trade flow depends on the importer's real growth as well as eight quarterly lags of the bilateral and cross-country terms of trade. Model projections require the future paths of prices, real growth rates, and real exchange rates of relevant countries *as exogenous inputs*. A 1 percent real appreciation of the yen in 1993 is estimated to reduce Japan's current-account surplus by $3 billion to $4 billion. The range of 102–112 yen to the dollar (in mid-1993 prices) is considered to be consistent with the target current-account position of 1–2 percent of GDP by 1995–96. As do the IMF economists, Cline finds that trade volumes respond to price signals with a lag of about two years. The relationship looks particularly impressive when Japan's bilateral surplus with the United States since 1979 is plotted against the real yen-dollar rate lagged two years (but see section 7.4 and chapter 11 for a critique of this correlation).

Helkie and Hooper (1988) present their "partial-equilibrium current-account model" of the United States estimated over the period 1969–84. This model is actually the U.S. external block extracted from the Federal Reserve Board multicountry model (MCM). It divides the current account into merchandise trade and services. Merchandise exports are disaggregated into agricultural and nonagricultural exports, and merchandise imports consist of oil and non-oil imports. Each category has volume and price equations. Trade volume equations follow the standard specification of depending on income and the real exchange rate, with some additional variables. As always, the real exchange rate affects the trade volume with an approximate two-year lag. That is, a devaluation today is associated with an improved trade balance two years later. Trade price equations (other than the oil price) are variously estimated with domestic prices, foreign prices, exchange rate, commodity prices, and world GNP as arguments. Three types of service flows are each estimated with separate receipts and payments equations.

Certainly, commodity disaggregation and explicit treatment of trade prices are the sophisticated features of this model. However, the fundamental weakness of the elasticities approach remains intact. The authors go on to discuss the relative contributions of *proximate* determinants of the U.S. current account—prices, business cycles, exchange rates, and so on—during 1980–86, but they also recognize the "inherent difficulties of trying to allocate causal contributions among jointly determined endogenous variables" (Helkie and Hooper 1988, p. 42).

7.3 Fiscal Rigidity and Monetary Perversity in Exchange-Rate Determination

Determinants of exchange rates include both so-called fundamentals and nonfundamentals. Unfortunately, most of both are beyond the immediate reach of policy-making authorities because of their endogeneity. News about fundamental variables such as inflation, output growth, money supplies, fiscal deficits, nominal and real interest rates, and current-account balances[3] seems to be correlated with exchange rates, although the correlations are not very robust over time. Additionally, factors unrelated to fundamentals, say bubbles driven by market psychology, also influence—and at times may even dominate—foreign-exchange markets.

Given that the real exchange rate has an observed impact on the current account under a floating exchange-rate system, can policy makers engineer a sustained real depreciation without upsetting fundamental variables? Most authors would reply that exchange rates can be managed indirectly through fiscal restraint or monetary expansion. In a standard open macroeconomic framework, such as the Mundell-Fleming model with imperfect capital mobility, either policy would lower domestic interest rates, encourage capital outflow, and depreciate the home currency.

Of the two macro policies, fiscal restraint is superior because it would reduce absorption directly, leading to a certain improvement in external balance. This point is widely recognized. For example, in the paper we have quoted, Helkie and Hooper (1988) simulate the full MCM model to examine the impact of fiscal and monetary policies on the current account. It is interesting to note that domestic and foreign fiscal policies explain 66 percent of the deterioration in the U.S. current account during 1980–86, whereas a shift in U.S. money growth "would have only a negligible impact on the current account" (p. 50) because of its offsetting effects. A U.S. monetary tightening—and the higher domestic interest rates associated with it—would lead to a higher dollar and lower income. The higher dollar would worsen the external balance, while lower U.S. income (and therefore absorption) would improve it.

In a similar vein, Cline (1993a) suggests that a recovery of the Japanese economy generated by its fiscal expansion would contribute to a reduction of Japan's trade surplus. Cline predicts that if, instead, easy monetary policy were adopted by the Bank of Japan to stimulate the economy, the yen would depreciate—which is undesirable from his viewpoint because it would augment the surplus. To keep the yen at a high level, he recommends fiscal stimuli combined with relatively tight money.

In the political reality of advanced industrial countries, however, fiscal policy is hardly a flexible tool. On the contrary, fiscal rigidity due to interest-group politics and bureaucratic resistance has become a large part of the problem, rather than a solution. Certainly, a drastic improvement in the U.S. fiscal balance over the next several years would significantly reduce its external deficit—and this, coupled with a rise in private savings, would be our preferred solution to the American trade deficit problem. But, in the current political landscape, this is unlikely to happen quickly (if at all)—see chapter 4, page 92. And, over such a long time horizon, real exchange-rate changes are neither necessary nor sustainable—once offsetting internal price inflation is considered.

Under the circumstances, the burden of managing the nominal exchange rate in the short and medium terms falls heavily on the monetary authority—and the Federal Reserve Board and BoJ are no exceptions. The only practical way for a central bank to depreciate (appreciate) the home currency is to adopt easy (tight) monetary policy relative to its major trading partners. However, central banks are usually also saddled with domestic macroeconomic management, and the two goals often conflict. For example, the desire to prevent domestic overheating requires higher interest rates, whereas keeping the currency down demands lower interest rates. All a central bank can do is to navigate between the two goals as best it can. When policy goals coincide, policies can be fully executed; otherwise, a compromise must be found. Relative weights given to domestic and external targets vary. Traditionally, the BoJ appears to have placed a greater weight on the exchange rate, compared with what the Fed does.[4]

The perpetual call for a lower dollar against the yen, notwithstanding (or with full knowledge of) the bleak fiscal reality, is tantamount to pressure for bilateral monetary adjustment. It imparts a subtle but continuous expansionary bias on the Fed's decision making and a similar, long-term contractionary bias on the Bank of Japan. But, as we show in chapters 1 and 9, the BoJ has done virtually all the adjusting through its relatively deflationary monetary policy.

Using monetary policy for exchange management entails several drawbacks. In the short run, as Cline and Helkie and Hooper recognize, the adverse absorption effect would offset the relative price effect of a real depreciation, as shown by our open-economy model in chapter 6. Because appreciation shocks affect domestic investment in a way that enhances—rather than reduces—the trade surplus, the initial impact may well be the opposite of what policy makers intend.

What about the long-run impact of yen appreciation on the trade balance? After its short-term impact works itself out, the consequence of tight money in Japan and easy money in the United States is relative deflation and inflation in the respective countries. This would accommodate American fiscal expansionism, which caused the persistent trade deficit in the first place, while contributing to *endaka fukyo* and low spending in Japan.

In the very long run, the impact of nominal yen appreciation on the real exchange rate simply washes out because of the fall in the Japanese price level relative to the American (see figure 1.4). In section 7.4, we estimate how fast relative domestic price levels adjust to offset changes in the nominal yen-dollar exchange rate.

7.4   The Real Exchange Rate and the Structural Trade Gap

First, let us return to the empirical observation that a real yen appreciation reduces Japan's trade surplus after a two-year lag. Using data since the end of the 1970s, Cline (1993a) showed a remarkable correlation of the Japan–U.S. bilateral trade gap with the real yen-dollar rate lagged two years. Bergsten and Noland (1993) reprint Cline's diagram to make the same point. In figure 7.1, we have replicated this diagram, extending it with our own data to include earlier years. Following Cline, the bilateral trade balance (T) is defined as a percentage of total bilateral trade; that is,

$$T = \frac{X - M}{X + M},\qquad\qquad(7.4)$$

where X represents Japan's exports to the United States and M represents Japan's imports from the United States. Here the real exchange rate is defined as the relative price of tradables between the two countries (deflated by bilateral wholesale prices).

We immediately notice that the cyclical movements of the bilateral trade balance and the real yen-dollar rate were indeed highly synchro-

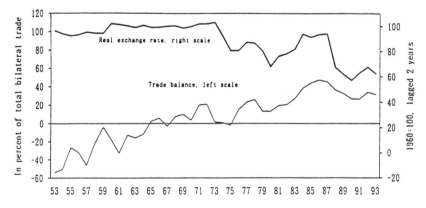

Figure 7.1
Japan–U.S. trade balance and the real yen-dollar rate.

nized during the floating-rate years. However, figure 7.1 also reveals two
facts that are not favorable to Cline's conclusion: (1) Apart from cyclical
movements, the long-term declining trend in the real exchange rate has
no explanatory power over the rising structural surplus of Japan vis-à-vis
the United States;[5] and perhaps more important, (2) in earlier years of the
Bretton Woods fixed-dollar standard, movements in the trade balance occurred without any perceptible changes in the real exchange rate. Clearly,
a persistent upward trend in the bilateral trade balance existed from the
early 1950s at least to 1994, spanning two different international monetary regimes. All this points to the strong possibility that changes in the
trade balance need not always be triggered by movements in the real
exchange rate.[6] In particular, the *structural* trade balance can shift independently of the real exchange rate.

To illustrate this point numerically, consider a simple model in which a
deviation from PPP exerts pressure on bilateral prices: a country with an
overvalued currency will have a relative deflation vis-à-vis a country with
an undervalued currency. In the spirit of the open economy model developed in chapter 6 and the syndrome of the ever-higher yen analyzed in
chapter 1, we reverse the causality and regard the nominal exchange rate
as a forcing variable. Figure 7.2, plotting the relative tradable price movement between Japan and the United States, confirms that this assumption
is a plausible one. Although the figure does not prove causality, we can
observe that the almost perfect price alignment of the 1960s was followed

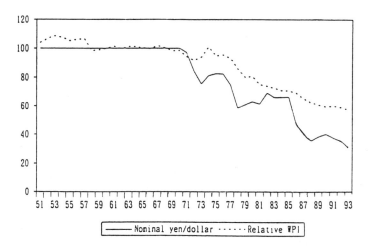

Figure 7.2
Yen-dollar rate and relative prices (1960 = 100).

by a trend of relative Japanese deflation that (partially) offset periodic yen appreciation against the dollar.

Let

$$\pi = p - p^* + \theta \tag{7.5}$$

be the PPP yen-dollar exchange rate, where p and p^* are published Japanese and U.S. tradable price indices. θ is an unknown parameter because price indices have arbitrary base years,[7] but it can be estimated. All lowercase variables except t (time) below are in logarithms. We can write our price equation as follows:

$$\Delta\pi = \phi(e - \pi), \tag{7.6}$$

where $\phi > 0$ is the adjustment speed and e is the nominal yen-dollar exchange rate. Unlike the conventional formulation, deviation from PPP generated by a forced yen appreciation is eliminated by adjustment in the relative price (π) rather than through regression in the yen-dollar rate. This occurs partly through imported inflation (i.e., pass-through effect) but mainly through accommodative monetary policy, which causes domestic inflation (deflation in the Japanese case) in due course.

We also propose a trade-balance equation that depends on home and foreign income (y and y^*), the real exchange rate lagged two years ($e_{-2} - \pi_{-2}$), and an exogenous shift in international lending (Γ):

$$T = F(y, y^*, e_{-2} - \pi_{-2}, \Gamma) = \alpha y + \beta y^* + \lambda(e_{-2} - \pi_{-2}) + \gamma_0 + \gamma_1 t. \tag{7.7}$$

Γ (equal to $\gamma_0 + \gamma_1 t$) represents the long-term under- or overspending propensity of this country under normal business conditions and PPP. Financially open economies would lend or borrow even if the real exchange rate remained constant. For simplicity, we assume Γ to be a linear trend, but it can be modeled in other forms as well.[8]

After substituting the definition of π in equation 7.5 into equations 7.6 and 7.7, these two equations are estimated simultaneously for 1954–93 by the nonlinear maximum likelihood method.[9] The results are reported in table 7.2. The estimated value of ϕ suggests that bilateral price movements close 7.7 percent of the deviation from PPP each year. This relatively slow adjustment speed is perhaps due to the fact that we are using the *overall* WPI as our Japanese tradable price index. (The overall WPI is a weighted average of domestic, export, and import prices.) Especially in Japan, various components of tradable prices diverge as the yen appreciates; see chapter 3. If bilateral export price indices were avail-

Table 7.2
Estimation of price and trade balance equations

ϕ	θ	α	β	λ	γ_0	γ_1
0.077	0.071	−0.141	0.962	0.535	−0.319	0.025
(2.53)	(0.62)	(−1.00)	(1.96)	(4.07)	(−4.30)	(14.8)
Price equation—adjusted $R^2 = 0.107$		SE = 0.034		DW = 2.12		
Trade equation—adjusted $R^2 = 0.900$		SE = 0.079		DW = 1.68		

Note: t-statistics are in parentheses. Maximum-likelihood nonlinear least squares estimation is performed over the sample period of 1954–93.

able, using them would have produced a much higher estimated speed of adjustment.[10]

Estimated α and β have the expected signs, although α (Japanese income elasticity) is not statistically significant. By contrast, U.S. income has a systematic impact on the bilateral trade balance; its 1 percent rise will lead to nearly a full percentage point increase in Japan's surplus with the United States. As for the real exchange rate, a 1 percent real appreciation of the yen vis-à-vis the dollar would reduce the bilateral trade gap by roughly 0.5 percentage point after two years. Finally, the model detects a long-term increase in the Japanese surplus at the rate of 2.5 percentage points per year, which is highly significant statistically and is independent of the real exchange rate.

This model clearly illustrates the futility of a commercially oriented exchange-rate policy when the trade imbalance is structural—that is, when it arises not from the levels of y and y^* but from the (trend) propensity to spend out of income (summarized by Γ). Because bilateral prices adjust to close the international price gap generated by an engineered depreciation, the impact of such policy on the real exchange rate is temporary. In the long run, a country pursuing a depreciation policy will have a higher inflation and an unchanged trend in the trade balance.

As a further illustration, the model is simulated with the estimated values of λ and γ_1, and $\phi = 0.2$ (instead of the estimated 0.077, to allow for a faster price adjustment of exportable products). Additionally, after $t = 0$, it is assumed that mercantile pressure from American policy makers episodically depreciates the dollar to a 30 percent undervaluation against the yen whenever the existing undervaluation falls below 10 percent. Under this hypothetical but not implausible simulation scenario for the nominal exchange rate, figures 7.3 and 7.4 display the simulated real exchange rate, trade balance, and actual and PPP yen-dollar rates. In our

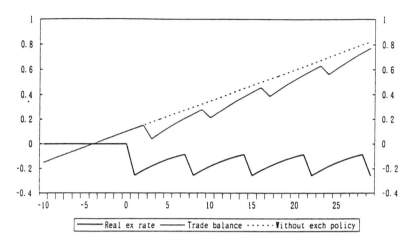

Figure 7.3
Real exchange rate and trade balance simulation.

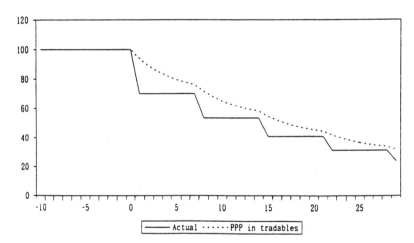

Figure 7.4
Actual and PPP yen-dollar rate simulation.

simulation, a cheap-dollar policy is triggered every seven years without fundamentally altering the rising trend of the bilateral trade balance. Similarities with the actual behavior of exchange rates, prices, and trade balances in figures 7.1 and 7.2 are striking.

This situation is analogous to the case of the augmented Phillips curve. The Phillips curve is an empirically observed negative relationship between price (or wage) inflation and unemployment. However, as Friedman argued, that relationship is based on short-term errors in inflation expectations and thus cannot be exploited by policy makers in the long run. A monetary surprise is useless to keep unemployment below its natural level (except temporarily) because expectations will sooner or later catch up with reality.

Similarly, in the case of cheap-dollar policy, correlation between depreciation and the trade balance two years later arises because prices are slow to adjust. (Because income and imports into Japan are abnormally depressed when the yen is overvalued (the reverse absorption effect), there is no presumption that the cumulative trade surplus of Japan over the whole exchange-rate cycle is reduced even if we observe the two-year lag.) However, over time, commodity arbitrage will eventually eliminate any bilateral price gap in tradable goods, and the trade balance will return to the level determined by the long-run savings and investment propensities. When the economy is open to trade, it is impossible to keep all the commodities overvalued all the time.[11] In both cases, the mistake consists in assigning a nominal policy to a real goal. The lagged effect on the trade balance does exist but is short-lived and inconclusive, but the long-term consequence is macroeconomic instability.

7.5   Theory, Policy, and Expectations

Unlike meteorology or seismology, where theories can only predict but not cause future events, in economics, theories can influence the very events they attempt to explain. This is because economic theories are an informational input to policy making as well as to the formation of expectations. The theory-to-reality feedback is especially evident in asset markets (including the foreign-exchange market), where all information must be filtered through expectations before it is allowed to influence the price. A defective cold-front model will not change tomorrow's weather, but a popular (but wrong) exchange-rate model will surely affect tomorrow's yen-dollar rates, which are then telescoped back to what we observe today.

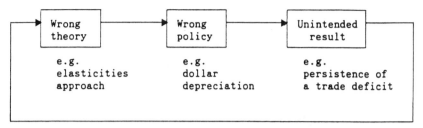

Reinforcement through failure

Figure 7.5
A policy trap.

In such an environment, the role of an exchange-rate theory is complex and goes beyond explanation of the past and prediction of the future. First, the validity of a theory becomes harder to ascertain because of its self-fulfilling nature. When market traders read the *Wall Street Journal* and the *Nikkei Shimbun* before placing an order, apparent agreement between reality and theory arises partly because the reality conforms to the theory and not vice versa. Second, for this reason a wrong theory can survive (and dominate) for a long time even though it continuously fails in its ultimate policy objective. Third, when a wrong theory is guiding public policy, private traders will employ their best knowledge of the prevailing policy reaction function to form expectations. Rational expectations in this sense does not imply effectiveness of the adopted policy. It only ensures efficient information processing on the part of the public.

Hence the possibility of a persistent policy trap, in which a resilient theory gets the upper hand on reality (figure 7.5). Implementation of an improper policy not only fails to attain a desired outcome but often creates new problems. But this does not prompt an immediate review of either theory or policy. The impotence of the prescribed measure is explained away by reference to inconsistent implementation ("it was not really tried") or other adverse effects ("things would have been worse without it"). In each subsequent round, an ever-increasing dose of the same medicine is administered to overcome the alleged difficulties. The vicious circle takes the economy in a downward spiral until things fall apart. Our hypothesis is that misapplication of the elasticities approach to the trade balance has been causing such a policy trap since the 1970s at least through to the summer of 1995.

A mistaken theory can take many forms. In Japan, the current version seems to be that three policy options can reduce the huge surplus: (1)

trade measures such as market opening and acceptance of numerical import targets; (2) fiscal expansion; and (3) a further yen appreciation. Among these, fiscal expansion is the only effective measure for trade adjustment, as discussed above. As Komiya (1994) correctly argues, the other two will have little or ambiguous impact on the current account.

Nevertheless, it is thought that these actions can be traded off against one another. With this mind-set, news of a deadlock in bilateral trade talks, an angry U.S. official, fiscal immobility, or the like, immediately appreciates the yen, because the market foresees impending political pressure to push up the yen to compensate for these so-called failures. This represents a conditioned reflex of market traders, not a reasoned analysis of the true economic structure. Economists who preach a cheaper dollar as an alternative remedy play an instrumental role in sustaining the trap, that is, the syndrome of the ever-higher yen.

Note that actual monetary easing is not even needed for a currency to depreciate in a forward-looking market. All the government has to do is to send a credible signal that it will happen. A statement by a high official or a concerted foreign-exchange intervention by central banks will do nicely.[12] As long as they are systematically followed by monetary adjustment, the market will react to such signals.

But reality has gone a step further. In the bilateral relationship between Japan and the United States, these foreign-exchange signals are often used to force the hand of monetary authorities at home and abroad. When a U.S. Treasury secretary says he wants to see a lower dollar, the market reacts—and, in time, the dollar actually falls. To keep it down, the Fed is obliged to maintain an easy money policy relative to the BoJ, which must also cooperate. Indeed, it is the BoJ that does almost all the adjusting (chapter 9). As long as central banks, willy-nilly, validate a preceding fall of the dollar, the signal remains a credible one. In this preemptive scenario, the exchange rate is not just a forward-looking variable but a *forcing* variable. It does not adjust in anticipation of future changes in money and prices; rather it compels these changes.

The persistence of the exchange policy trap cannot be blamed on market traders, who correctly see through the (wrong) policy-making process. In our opinion, the problem cannot be attributed to provocative media reports or even to policy makers who pursue a cheap-dollar policy. The ultimate responsibility must be borne by economists who promote the idea that currency depreciation will improve the trade balance even though public overspending and the private savings shortage remain as great as ever in the United States. This opens the floodgates for industrial lobbies in the United States to exert mercantile pressure on the U.S. government to keep "talking the yen up" to enhance their own profit margins, at least in the short run.

Appendix: A Critical Analysis of Cline's Reduced-Form Model

William Cline's book *Predicting External Imbalances for the United States and Japan* (1995) is one product in a series of influential policy studies by the Institute of International Economics (IIE). His earlier work analyzed the bilateral trade balance between the two countries, but this volume focuses separately on each country's global current-account balance. As in his earlier work, Cline stresses the importance of the real exchange rate for adjusting the current account of each country. His model provides a good example of the elasticities approach applied to the real-world problem of how to reduce the bilateral current-account gap.

Cline argues that ongoing dollar devaluation will be necessary to prevent the U.S. current-account deficit from widening to unacceptable levels in 1996 and beyond. Improvement in U.S. fiscal policy would also be helpful, but he sees it as a complement to, rather than a substitute for, real dollar devaluation. Consequently, he had severe reservations about the successful joint operations by the Federal Reserve System, the Bank of Japan, and the Bundesbank in August 1995 to bolster the dollar significantly against the yen and the mark. In an IIE news release for his book (September 20, 1995), Cline predicted that, had the exchange rate stayed at its mid-April 1995 level of 85 yen to the dollar, Japan's current-account surplus would have fallen from about $130 billion in 1994 to less than $90 billion (about 1.5 percent of GDP) by 1997. "However," he continues, "the recent rebound of the dollar to over 100 yen means that Japan's trade surplus is likely to remain above $115 billion, or more than 2 percent of GDP."

Into the late 1990s, Cline also wants the dollar to be devalued against the currencies of many developing countries (particularly those of the newly industrialized Asian economies and of China) with burgeoning current-account surpluses with the United States.

The Reduced-Form Model

What are the essential aspects of the underlying model, applied separately to the United States and Japan, that lead Cline to project ever-larger current-account deficits for the United States—and then to project the need for an ever-lower dollar and an ever-higher yen to offset these deficits?

Cline's arguments are centered around his reduced-form model (RFM) of the current account.[13] As with other models based on the elasticities approach, the RFM does not explicitly consider the saving-investment balance in each country or how its components might change through time. (U.S. fiscal policy is considered in Cline's concluding chapter, but only insofar as it affects U.S. interest rates and, hence, the exchange rate.) For example, the model does not directly address the dramatic effects of the Reagan fiscal deficits, which caused U.S. absorption to begin rising above its income in the 1980s.

Instead, Cline elects to follow the old Houthakker-MaGee (1969) tradition of explaining the real trade balance (and eventually the nominal current account) by the lagged real exchange rate (denoted by R_L^* against OECD countries and by r_L^* against developing countries) on the one hand, and by real GDP at home (Y_d) and abroad (Y_f) on the other. In his single-equation regression analysis, these values are treated as if they were exogenous determinants of real trade flows (table 7.3).

Let us ignore complex exchange-rate pass-through effects, which Cline denotes by R_L and R in table 7.3, but which turn out to be statistically insignificant for the United States. Then, his basic equation for the U.S. trade deficit with the developed (OECD) countries boils down to

$$\ln[M^v/X^v] - \ln[P_f/P_d] = \pi_0 + \pi_1 \ln R_L^* + \pi_3 \ln Y_d + \pi_4 \ln Y_f + \pi_6 \ln r_L^*. \quad (7.8)$$

On the left-hand side, the ratio of the value of imports of non-oil goods and nonfactor services (M^v) to the similarly constructed value of exports (X^v) is deflated by the ratio of the foreign (P_f) to the domestic (P_d) price level. This is Cline's measure of the real trade deficit. This real trade ratio is assumed to depend on the real variables on the right-hand side, which we have already discussed.

To forecast future trade deficits, Cline first assumes alternative paths of the right-hand side variables—real exchange rates and levels of GDP—*as if they could be determined independently of each other.* For example, he uses consensus forecasts (by the IMF or other august bodies) of Y_d and Y_f to calculate their impact on the real trade ratio according to the estimated parameters π_3 and π_4. Next, he picks alternative values for the future real exchange rates R^* (and r^*), each of which he holds constant through time while taking past lags into account, in order to compute alternative

Table 7.3
Estimation of Cline's "reduced-form model"

Dependent variable	Coefficient[a]										
	π_0	π_1	π_2	π_3	π_4	π_5	π_6				
Independent variable:	constant	$\ln R_L^*$	$\ln R_L$	$\ln Y_d$	$\ln Y_f$	$\ln R$	$\ln r_L^*$	RHO	$\bar{R}^2$	DW	Q
Analytical:	$\ln(\delta/\alpha)$	$\phi - \beta\,(\psi - \Omega)$	$-[\phi(1+\rho) + \beta\varepsilon]$	θ	$-\gamma$	$\rho - \varepsilon$	$\psi - \Omega\,(\phi - \beta)$				
United States											
Developed countries											
$\ln[M^v/X^v] -$	-6.682	0.827	-0.183	1.526	-1.379	0.033	0.709	0.502	0.960	1.93	22.2
$\ln[P_f/P_d]$	(8.7)	(2.0)	(0.4)	(3.4)	(3.6)	(0.3)	(3.0)	(4.7)			
Developing countries											
$\ln[M^v/X^v]$	0.634	0.816	—	1	−1	—	1.316	0.989	0.982	2.06	18.1
$+ \ln r^*$	(0.2)	(2.9)	—	b	b	—	(2.2)	(44.6)			
Japan											
Total											
$\ln[M^v/X^v] -$	-3.42	1.989	-1.035	0.919	-0.994	-0.260	—	0.491	0.892	1.95	26.1
$\ln[P_f/P_d]$	(1.5)	(7.7)	(2.9)	(1.9)	(1.0)	(1.7)		(3.8)			

Source: Reproduced from Cline 1995, 22.
Note: For Japan, Y_d is lagged one quarter.
a. t-statistics are shown in parentheses.
b. Constrained to be unity.

exchange-rate effects according to the estimated parameter π_1. These exchange-rate effects are multiplicable (additive in log) with the income effects.

The Critique

What is wrong with Cline's projection procedure? We would like to underscore three major problems.

First, the future paths of real exchange rates and GDP cannot be assumed independently. Interaction between them is particularly acute in the case of Japan, with its high-yen-induced recession (*endaka fukyo*). Overvaluation of the home currency is known to reduce domestic spending (especially investment in tradable industries) and therefore the level of real output. To be consistent, higher projections for the yen, say 85 yen to the dollar (suitably deflated in real terms), should be accompanied by lower projections of real growth in Japan. More properly, such macroeconomic interdependence should be examined within a general-equilibrium model. A partial-equilibrium single-equation model is inherently ill suited for handling this type of mutual interdependence.

Second, the focus on the real trade adjustment misses the important aspect of the persistent U.S. current-account deficit. That real exports and real imports adjust to exchange-rate shocks is beyond dispute. What is not settled is whether these real adjustments will actually amount to nominal adjustment in the current account after all macroeconomic repercussions are taken into account. In a financially open economy, the current account largely reflects the saving-investment gap of both the public and private sectors. This financing gap must be filled *nominally* (i.e., in terms of billions of current dollars). Even with exchange adjustment, the nominal need for the United States to find adequate foreign savings should not change substantially if the saving and spending propensities of the domestic sectors have not changed.

Third, projecting arbitrary values for the real exchange rate, R_L^* in equation 7.8, is not generally sustainable. For example, projecting some very low value for the yen, say 85 to the dollar in real (1995) terms, can only be sustained with increasing inflation in the United States or (more likely) accelerating deflation in Japan. Indeed, in this chapter, we provide empirical estimates of how fast the domestic price level in Japan falls in response to setting the yen-dollar rate below PPP, that is, overvaluing the yen, when the American price level remains fairly stable.

8

Monetary and Exchange-
Rate Regimes, Inflation
Persistence, and the
Volatility of Long-term
Interest Rates

We have seen how exchange volatility that emerges naturally from an unanchored international monetary system directly damages the real economy by confounding price signals and upsetting international competitiveness. But that is not all. This chapter examines how floating exchange rates affect economic efficiency indirectly by influencing the volatility of long-term interest rates, which in turn impinges upon long-term physical investment and output growth.

Since yen- and dollar-denominated assets are competing financial instruments that can be bought and sold electronically, their *expected* returns (adjusted for the risk premium that compensates foreign asset holders for uncertain future exchange rates) must be similar. Otherwise, there will be a stampede across currencies until such relationship again holds. Thus, after interest arbitrage, we have

$$i = i^* + \hat{x} - \rho, \tag{8.1}$$

where i is the yen interest rate, i^* is the dollar interest rate, $\hat{x}$ is the expected change in the yen-dollar exchange rate, and ρ is the risk premium. This relationship, known as uncovered interest parity, is a common building block of open macroeconomic models, including the portfolio balance exchange-rate determination model and the Dornbusch overshooting model.

In this equation, do interest rates determine the exchange rate, or does the exchange rate drive interest rates? The popular models tend to assume the former. But uncovered interest parity per se does not tell us the direction of causality. Most endogenous variables are mutually determined. We suspect that the dominant causality runs from the nature of the exchange-rate regime to the volatility of interest rates.

8.1 Behavior of Interest Rates: An Overview

Let us examine the characteristic behavior of interest rates in the major industrial countries under three different international monetary systems of the past: the classical international gold standard (1880–1913), the Bretton Woods international dollar standard (1950s–1970), and the present floating-rate system (1973 onward). The last system—which some would call a nonsystem—may be further divided at 1985 into the pre– and post–Plaza Agreement subperiods.

The classical gold standard was truly international, because all major European countries and the United States were in it. The United Kingdom was officially under the gold standard beginning in 1821, but it was during the late 1870s that other European countries adopted in droves the U.K.–centered yellow metal standard.[1] In 1879, the United States rejoined the gold standard after a suspension caused by the Civil War. From then until the outbreak of World War I in 1914, major currencies were linked to each other at fixed parities without a single realignment. Japan, situated at the fringe of the "civilized" world, also moved to the gold standard in 1897, using the gold reserves obtained from China as a reparation of the Sino-Japanese War (1894–95).

Figures 8.1 and 8.2, respectively, show the movements of wholesale prices and long-term interest rates for the three periods. (Different choices of countries across the three periods reflect data availability.) The remarkable thing about the pre–World War I period is that tradable prices were highly stable in the long run (by today's standard) and that they were also internationally well aligned. True, they exhibited a modest declining trend until 1896 and then rose modestly during the years leading to 1914. Medium-term cycles with peaks around 1882, 1891, 1900, and 1907 are too small to be seen in the figure. But every country participating in the international gold standard shared these movements. Japanese prices also began to move with the rest after Japan joined the gold-based international monetary system.

During the heyday of the gold standard, virtually no restrictions were placed on capital mobility. For example, British citizens were free to invest in American railroad bonds or South African mining stocks.[2] Long-term interest rates were internationally linked and extremely stable in all major countries (figure 8.2). This was by no means a reflection of stable short-term fundamentals. On the contrary, besides the aforementioned short-term price fluctuations, synchronized business cycles were severe and banking crises were frequent. Unlike long-term interest rates, short-

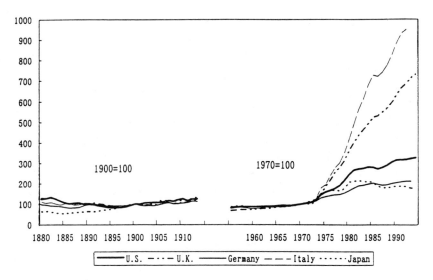

Figure 8.1
Wholesale prices, 1880–1913 and 1955–1994.

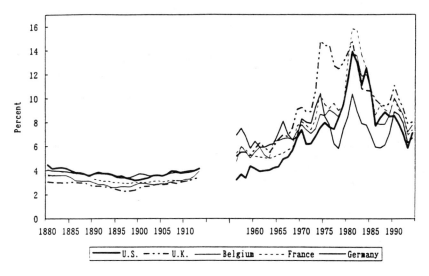

Figure 8.2
Long-term interest rates, 1880–1913 and 1956–1994.

term ones were highly volatile and also synchronous across countries. Against this rough background, it is truly amazing that long-term rates hardly budged for as long as thirty-five years—with the British rate always providing the floor.

The Bretton Woods system of the early post–World War II period was also a gold-exchange standard featuring fixed major exchange rates, but it differed from the classical gold standard in certain important aspects (McKinnon 1993 and 1996). First, relatively speaking, global price stability depended more on the policy discipline of the United States (center country) than on the market condition of gold. Second, it contained a mechanism to allow individual countries other than the United States to re-peg exchange parities—though this was resorted to rather infrequently. Third, unlike under the classical gold standard, capital mobility was highly restricted. (By contrast, integration of goods markets was vigorously sought through a series of GATT trade rounds.)

With respect to prices, the United States was a very successful nominal anchor during the 1950s and much of the 1960s. This is clear in the historically unprecedented stability of global tradable prices (figure 8.1; see also chapter 2).[3] Such price stability in the short-term was not seen even under the classical gold standard. As for long-term interest rates, stability was less spectacular (figure 8.2): financial markets were internationally segmented and, in some countries, including Japan, there was heavy government intervention on financial transactions and interest rates. Thus interest rates were domestically (and often officially) determined. Yet, since inflation was low or even nil, long-term interest rates were relatively stable compared with the period to come. The dollar interest rate was consistently the lowest, reflecting the confidence in and the efficiency of American financial markets.

Finally, the current international monetary system is characterized by floating exchange rates (since 1971–73) and free capital mobility (especially since the early 1980s). Tradable prices are less stable and tend to diverge internationally; the United States is now a middle performer instead of an anchor for global price stability (figure 8.1). Correspondingly, long-term interest rates are volatile, in sharp contrast to those under the classical gold standard, which also permitted free capital mobility (figure 8.2).[4]

Volatility in long- and short-term interest rates for four industrial countries, as measured by the mean absolute monthly change, is summarized in figures 8.3 and 8.4. Under the classical gold standard, as already noted, short-term rates were fairly volatile but long-term rates were extraordi-

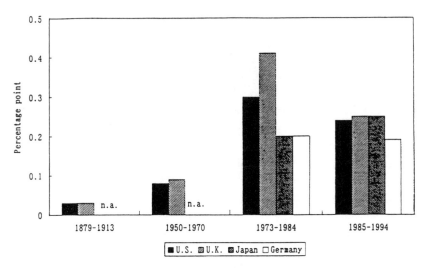

Figure 8.3
Volatility in long-term interest rates, mean absolute monthly changes.

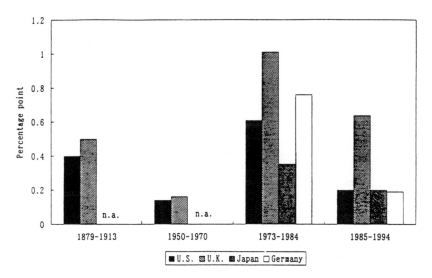

Figure 8.4
Volatility in short-term interest rates, mean absolute monthly changes.

narily stable. (Note that the scales are different in the two diagrams.) In contrast, both rates became highly volatile with the advent of floating exchange rates. After the Plaza Agreement of 1985, however, short-term rates became more subdued—except for the British short-term interest rate—and are now more tranquil than during 1879–1913. However long-term rates have remained very volatile since floating began. (Results for the Bretton Woods period should be evaluated carefully, because financial markets were controlled and segmented during that time.)

Why do long-term interest rates behave so differently across alternative international monetary regimes—the classical gold standard versus the current floating rate system—with equally free capital mobility? The advancement of global communication technology from transoceanic cables to computer networks, though spectacular, is unlikely to be the chief culprit. It is also difficult to argue seriously that fundamentals are strikingly more volatile today than around the turn of the last century. The solution to the puzzle lies in the difference in the monetary policy rules that support these alternative regimes under which global financial markets must operate.

8.2 Global Economic Regimes and Inflation Persistence

The well-known Lucas critique says that any policy change will induce a corresponding change in economic structure as people adjust, sooner or later, to a new policy regime. When the government adopts a new policy rule, therefore, it cannot assume that everything else will remain just the same. As a consequence of the new policy, it must deal with an economy with new characteristics and responses. Few policy changes are more dramatic and unequivocal than changes in the international exchange-rate obligations of national governments.

Measuring Inflation Persistence

Alogoskoufis and Smith (1991) and Alogoskoufis (1992) show that the persistence of national inflation differs under alternative international monetary regimes. Under a floating exchange-rate system, the possibility of exchange-rate adjustment allows monetary authorities to accommodate price shocks more fully than otherwise. The intended purpose of such accommodation is to lessen the adverse output effect of a positive price shock by accepting some inflation à la Phillips curve. In the economics profession, naive thinking along an immovable Phillips curve has been out of vogue ever since Friedman pointed out its logical defect in 1968. Rather than disinflate immediately, however, the monetary authority is still under political pressure to temporarily accommodate unexpected price inflation—even at the cost of long-term price instability.

With floating exchange rates, therefore, monetary policies tend to be expansionary and divergent across countries because national central banks are more independent. By contrast, participation in a fixed exchange-rate regime will bind monetary authorities so severely that they have little room for individual action to exploit the inflation-unemployment trade-off. Instead, they are forced to adopt a globally common monetary policy. This straitjacket requirement of fixed exchange rates is a blessing if the common monetary standard provided by the center country is itself stable. Then the time-inconsistent monetary policy is prevented, and the country is better off being tied to the center and importing price stability from it.[5] To repeat, the crucial difference in policy rules between the two exchange regimes is whether monetary accommodation of a price shock is high or low.

In their paper, Alogoskoufis and Smith make the theoretical point using a complete macroeconomic model—featuring IS–LM, uncovered interest parity, monopolistically competitive firms, convex price-adjustment costs, wage-setting assumptions, and rational expectations. Without replicating their model (for which we do not have the space), however, we can state that their assertion is intuitively plausible. In fact, this is exactly the traditional argument about the disciplinary effect of a fixed exchange rate. Commitment to a fixed parity deprives the government of the power to conduct independent monetary policy—and when the central bank lacks independence from the political authority, a fixed parity will improve the economic situation.

Even more remarkable is the convincing evidence the authors present to support their theoretical conclusions. Using the U.S.–U.K. data spanning more than a century (Alogoskoufis and Smith 1991) and the data for twenty-one OECD member countries in the postwar period (Alogoskoufis 1992), they show that monetary accommodation and inflation persistence are both much higher during the floating-rate periods compared with those during the fixed-rate periods.

We follow the statistical method of Alogoskoufis and Smith and estimate inflation persistence for Japan and the United States during 1882–1994. Three alternative dependent variables are used: U.S. wholesale price inflation, Japanese wholesale price inflation, and their difference ("relative inflation"). The four explanatory variables on the right-hand side are a

Table 8.1
The persistence of U.S., Japanese, and relative inflation, 1882–1994

	OLS			IV		
	U.S.	Japan	Relative	U.S.	Japan	Relative
Constant	0.013	0.025	0.022	0.013	0.038	0.024
	(0.009)	(0.017)	(0.016)	(0.013)	(0.025)	(0.023)
F dummy	0.010	−0.011	−0.022	−0.027	−0.056	−0.034
	(0.017)	(0.031)	(0.028)	(0.048)	(0.074)	(0.052)
π_{t-1}^{F}	−0.188	0.265	0.206	1.964	1.078	0.687
	(0.345)	(0.253)	(0.215)	(2.635)	(1.344)	(1.294)
π_{t-1}^{NF}	0.348*	0.766*	0.753*	0.321	0.604*	0.733*
	(0.093)	(0.065)	(0.069)	(0.316)	(0.210)	(0.280)
Number of observations	113	113	113	113	113	113
R^2	0.115	0.568	0.537	0.017	0.506	0.516
SE	0.079	0.144	0.134	0.092	0.154	0.138
DW	1.986	1.890	2.139	2.217	1.584	2.091

Note: The dependent variable is wholesale price inflation π for the United States, Japan, or their difference ("relative"). Standard errors are in parentheses, and * indicates significance at the 5 percent level. "F dummy," corresponding to the periods when the yen-dollar exchange rate was fixed, takes the value 1 for 1899–1913 and 1950–70, and 0 elsewhere. The superscript F denotes that lagged inflation has been multiplied by F dummy, and the superscript NF denotes that it has been multiplied by 1 minus F dummy. For instrumental variable (IV) estimation, instruments used are the constant, F dummy, π_{t-2}^{F}, and π_{t-2}^{NF}. For the theoretical model underlying these regressions, see Alogoskoufis and Smith 1991 and Alogoskoufis 1992.

constant, an "F dummy," which takes the value 1 when there was an official yen-dollar parity (1898–1913 and 1950–1970) and 0 otherwise,[6] and lagged inflation π_{t-1}^{F} and π_{t-1}^{NF}. π_{t-1}^{F} is lagged inflation during the fixed-rate period and takes the value 0 during the nonfixed-rate period. π_{t-1}^{NF}, lagged inflation when the yen-dollar rate was not fixed, is similarly defined.

The results are reported in table 8.1. Both ordinary least squares (OLS) and instrumental variables (IV) estimation are tried.[7] None of the coefficients on lagged inflation during the fixed-rate periods is statistically significant, and thus we cannot reject the hypothesis that inflation did not persist when the exchange rate was officially fixed. By contrast, the coefficients on lagged inflation during the nonfixed-rate periods are positive and significant: the persistence of U.S. inflation is about 0.33, whereas the persistence of Japanese inflation ranges from 0.60 to 0.77. The persistence of relative inflation is also about 0.75. (Note however that the U.S. coefficient estimated by the IV method is statistically insignificant.)[8] Overall, these results are very similar to those of Alogoskoufis and Smith, confirming the remarkable persistence of inflation during the periods when there was no official exchange-rate parity.

We conclude that the disciplinary effect of fixed exchange rates does exist and is practically important. When we compare economic performance under alternative international monetary regimes, inflation cannot be assumed to be equally persistent under each regime. Some regimes permit a slippage of monetary discipline, giving rise to persistent inflation; other regimes do not. The terms of the Phillips curve trade-off are critically dependent on the type of monetary and exchange regime that is in place.

Independent versus Forced Monetary Accommodation

However, we must be careful in evaluating monetary accommodation and inflation persistence in recent years. Alogoskoufis and Smith implicitly assume that each central bank willingly selects a desired rate of domestic inflation without any international constraint. This insular perspective is inadequate for understanding the true policy intention of the Bank of Japan under the current no-par system.

Because American monetary policy has been more or less independently determined since 1973, the persistence of inflation in the United States has been the direct result of the deliberate Fed policy to accommodate price shocks domestically. But the case of Japan is somewhat different. The yen-dollar exchange rate has not been floating passively, which would give Japan the option of following an independent monetary policy. Rather, the yen has been talked up—sometimes directly, but also indirectly through American mercantile threats—to make Japan less price-competitive and to "correct" the trade imbalance. We have shown that this idea is wrong-headed (chapters 6 and 7). But the markets see yen appreciation as a political alternative to American protectionism—whether or not it is economically meaningful—and that forces relative deflation in Japan.

In this bilateral policy game, the U.S. Fed has been the prime mover in choosing its own monetary policy while the BoJ is continually forced to follow a relatively deflationary policy vis-à-vis the United States. During the 1970s when global inflation was rampant, this accidentally brought the benefit of lower inflation to Japan, and the dilemma was not apparent. However, since the mid-1980s when inflation in the United States was greatly reduced, absolute deflation has persisted in Japan—contrary to what the Japanese government would have wanted. Thus, to a large extent, monetary accommodation of inflation (rather, deflation) in Japan has been imposed from outside.

8.3   The Fisher Effect and Interest-Rate Volatility

Inflation persistence gives us the first vital clue to understand the very different movements of long-term interest rates under the classical gold standard in comparison to the floating-rate system. Let us begin with the famous Fisher equation of the interest rate. Irving Fisher argued that the nominal interest rate (denoted by i) contains the real (i.e., inflation-adjusted) part (r) and the part reflecting people's expectations about future inflation (π) for the duration of the financial contract. The short-term interest rate (with the maturity of one period) can be written as follows:

$$i^S(t) = r^S(t) + \pi(t+1|t), \tag{8.2}$$

where the superscript S denotes the short term. The last term is inflation at time $t+1$ expected from the information available at time t. All variables in this and the following equations are expressed in terms of deviation from the historical norm.

According to the expectation theory of the term structure of interest rates, the long-term interest rate with the maturity of n periods can be written, in turn,

$$
\begin{aligned}
i^L(t) &= \frac{1}{n} \cdot \sum_{k=1}^{n} i^S(t+k-1|t) \\
&= \frac{1}{n} \cdot \sum_{k=1}^{n} r^S(t+k-1|t) + \frac{1}{n} \cdot \sum_{k=1}^{n} \pi(t+k|t).
\end{aligned}
\tag{8.3}
$$

Let us assume that the short-term real interest rate and inflation each follow an autogressive process lagged one period:

$$r^S(t) = \lambda r^S(t-1) + \varepsilon(t), \qquad 0 < \lambda < 1 \tag{8.4}$$

$$\pi(t) = \phi \pi(t-1) + \eta(t), \qquad 0 < \eta < 1 \tag{8.5}$$

We further assume, for simplicity, that these two processes are mutually independent. We may call this the assumption of "classical dichotomy" in the determination of the interest rate. Then, it can be shown that the variances of the nominal short- and long-term interest rates are, respectively,

$$\mathrm{Var}(i^S) = \frac{\sigma_\varepsilon^2}{1-\lambda^2} + \frac{\sigma_\eta^2}{1-\phi^2} \tag{8.6}$$

and

$$\text{Var}(i^L) = \frac{1}{n}\left(\sum_{h=1}^{n} \lambda^{h-1}\right)\frac{\sigma_\varepsilon^2}{1-\lambda^2} + \frac{1}{n}\left(\sum_{j=1}^{n} \phi^j\right)\frac{\sigma_\eta^2}{1-\phi^2}, \tag{8.7}$$

where σ_ε^2 and σ_η^2 are the variances of the two error terms. In each case, the first term on the right is the volatility due to the real interest rate and the second term is due to the inflation premium.[9]

Now consider the relative volatility of Fisher effects (second term). The variance of the long-term inflation premium is that of the short-term inflation premium multiplied by $(1/n)\sum_{j=1}^{n} \phi^j$. This is less than 1 for an inflation persistence ϕ that is not too close to 1, and for maturity n which is sufficiently long. In other words, long-term interest rates tend to be more stable than short-term rates partly because the inflation premium a long-term rate contains is more stable than that of a short-term rate. The price shock observed today may have a significant impact on the expected inflation of next year, but it will not change the expected inflation over the long run as much.

But how much smaller is the volatility of the long-term inflation premium relative to that of the short-term inflation premium? This depends on the value of ϕ—the more persistent the inflation rate, the less will be the proportional difference between the two variances. If every inflation is temporary and the long-term price level is known to be little affected by it, observed inflation today influences neither the inflation premium nor the long-term interest rate. On the other hand, if current inflation is a herald of more inflation to come, people will demand a higher long-term inflation premium—and along with it, a higher long-term interest rate.

Using equations 8.6 and 8.7 and comparing a hypothetical one-year bill rate versus a ten-year bond rate, the ratio of the two variances are found to be as follows:

Inflation persistence (ϕ)	Ratio of variances in inflation premium (long-term versus short-term)
0.1	0.01
0.3	0.04
0.5	0.10
0.7	0.23
0.9	0.59

This calculation suggests that under an international monetary regime with persistent inflation, long-term interest rates become increasingly volatile relative to short-term rates because of volatile inflation premia. If inflation persistence is 0.75 (as in the cases of Japanese and relative inflation during the nonfixed-rate periods; see table 8.1), the ratio of the variances between long- and short-term rates will be 0.28.

Thus, inflation persistence alone can go a long way to explain the striking difference in the volatility of long-term interest rates across alternative regimes. Suppose real interest rates behave similarly and the size and frequency of (initial) price shocks is also comparable. Then, because of the greater persistence of inflation under floating exchange rates, the Fisher effect will significantly destabilize long-term interest rates.

8.4 Multiple Portfolio Risk for International Investors

Inflation persistence and associated Fisher effects explain the volatility of long-term interest rates in terms of the evolution of domestic prices: speculators determine long-term nominal rates by arbitraging between commodities and domestic long-term bonds as inflationary expectations change. As such, our analysis so far did not consider any direct interactions through international financial markets.

Among financially open industrial countries, however, there is a further reason why long-term rates are even more volatile than shifting inflation premia would justify. In these economies, the dominant form of arbitrage at the long end of the maturity spectrum is between, say, yen bonds and dollar bonds. Speculators find it much easier to switch between dollar and yen financial assets in response to changing expectations about the long-run evolution of the yen-dollar exchange rate than to switch between domestic bonds and commodities in response to changing expectations about the long-run evolution of the domestic price level. When a domestic inflation scare arises, speculators would prefer to relocate their financial assets across countries rather than run into real assets—inventories, fixed assets, real estate, and the like—which are much less liquid.

As investors are given a broader menu of inflation hedges, the scope of information that needs to be monitored is enlarged correspondingly. In contrast, if exchange controls prevent international portfolio diversification, about the only information required for sensible domestic investors is the monetary policy stance of the home country, which would determine future domestic inflation. The higher the expected domestic inflation, the faster they should shift out of monetary instruments and into real assets. Once the economy is opened up financially, however, the game becomes much more complex, and investors need to be highly alert. Besides the stance of the domestic central bank, the relative monetary policies of a number of key industrial countries must be constantly observed and anticipated. Political instability, banking crises, new announcements, and other signs of monetary change in foreign countries become important.

In addition, international investors know that, under floating exchange rates, relative inflation is by no means the only cause of exchange fluctuations. In fact, deviation from purchasing power parity is the rule rather than the exception, especially in the short to medium run.[10] To the extent that people have doubts as to whether PPP will hold in the future, a new dimension of instability is introduced in their portfolio returns. People must anticipate not only relative inflation but also real exchange rates far into the future. The information requirement multiplies as news that is not directly concerned with monetary policies but may nonetheless affect exchange rates (i.e., potentially *any* incoming news) becomes relevant. Because international financial assets can be bought and sold more swiftly and conveniently than an inventory of commodities or real estate, market traders behave as if they are hypersensitive to global news of all sorts. Shifting expectations based on statements, business indicators, and even conjectures and rumors—will come to dominate the foreign-exchange market and interest rates.

By contrast, if countries are bound together under a common monetary standard and exchange rates are credibly fixed in the long run, volatility in long-term rates should diminish significantly even if the evolution of the common price level is uncertain. The pre-1914 classical gold standard gives some flavor of this. Although the relative price of gold—and its inverse, which is the general price level—were not perfectly anchored, speculators did not continuously switch among British, French, American, and other bonds, because all economies shared the same long-run inflation in tradable commodities with no long-term exchange risk.

In the final analysis, the observed high volatility of long-term interest rates when exchange rates float is a combined result of monetary accommodation of price inflation and price divergence (Fisher effect) on the one hand, and the unpredictability of unanchored nominal exchange rates in a financially linked world without a common monetary standard on the other. Neither the adventurousness of market traders nor the development of global electronic communications is the primary culprit.

9   Price Deflation and Purchasing Power Parity: A Causality Analysis of Yen Appreciation and Japanese Monetary Policy

Central to the main theme of our book is the hypothesis that the appreciating yen was a *forcing variable* in determining the Japanese price level. This view has been controversial. The alternative interpretation is that, under floating exchange rates after 1971, the Bank of Japan (BoJ) freely determined Japanese monetary policy and the Japanese price level according to domestic economic conditions. In this more traditional view, the yen-dollar rate would then adjust passively to be consistent with the independently chosen Japanese (and American) monetary policy.

Under either hypothesis, we know that purchasing power parity (PPP), for broad baskets of tradable goods, holds in the long run. The exchange rate and the relative price level in the two countries are both endogenous and, in response to any short-run macroeconomic disturbance, they eventually realign themselves to restore PPP (chapter 7). However, causality between these two endogenous variables is generally mutual. Thus, the relative strength of the two causal directions—from the exchange rate to prices, or from prices to the exchange rate—cannot be assumed a priori but must be ascertained empirically.

This chapter presents a new set of causality tests using the yen-dollar exchange rate together with Japanese price-level and interest-rate data. Section 9.1 introduces three alternative interpretations, with mutually incompatible policy conclusions, of how PPP reestablishes itself. Section 9.2 tests whether Japanese price movements originated mainly domestically or abroad for the period from 1985 through 1994. Section 9.3 estimates the monetary reaction function of the BoJ in response to movements in the yen-dollar rate and to domestic inflationary (deflationary) pressure over the same period. Section 9.4 summarizes the evidence on whether the exchange-rate and price movements are the cause or the result of the BoJ's policies. An appendix discusses alternative methods of computing the PPP yen-dollar rate at any point in time.

9.1   Causality in Long-Term Purchasing Power Parity

Suppose that price inflation in American tradable goods is largely exogenous, as is American monetary policy more generally. In the postwar period, the U.S. Federal Reserve Bank's formal intermediate monetary targets have changed continually: from interest rates, to nonborrowed reserves, to various monetary aggregates like M1 and then M2, to no official intermediate targets at all at the present time. Because of America's central role in the world's monetary system, however, the dollar exchange rate has seldom appeared on this list—and it has received almost no weight in the actual conduct of American monetary policy (McKinnon 1996).

Instead, over the past decade or so, the best empirically fitted model of the Fed's reaction function is "Taylor's rule" (Taylor 1992). According to Taylor, the Fed tends to increase U.S short-term interest rates when inflation increases above a norm of 2 percent in the U.S. GDP deflator, or when American real output increases above its sustainable full-employment growth path. Because the United States remains the reserve-currency country without effective foreign-exchange constraints (chapter 5), Taylor's rule continues as a purely inward-looking—or insular—reaction mechanism, quite independent of the exchange rate or monetary events in other countries. The upshot is that, in our analysis of the direction of causation between the yen-dollar rate and Japan's price level, we take the U.S rate of price inflation, and Fed policy, to be a given.

(In contrast for many, if not most, other countries, pressure on their exchange rate, for or against the dollar, quickly gets the attention of national monetary authorities. Indeed, in the case of Japan, we show in section 9.3 that the BoJ responds actively to fluctuations in the yen-dollar rate. In chapter 10, we argue for greater symmetry in the conduct of BoJ and Fed monetary policies in the future.)

Consider then the question of causality in long-term purchasing power parity (PPP). The concept of PPP was originally proposed by Gustav Cassel in the early twentieth century. According to his formulation, the exchange rate is determined by the ratio of the "purchasing powers" of two national currencies. The purchasing power of a currency, in turn, is determined by the inverse of the price of a typical goods basket. Thus, the PPP exchange rate (E^{PPP}) is shown as:

$$E^{PPP} = P/P^* \qquad\qquad (9.1)$$

where P is the price level in the home country and P^* is the price level in the foreign country. Suppose Japan is the home country and the United

States is the foreign country, and (for example) let the price of a certain goods basket be 100,000 yen in Japan and $1,000 in the United States. Then the PPP yen-dollar exchange rate for this basket is 100 (100,000/ 1,000). According to Cassel's original interpretation of PPP, an increase in the Japanese price level would proportionally depreciate the yen against the dollar, and an increase in the American price level would proportionately depreciate the dollar against the yen.

It is important to distinguish tradable goods from nontradable goods when we discuss PPP. For tradable goods, PPP holds in the long run— aside from temporary deviations and when transportation costs, tariffs, and other frictional factors are taken into account. Because industrially diversified economies like Japan and the United States each produce thousands of similar goods and are not specialized in a few products, persistent shifts in their overall terms of trade are unimportant. Thus, in the long run, commodity arbitrage will align their average price *levels*—as represented by P and P^*—internationally. In contrast and by definition, such commodity arbitrage does not occur over nontradable goods and services. Therefore, internationally divergent movements of nontradable prices do not necessarily indicate disequilibrium in the market for goods— see the discussion of the Balassa-Samuelson effect in chapters 2 and 4. In what follows, we focus on the PPP relationship among tradable goods.

Under floating exchange rates since the early 1970s, *short-term* PPP seldom holds. Frequent exchange-rate bubbles and overshooting keep the actual exchange rate mostly away from the PPP level. For the yen-dollar exchange rate, the short-term violation and the long-term validity of PPP is depicted in figure 9.1. (For alternative methods of computing PPP rates, see the appendix to this chapter.). During the past two decades, both the actual and PPP yen-dollar exchange rates showed declining trends (figure 9.1), reflecting the long-term yen appreciation against the dollar and the relative fall in the Japanese price level.[1] In the short run, however, deviations occur because the actual exchange rate changes much more rapidly than the PPP rate, whose movement depends on the more slowly evolving national price levels.

Three Hypotheses

Although many studies on the validity of long-term PPP exist, a method to investigate the mechanism by which such a relationship holds between major currencies has not been fully established. Generally speaking, the causality between two endogenous variables, such as the exchange rate

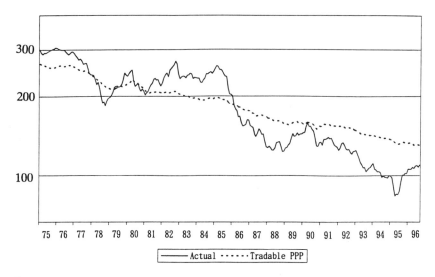

Figure 9.1
Actual and PPP yen-dollar exchange rate (semilog scale). *Note:* Tradable purchasing power
parity is based on the price survey of manufactured goods conducted by the Research Institute for International Price Mechanism (1993). For the fourth quarter of 1992, its estimate of
the tradable PPP yen-dollar exchange rate was 150.5. This benchmark has been updated and
backdated using the Japanese overall wholesale price index and the U.S. producer price
index.

and the relative price, i.e., the ratio of relative price levels P/P^*, is mutual.
The empirical observation of long-term PPP only demonstrates correlation, but does not prove causality. Understanding the dominant causality, which is unlikely to be unilateral, requires another set of empirical
inquiries.

Following Cassel, the traditional interpretation of PPP presupposes
that the main causality runs from prices to the exchange rate: autonomous changes in domestic price levels induce proportional changes in the
exchange rate. The assumption of such one-way causality is still widely
accepted. Dornbusch (1988) defines the concept of PPP thus: "Purchasing
power parity (PPP) is a theory of exchange rate determination. It asserts
(in the most common form) that the exchange rate change between two
currencies over any period of time is determined by the change between
the two countries' relative price levels" (p. 265).

However, the exchange rate may also cause the movement of relative
national price levels. In this case, the PPP relationship becomes an equation determining domestic prices. If the home currency appreciates inde-

pendently from the current monetary fundamentals, the residents will find that imported goods are now cheaper—and this will exert downward pressure on the domestic price level. Causality is reversed from the previous case: the exchange-rate movement causes the changes in the fundamentals. For instance, empirical studies by Helkie and Hooper (1988) and Ohno (1990) treat the exchange rate as an explanatory variable that determines domestic prices. In addition, practically all contributions to the literature on exchange-rate pass-through treat the exchange rate as an exogenous shock.

Because the exchange rate is an asset price dominated by expectations, it could also *anticipate* future changes in the fundamental variables and move first. In that case, true causality runs from Japanese monetary policy to the yen-dollar rate—although the time sequence is reversed from the traditional Cassel case.

In sum, there are three alternative and mutually exclusive interpretations of the fact that the nominal exchange rate and relative national price levels move in the same direction in the long run.

Hypothesis 1   The exchange rate is an *adjusting variable* that passively accommodates current changes in the fundamentals (prices, monetary policy, etc.). In this case, the flexibility of the exchange rate—despite short-term volatility—contributes to economic adjustment in the medium to long run. Causality runs from the fundamentals to the exchange rate.

Hypothesis 2   The exchange rate is a *forward-looking variable* that anticipates future autonomous changes in the fundamentals. In this case, the true causality is from the fundamentals to the exchange rate, but the movement of the exchange rate precedes that of the fundamentals in the observed time-series sequence.

Hypothesis 3   The exchange rate is a *forcing variable* that produces changes in relative national price levels, monetary policies, and so on. In this case, the exchange rate is causal in the true as well as the time-series sense. These changes in the fundamentals would not occur without the initial change in the exchange rate.

Under the maintained assumption that the U.S. price level is independently determined by the Fed, hypothesis 3 corresponds to our basic proposition that the appreciating yen caused the Japanese price level (rate of relative price deflation) and the BoJ's long-run monetary policy.

Existing Causality Tests

Many of the existing causality tests—Granger test, Sims test, variable autoregression (VAR)—are based on the concept of causality in the sense of Granger (Ohno 1989b; Manning and Andrianacos 1993). For example, Ohno's (1989b) causality test using VAR concludes that the exchange rate is an exogenous variable in the Granger sense.

It is also common to use the instrumental-variable (IV) estimation method in order to address the simultaneous equation bias problem, recognizing that the exchange rate and prices are mutually causative. For example, in estimating the standard PPP equation regressing the exchange rate on the relative price, Krugman (1978) notes that the IV estimation yields better results than the ordinary least squares (OLS) estimation in the sense that the estimated coefficient is close to unity. However, the IV estimation cannot directly test the direction of causality. In the case where the reverse causality (from the exchange rate to prices) is dominant, even the correction by the IV estimation may not produce meaningful results.

Because the tests based on Granger causality examine the time sequence of the two variables, they are able to distinguish hypothesis 1 (fundamentals precede) from hypotheses 2 and 3 (the exchange rate precedes). However, in the latter cases, these tests cannot distinguish whether the true cause lies with the fundamentals (hypothesis 2) or with the exchange rate (hypothesis 3). Nevertheless, the economically more interesting distinction is between hypotheses 2 and 3.

Different Policy Implications

The alternative assumptions about the true causality lead to sharply different interpretations and policy implications of (long-term) PPP. For the decade following the Plaza Agreement of September 1985, the yen tended to appreciate against the dollar, albeit with temporary reversals. If we consider the exchange rate to be a passively adjusting variable (hypothesis 1), this yen appreciation was nothing but a reflection of the Japanese and American fundamentals, and therefore contributed to economic adjustment and stability. This leads us to conclude that exchange-rate flexibility is desirable. The conclusion will essentially be the same even if the exchange rate is a forward-looking, but still passive, variable (hypothesis 2).

However, if the yen-dollar exchange rate is a forcing variable causing exogenous shocks to the Japanese economy (hypothesis 3), exchange-rate flexibility is by no means an unqualified blessing. Since the mid-1980s, inflations in the United States and Europe have abated. Under global price stability, if the yen appreciates greatly, driven by market sentiment unrelated to either American or Japanese price trends, the consequent deflationary pressure on Japanese prices will cause difficulties in the real economy—including *endaka fukyo* (high-yen-induced recession) and the hollowing out of the manufacturing base. Under such circumstances, the crucial policy question is how to stabilize the nominal exchange rate.

Let us summarize. Causality between the exchange rate and prices cannot be deduced a priori but should be determined empirically for each individual case. Neither the exchange-rate policy nor the international monetary system can be properly evaluated unless such causal relations are quantitatively ascertained. Policy actions based on the inaccurate causal relationship will only destabilize the macroeconomy.

9.2 Domestic versus Foreign-Exchange Determination of the Japanese Price Level

In this section, we first model the causal relationship between the yen-dollar rate and Japanese prices (hypothesis 1 versus hypotheses 2 and 3) theoretically by positing an economic structure unique to the problem at hand—unlike the popular Granger and Sims tests or VAR methodology. We then test the model empirically by looking at the price behavior of Japanese manufactured goods. We ask the question: when general inflation or deflation occurs, did domestic prices or internationally exposed prices change first? By comparing the prices of similar goods destined for home or foreign markets, we can show whether recent Japanese inflation—or, more often, deflation—is homemade or externally imposed.

The Model

The model can be construed to describe either the entire economy or individual industries. (We do both in our data analysis below.) Like us, Marston (1991) also uses Japanese sectoral data to see how yen appreciations affect the relative price structure—namely, how Japanese firms set their export price relative to the domestic price of the same product. Marston defines this exchange-rate-induced price discrimination as the "pricing-to-market" effect. Although his and our studies share a similar data set, Marston begins his investigation by assuming causation from the exchange rate to prices. In contrast, our aim is to test for the direction of causality itself.

All goods are assumed to be tradable, differing only in degree. All variables are in logarithms and refer to the manufacturing sector of the Japanese economy.

Let the *average* (i.e., domestic sales and exports combined) price level be:

$$P = \theta P_D + (1 - \theta)P_X, \qquad\qquad (9.2)$$

where P_D is the domestic sales price, P_X is the external price (export or import price, depending on whether the good is mostly exported or imported), and θ is the share of domestic sales in total sales. Assuming for simplicity that PPP always holds for the external price, we have

$$P_X = E + P_X^*, \qquad\qquad (9.3)$$

where E is the nominal exchange rate (domestic currency/foreign currency). P_X^* is the foreign (dollar) price, which is assumed—or controlled—to be given.

We assume the domestic price to be determined by the interaction of domestic aggregate demand and aggregate supply as in the standard macroeconomic model, where the price and output levels are determined at the intersection of the aggregate demand and supply functions. Thus, the domestic price can be written in a reduced form,

$$P_D = P_D(\alpha, \gamma), \qquad\qquad (9.4)$$

where α and γ are various shift parameters of the aggregate demand and supply functions, respectively. For example, α includes fiscal and monetary policies and autonomous changes in consumption and investment. γ includes productivity shocks, wage push, and so forth.

In this simplified framework, let us consider whether domestic price changes are driven mainly by domestic shocks or by exchange-rate shocks. Two cases are examined: (1) price changes precede exchange-rate changes; and (2) exchange-rate changes precede price changes. The analysis of these two cases will enable us to distinguish hypothesis 1 from hypotheses 2 and 3. In the discussion that follows, the situation of yen appreciation and Japanese price deflation is supposed, as per figures 1.1 and 1.4 (chapter 1) for 1985 to mid-1995.

Case 1: $P \to E$

In this case, an initial shift in the domestic parameter (either α or γ) lowers the domestic price. Subsequently, the exchange rate gradually adjusts to reflect the new relative price between home and abroad: the change in P precedes the change in E (hypothesis 1).

The exchange-rate dynamics can be described as follows:

$$\dot{E} = \lambda(P - E), \qquad \lambda > 0, \tag{9.5}$$

where $(P - E)$ is the deviation from tradable PPP and λ is the adjustment speed. (Recall that the foreign price is assumed to be fixed throughout.) Suppose, for instance, that monetary tightening causes absorption (total domestic spending) to contract. This will lower P_D according to equation 9.4. Because P_D is part of P (equation 9.2), P also declines. This creates a temporary deviation from PPP ($P - E < 0$), prompting E to adjust passively and gradually to the new relative price between home and abroad. P_X also moves in tandem with E, because of equation 9.3.

The entire sequence can be summarized as follows:

$$(\alpha, \gamma) \rightarrow P_D\downarrow \rightarrow P\downarrow \Rightarrow E\downarrow \rightarrow P_X\downarrow,$$

where $\rightarrow$ indicates an immediate effect and $\Rightarrow$ a lagged effect. Figure 9.2 depicts the movement of each variable after the occurrence of a domestic shock leading to domestic price deflation. Note that the average price

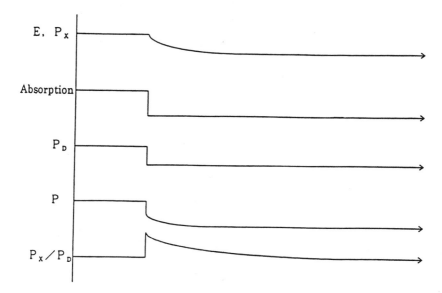

Figure 9.2
P precedes E.

level (P) and the internal relative price (P_X/P_D) move in opposite directions—that is, they are negatively correlated.

Case 2: $E \to P$

In this case, the exchange rate first appreciates independently from the fundamentals, lowering P_X according to equation 9.3. Because the reduction in P is proportionally not as large as the appreciation of E, this creates an overvaluation of the home currency ($P - E > 0$). Assuming Japan to be the home country, the yen's overvaluation leads to *endaka fukyo* and the hollowing out of domestic industries, both of which reduce absorption (especially investment):

$$\dot{A} = -\mu(P - E), \qquad \mu > 0, \tag{9.6}$$

where A is absorption. As A declines, P_D also falls due to equation 9.4—currency overvaluation is part of the demand shift parameter α.

The causal sequence can be summed up as follows:

$$E\downarrow \to P_X\downarrow \to P\downarrow \Rightarrow A\downarrow \to P_D\downarrow .$$

This is consistent with hypothesis 3. Solid lines in figure 9.3 describe the changes in the key variables after an exogenous exchange-rate shock.

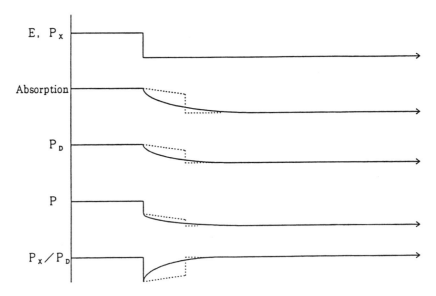

Figure 9.3
E precedes *P*.

Unlike the previous case, at the time of the shock, the movements of the average price level (P) and the internal relative price (P_X/P_D) are positively correlated.

Alternatively, if hypothesis 2 is true, the key variables are expected to behave according to the dotted lines in figure 9.3. In this case, the exchange rate changes in anticipation of the future downward jumps in A and P_D. With the change in the exchange rate, P_X also declines proportionally, while the domestic price does not change very much until the fundamentals actually change later. (However, with the initial overvaluation, absorption and P_D begin to adjust downward slowly.) In this case also, the average price level and the internal relative price are positively correlated.

The Dornbusch overshooting model is perhaps the most famous as the standard model of the exchange rate as a forward-looking variable. However, the assumptions of our model differ from Dornbusch's. Most important, prices are sticky in his model but are assumed to be flexible in response to an initial shock in ours. The dynamics of our model are provided by the lagged response of the exchange rate to the relative price, as per equation 9.5, or by the slow change in absorption due to exchange-rate overvaluation, as per equation 9.6. The assumption that prices can change fairly quickly is not entirely inconsistent with Japanese data. It is observed that a large movement of the yen-dollar exchange rate is passed through—albeit incompletely—to domestic prices within a few months.

Data Analysis

From the foregoing economic model, we should be able to distinguish hypothesis 1 from hypotheses 2 or 3 by examining the correlation between the average price level (P) and the ratio of the export price relative to the domestic price in the same product category (P_X/P_D).

In order to remove global price drift, the Japanese "average" price level, including both domestic and export goods as per equation 9.3, is deflated by the U.S. producer price index for the corresponding industry. Thus, the corrected P, now really P/P^*, measures Japanese inflation relative to U.S. inflation. If P/P^* and P_X/P_D are negatively correlated, hypothesis 1 is accepted. If they are positively correlated, we accept hypotheses 2 or 3.

The wholesale price index (WPI) for the entire manufacturing industry, as well as WPIs for seven two-digit-level industries (food, wood products, chemicals, general machinery, electrical machinery, transport machinery,

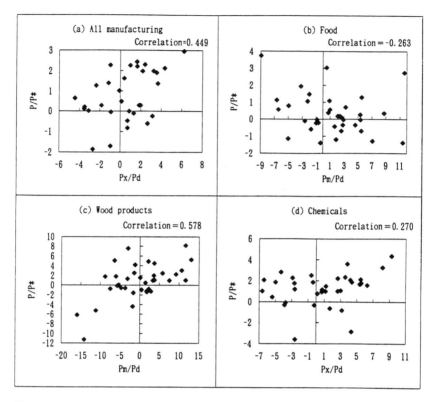

Figure 9.4
Correlation between price movements and internal relative price. On the vertical axis, Japanese price movement relative to global inflation (Japanese overall WPI deflated by U.S. Producer Price Index) is measured. "Overall" here means the weighted average of domestic, export, and import prices. On the horizontal axis, the change in the internal relative price (the ratio of export WPI (or import WPI in the case of mainly imported products) to domestic WPI) is measured. Quarterly data for 1986:Q1–1994:Q4 are used. The change is from the last month of the previous quarter to the last month of the current quarter.

and precision machinery) are examined. Selection of individual industries is dictated by the comparability of Japanese and U.S. price indices.

The domestic price data are taken from the BoJ's Domestic Wholesale Price Index. For the external price, the BoJ's Export Price Index is used. Because imports are greater than exports for food and wood products, we use instead the BoJ's Import Price Index, P_m, for those industries.

To capture causality between the yen-dollar rate and Japanese prices when deflationary pressure on Japan was greatest, that is, after the Plaza Agreement, the sample period is 1985:Q4–1994:Q4. Observations are based on quarterly rates of price change, from the last month of the pre-

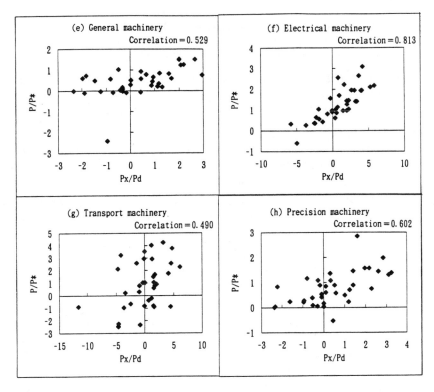

Figure 9.4 (cont.)

vious quarter to that of the current quarter. Figure 9.4 plots P/P^* against P_X/P_D for all these time-series observations, and also displays the overall correlation coefficient between the two within each product category.

Figure 9.4a shows the plot for the whole of Japanese manufacturing industry, while figures 9.4b through 9.4h show those for individual industries. For all industries except food and chemicals, the correlation between P/P^* and P_X/P_D is positive and statistically significant at the 5 percent level (the critical value is ± 0.35). In particular, electrical machinery—a key export industry of Japan—carries a high positive correlation coefficient of 0.813.

These results confirm the existence of positive correlation between the Japanese price level and its internal relative price (with a few exceptions), and thus are supportive of hypotheses 2 or 3. In the decade before 1995, a large part of Japanese price instability originated in externally exposed prices, and major inflations and deflations rarely began with domestic price changes. Thus we can safely reject hypothesis I.

9.3   The Monetary Reaction Function of the Bank of Japan

But is the true causation from anticipated domestic prices (as determined by future fundamentals such as monetary policy) to the exchange rate under hypothesis 2, or from the exchange rate to future prices under hypothesis 3? In other words, is the yen-dollar rate an *anticipatory* variable or a *forcing* one?

To answer this question, we focus on the monetary policy of the BoJ as the key fundamental variable. Although there are other fundamentals (fiscal policy, current-account balance, product innovation, demand shift, etc.), it is not unreasonable to single out the BoJ's monetary policy because (1) it is widely recognized that monetary policy is one of the most important determinants of the exchange rate; (2) monetary policy is more flexibly implemented than fiscal policy; and (3) changes in the monetary stance of the BoJ can be measured, albeit imperfectly.

Monetary policy is part of α (the shift parameter in the aggregate demand function) represented in equation 9.4 above. If the exchange rate moves in anticipation of a future change in monetary policy, the subsequent change in monetary policy must be consistent with the initial exchange-rate movement. For example, if the market expects a monetary tightening by the BoJ and therefore appreciates the yen, and assuming that expectations are on average correct, we should see an actual tightening. When the policy is later implemented, short-term interest rates will rise and prices will fall. These movements reinforce and validate the initial exchange-rate appreciation.

In contrast, if the exchange rate is an exogenous shock that truly causes undesirable price variation, the subsequent monetary policy should tend to offset the exchange rates impact on the macroeconomy. In this case, the exchange rate is the cause and monetary policy the effect.

We propose to distinguish hypothesis 2 from hypothesis 3 by observing the typical monetary policy reaction immediately after a large change in the yen-dollar exchange rate. More specifically, we will first investigate informally the policy intentions of the BoJ when it changes the official discount rate. Second, we statistically estimate the monetary reaction function of the BoJ to see whether its policy tends to validate or to offset the yen's preceding movement.

The existing literature (Yoshino and Yoshimura 1995) shows that the BoJ's principal policy instrument is the manipulation of short-term interest rates through changes in the official discount rate and through guidance of the call money rate. Nor, according to Takatoshi Ito (1992, p. 132), did

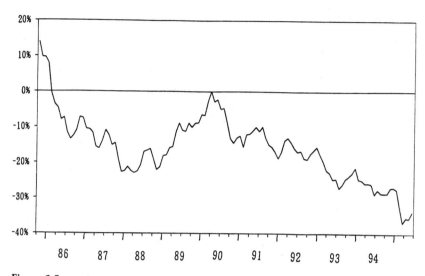

Figure 9.5
Real exchange rate (deviation of the yen-dollar rate from tradable PPP).

the BoJ aim in practice to control systematically any monetary aggregate as an intermediate target—even the "official" target of growth in M2 plus CDs. Our study also accepts that changes in short-term interest rates are the best representation of the BoJ's policy intentions, and examines their correlation with the exchange rate.

(In analyzing the reaction function of the BoJ, we dispense with the popular but empirically tenuous assumption of uncovered interest parity in short-term interest rates. However, as discussed in chapters 1 and 5, long-term interest rates in Japan have fallen systematically below their American counterparts—reflecting the expectation of an ever-higher yen and representing an important aspect of the syndrome. Furthermore, when the exchange rate moves independently, interest rates may accommodate the expected change in the exchange rate—see chapter 8—and not vice versa.)

Figure 9.1 plots the actual and PPP yen-dollar exchange rates since 1975, and figure 9.5 displays the divergence between those two exchange rates since October 1985. The decade 1985–94 can be divided into three distinct periods: the first, beginning in the spring of 1985, in which the yen appreciated sharply above PPP and continued appreciating into 1988; the second period of moderate yen depreciation from 1989 to the brief return to PPP by mid-1990; and the third period of prolonged yen appreciation from 1990 through 1994, taking the yen even further above PPP

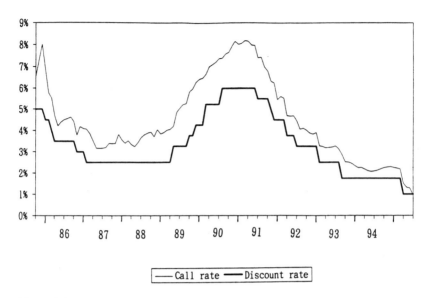

Figure 9.6
Discount rate and call rate.

until the joint interventions of May–August 1995 finally reversed this trend (figure 1.1).

Over the same decade, the BoJ's policy toward the discount rate and the call rate was correlated with these large movements in the yen-dollar exchange rate. Between 1986 and 1995, the discount rate was changed nineteen times. The call rate was also guided to trace the changes in the discount rate, as can be seen in figure 9.6. The discount rate was lowered in steps from 1986 to early 1987, then kept constant at a low level until mid-1989 (it was maintained at 2.5 percent for twenty-seven months). Rapid increases followed, up to the summer of 1990. After that, a long period of discount-rate reduction ensued.

Comparing figures 9.5 and 9.6, yen appreciation and the falling discount rate roughly coincide, as do yen depreciation and the rising discount rate. Moreover, turning points in the real exchange rate precede those in short-term interest rates by a few months to a year. We conclude from these data that, since the Plaza Agreement, the BoJ conducted interest-rate policy to offset, rather than to validate, movements in the yen-dollar rate. It has attempted to slow down or reverse sharp movements in the yen and to alleviate the deflationary impact of yen appreciation on the macroeconomy.

Table 9.1
Changes in the discount rate

Date	New rate (%)	Reason(s) for change
30 Jan. 1986	4.50	To stimulate domestic demand
7 Mar. 1986	4	To counter yen appreciation, stimulate domestic economy
19 Apr. 1986	3.50	To counter yen appreciation, participate in global monetary coordination
1 Nov. 1986	3	To counter yen appreciation, stimulate domestic economy
21 Feb. 1987	2.50	To counter yen appreciation, stimulate domestic economy
31 May 1989	3.25	To check inflation in advance
11 Oct. 1989	3.75	To check inflation caused by yen depreciation in advance
25 Dec. 1989	4.25	To check inflation in advance
20 Mar. 1990	5.25	To check inflation in advance, calm financial and security markets
30 Aug. 1990	6	To check inflation in advance
1 July 1991	5.50	To stimulate domestic economy
14 Nov. 1991	5	To prevent recession
31 Dec. 1991	4.50	To stimulate domestic economy
1 Apr. 1992	3.75	To stimulate domestic economy
27 July 1992	3.25	To stimulate domestic economy
4 Feb. 1993	2.50	To stimulate domestic economy
21 Sept. 1993	1.75	To stimulate domestic economy
14 Apr. 1995	1	To stimulate domestic economy, counter yen appreciation
8 Sept. 1995	0.50	To stimulate domestic economy, promote yen depreciation and stock market recovery

Source: Japan Economic Journal, various issues.

The BoJ's concern over exchange-rate shocks is also documented by its official statements when the discount rate was changed (see table 9.1). During the period of yen appreciation in 1986–87, the BoJ sought to counter the high yen and weak domestic business conditions. Increased interest rates in 1989–90 were designed to prevent inflation caused by the then-lower yen. (This monetary tightening in the late 1980s was also intended to end the domestic asset bubble, which was the delayed consequence of the BoJ's trying to dampen the yen's appreciation in the mid-1980s and of the first *endaka fukyo*; Ueda 1992). Subsequently, discount-rate reductions, which took the entire interest-rate structure to historically low levels by 1994, were designed to stimulate a domestic economy that was reeling from the bursting of the asset bubble and the second *endaka fukyo*.

We conclude that the BoJ regards the movement of the yen-dollar rate to be an exogenous shock to the Japanese economy and reacts to stop its trend or to ameliorate its adverse effects—but without succeeding in preventing them altogether. These results support hypothesis 3. Indeed, it is difficult to believe hypothesis 2: that the BoJ intended to allow the WPI to fall from 1985 to 1995 (figure 1.4), and that the exchange rate was just anticipating this deflationary policy.

Estimating the Policy Reaction Function

To confirm our intuition we need a more precise statistical technique for showing how the BoJ reacts to, and tries to offset, what it regards as exogenous shocks in the yen-dollar rate. We shall directly estimate the policy reaction function of the BoJ to test whether it guides short-term interest rates to offset exchange-rate movements.

The policy reaction function, estimated by Yoshino and Yoshimura (1995), shows that the BoJ responded *both* to domestic business conditions and to the exchange rate. Ueda (1992, 1995) even accuses the BoJ of overreacting to the current-account surpluses and yen appreciations of the early 1970s and the mid-1980s by creating too much domestic liquidity, which ignited domestic inflation and the asset bubble.

Let us estimate the BoJ's policy reaction function using a slightly different specification from that of Yoshino and Yoshimura. Let the monetary policy reaction function be

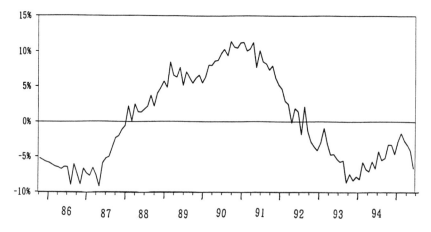

Figure 9.7
Output gap (industrial production index, deviation from trend).

$$i_t^s = \beta_0 + \beta_1 i_{t-1}^s + \beta_2 \pi_{t-1} + \beta_3 y_{t-1} + \beta_4 s_{t-1} + \eta_t, \qquad (9.7)$$

where i^s is the call rate, π is the inflation rate, y is the output gap, s is the real exchange rate, and η is the error term. The output gap is the deviation of the index of industrial production from its log-linear trend as shown in figure 9.7. The real exchange rate is measured as the deviation of the actual exchange from PPP, as shown in figure 9.5. An increase in s indicates yen depreciation against the dollar, and vice versa.

Monthly data are used, and all explanatory variables are lagged one month in equation 9.7. Alternatively, if two-month lags are taken for the explanatory variables (except the lagged call rate itself), we have

$$i_t^s = \delta_0 + \delta_1 i_{t-1}^s + \delta_2 \pi_{t-2} + \delta_3 y_{t-2} + \delta_4 s_{t-2} + v_t. \qquad (9.8)$$

The explanatory variables are lagged because of the delays in recognition and action associated with interest-rate policy. These lags reflect the time required for the BoJ to collect the data needed to initiate an action, and are perhaps a month or two in duration. Although inflation and business statistics are officially announced after two months or so, the BoJ usually has earlier access to preliminary data. As for the real exchange rate, the nominal exchange rate is known without delay, but the prices with which to deflate it also come with lags. Technically, these lags also enable us to lessen the simultaneous equation bias in the estimation of any policy reaction function.

For price data, the wholesale price index (WPI) and the consumer price index (CPI), up to $t-1$ or $t-2$, are used as alternatives. We posit that the BoJ does not react to a temporary blip, but does react to a sustained movement in the price level. The number of months that constitute such a sustained period cannot be determined a priori. Experimentation showed that monthly price variation contains too much noise, and a twelve-month movement would be too long because the BoJ reacts sooner. Somewhat arbitrarily, we choose the cumulative change over either three-month or six-month intervals to be the sustained price movement to which the BoJ reacts. For example, in equation 9.7, π_{t-1} is the cumulative price change from four months before to one month before, or from seven months before to one month before (see figure 9.8).

Tables 9.2 and 9.3 report the results of estimating equations 9.7 and 9.8, respectively, by the OLS method. In table 9.2, where the explanatory variables are lagged one month, parameters in all specifications carry the correct signs (they should all be positive) regardless of whether the WPI or CPI is used. In response to inflation, a business boom, or yen depre-

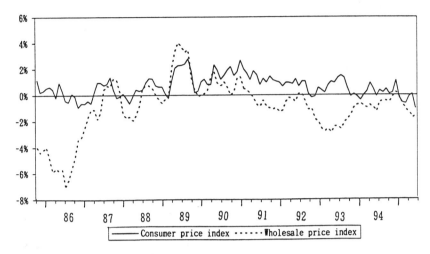

Figure 9.8
Inflation (six-month moving average).

ciation, the BoJ raises the short-term interest rate, and reduces interest rates in response to deflation, a business recession, or yen appreciation. Although the coefficients of the inflation indexes are statistically insignificant at the 5 percent level, the output coefficient is generally significant—except under specifications 1 and 2 (table 9.2), where the WPI, but not the real exchange rate, is included.

The outstanding feature of table 9.2 is that the real exchange rate induces a positive and significant policy reaction in all cases. The importance of the real exchange rate is also revealed in Durbin's h statistics. Without inclusion of the real exchange rate, h is significant at the 5 percent level (exceeding 1.96) and points to the possibilities of misspecification or a missing variable. The adjusted R^2 also improves slightly when the real exchange rate is included.

A possible reason for the insignificance of the inflation indexes in table 9.2 is that the real exchange rate already provides the information needed to forecast future price movements. Thus the actual (lagged) price data become superfluous. This interpretation is consistent with hypothesis 3, which states that exchange-rate shocks are the primary cause of (future) domestic inflation.

Table 9.3 extends the lags on the explanatory variables (except on the call rate itself) to two months, as per equation 9.8. Here, all parameters also carry the correct signs—except for the output gap in specification 2, which is insignificant. Inflation now seems to be more significant. How-

Table 9.2
Policy reaction function of the Bank of Japan (explanatory variables lagged one month; dependent variable: call rate)

	Using WPI inflation				Using CPI inflation			
	(1)	(2)	(3)	(4)	(5)	(6)	(7)	(8)
Constant	0.00086 [0.86]	0.00075 [0.74]	0.00954 [3.94]	0.00937 [3.93]	0.00134 [1.40]	0.00131 [1.37]	0.00997 [4.51]	0.00997 [4.50]
Call rate (−1)	0.977 [42.9]	0.981 [41.2]	0.848 [21.6]	0.854 [21.7]	0.955 [47.3]	0.950 [46.1]	0.835 [24.6]	0.830 [24.4]
Inflation (−1) 3-month moving average	0.0579 [1.91]		0.0230 [0.77]		0.0605 [1.61]		0.0520 [1.49]	
Inflation (−1) 6-month moving average		0.0387 [1.95]		0.0110 [1.03]		0.0705 [1.56]		0.0611 [1.45]
Output gap (−1)	0.0081 [1.03]	0.0049 [0.54]	0.0319 [3.32]	0.0290 [2.79]	0.0156 [2.53]	0.1350 [2.05]	0.0345 [4.75]	0.0328 [4.30]
Real exchange rate (−1)			0.0199 [3.90]	0.0198 [3.95]			0.0206 [4.27]	0.0207 [4.27]
$\bar{R}^2$	0.976	0.976	0.978	0.978	0.975	0.975	0.979	0.979
SE	0.00297	0.00297	0.00280	0.00279	0.00298	0.00299	0.00278	0.00278
h	1.872	1.878	1.546	1.490	2.249	2.116	1.600	1.426

Note: t-statistics in square brackets. The sample period is October 1985–July 1995 ($N = 118$). The call money rate is the dependent variable.

Table 9.3
Policy reaction function of the Bank of Japan (explanatory variables lagged two months, except call rate; dependent variable: call rate)

	Using WPI inflation				Using CPI inflation			
	(1)	(2)	(3)	(4)	(5)	(6)	(7)	(8)
Constant	0.00044 [0.44]	0.00040 [0.40]	0.00867 [3.49]	0.00887 [3.60]	0.00114 [1.17]	0.00104 [1.08]	0.0102 [4.36]	0.00991 [4.30]
Call rate (−1)	0.989 [43.47]	0.991 [42.20]	0.863 [21.06]	0.862 [21.03]	0.960 [46.25]	0.948 [45.15]	0.827 [22.37]	0.820 [22.41]
Inflation (−2) 3-month moving average	0.0812 [2.75]		0.0546 [1.88]		0.0634 [1.67]		0.0638 [1.80]	
Inflation (−2) 6-month moving average		0.0485 [2.51]		0.0342 [1.83]		0.117 [2.61]		0.112 [2.66]
Output gap (−2)	0.0017 [0.22]	−0.0009 [−0.097]	0.0261 [2.60]	0.0245 [2.28]	0.0130 [2.07]	0.0087 [1.33]	0.0357 [4.48]	0.0312 [3.84]
Real exchange rate (−2)			0.0182 [3.58]	0.0188 [3.74]			0.0207 [4.20]	0.0203 [4.18]
$\bar{R}^2$	0.976	0.976	0.978	0.978	0.975	0.976	0.978	0.979
SE	0.00295	0.00297	0.00281	0.00281	0.00301	0.00296	0.00282	0.00277
h	1.932	1.975	1.789	1.818	2.238	2.364	1.885	1.954

Note: t-statistics in square brackets. The sample period is October 1985–July 1995 ($N = 118$). The dependent variable is the call money rate.

ever, in the BoJ's reaction function, the main story again is the importance of the yen-dollar rate's deviations from PPP. Not only is the real exchange rate highly significant when measured by its t-statistics, but the adjusted R^2 and Durbin's h both improve—and the effects of the output gap become more positive—when the exchange rate is included.

Like the results found by Yoshino and Yoshimura (1995) and Ueda (1992, 1995), our results for the 1985–94 period also show that the BoJ reacts systematically to the exchange rate as well as to domestic output and inflation. In the short run, movements in the yen-dollar rate are not accommodated but instead are partially counteracted.

How, then, does our statistical study differ from the earlier ones? We consider these reactions of the BoJ *together with* our finding of positive correlation between P and P_X/P_D. Together, these confirm the validity of hypothesis 3: on net balance, the falling yen-dollar rate forced more deflationary pressure on the Japanese price level than the BoJ was happy with.

9.4 Conclusion

This chapter has presented a series of new causality tests for price movements and exchange-rate fluctuations based on Japanese monetary and price data after the Plaza Agreement in 1985. We discovered that exchange-rate movements precede changes in relative national price levels, and that any initial movement of the exchange rate not only anticipates the BoJ's long-run policy but actually causes it. True, in the short run, the BoJ reacted by adjusting its call money rate to resist these exchange-rate movements. But this resistance was insufficient to prevent a long-term downward trend in Japanese prices relative to those in the United States, with a parallel downward drift in the PPP value of the yen-dollar exchange rate, at least through 1995.

We showed that, on net balance, flexibility in the yen-dollar exchange rate was not an automatic stabilizer. Quite the contrary. The erratically appreciating yen has been an independent (or exogenous) source of disturbance. And since 1984, at least, it has imposed undue deflation on the Japanese economy.

Chapter 1 offered an explanation of why the yen should have risen in such a puzzling fashion since 1971, despite frequent bouts of resistance from the BoJ in the short run, particularly in the last decade. Mercantile pressure from the United States, consisting of commerical pressure from individual American companies impacted by Japanese competitors, and academic pressure to devalue the dollar (appreciate the yen) to "correct" American trade deficits, created a climate in which the yen would increase episodically. Caught up in this syndrome at least through-mid 1995, the Japanese authorities were too inhibited by mercantile pressure—that is, by threats of trade war—to act, or be able to act, decisively to stop the yen's appreciation.

Only after American mercantile pressure was relaxed in the summer of 1995, as we show in chapter 11, was the BoJ able to re-expand the Japanese economy while driving the yen down in the foreign exchanges. But this ad hoc policy shift need not be permanent. In chapter 10 we now discuss how mercantile and monetary relationships between the two countries could be put on a more stable and secure footing in the future.

Appendix: Estimating Tradable PPP

Estimating PPP exchange rates when exchange rates float poses a number of technical problems. First, if compiled price indices (rather than direct price surveys) are used to calculate PPP, the base year problem arises because the ratio of two countries' price indices contains an arbitrary multiplicative factor. This factor must somehow be estimated. Second, PPP exchange rates are not constant but drift over time if one country adopts expansionary monetary policy relative to another (PPP drift). Third, even among tradable goods, deviation from PPP and the speed with which prices adjust to exchange shocks differ depending on the tradability of each commodity (price diffusion). For these reasons, there is no single PPP exchange rate that would align all tradable prices individually and over time, and the exact specification of the commodity basket becomes important (see chapter 3).

The base year problem can be described as follows. If direct surveys of wholesale prices (for example) are conducted, the absolute PPP exchange rate can be calculated simply by

$$E^{PPP} = \frac{P_a}{P_a^*},$$ (9.9)

where P_a is the (absolute) yen price, and P_a^* is the dollar price, of the identical broad basket of manufactured goods at the factory gate before any indirect taxes or subsidies are imposed. Instead, price indices published by government agencies are price relatives—that is, indices relative to some arbitrarily chosen base. They are pure numbers rather than being denominated in yen or dollars. They lack a scale factor, yen/dollars, to make them comparable across countries. Thus, instead of (9.9), we have

Table 9.4
PPP estimates for 1996:Q3[a]

	Yen/Dollar	Mark/Dollar
Long-run averaging method (12-year moving average)	117	1.69
OECD price survey for machinery and equipment only[b]	125	1.90
RIIPM price survey on manufactured goods[c]	131	1.76
Price pressure method[d]	143	1.92
Economic Planning Agency price survey for consumer durables only[e]	136	2.19
OECD price survey adjusted for tradability[f]	153	2.26
Economist Big Mac index[g]	122	2.06

Note: Actual exchange rates in 1996:Q3 were 109 yen per dollar and 1.50 marks per dollar.
a. Estimates for periods other than 1996:Q3 are updated using the Cassel-Keynes method with wholesale price indices.
b. OECD 1992.
c. Research Institute 1993.
d. Ohno, 1991.
e. Economic Planning Agency, 1995.
f. Subject to upward biases, as the original data include net indirect taxes.
g. Based on *Economist*, April 27, 1996. The magazine surveys the price of McDonald's popular hamburger annually. Since the product contains both local labor and ingredients and imported materials, the results could be seen as a very limited and special PPP index.

$$E^{PPP} \approx \frac{\theta P}{P*}.$$ (9.10)

Here θ is an unknown scale factor that links the price relatives, P and P^*, and depends on the arbitrary sizes of these indices—say, 100 in 1990. The approximate equality reflects the fact that the weights of the two national baskets are similar but not identical.

Despite these problems, PPP exchange rates in tradable goods, based on several different methods for estimating θ over the same period, are rather close to each other. Table 9.4 shows various estimates of yen-dollar and mark-dollar PPP rates as of the third quarter of 1996. Table 9.4 also proves that baskets containing nontradables or net indirect taxes tend to overestimate PPP because of higher nontradable prices and/or indirect taxes in Japan and Germany compared with the United States. Alternative estimation methods are described in the following sections.

The Cassel-Keynes Method

The simple technique for estimating θ employed by Cassel (1922) and Keynes (1923) after World War I is still practiced widely. To estimate the postwar dollar-sterling PPP exchange rate, they chose one base year when it could reasonably be assumed that PPP had actually held, and then extrapolated the base year exchange rate using subsequent relative price movements.[2] The PPP exchange rate is estimated by

$$E_t^{PPP} \approx E_0 \cdot \frac{P_t/P_0}{P_t^*/P_0^*},$$ (9.11)

where E_0 is the actual (and PPP) exchange rate in the base period. θ in equation 9.10 is now $E_0 P_0^*/P_0$.

The validity of this method obviously depends on the certainty of PPP in the base period. The base period selected by both Cassel and Keynes was 1913, the year before World War I broke out. The assumption that PPP held then is justifiable because of the unparalleled exchange-rate stability and openness of the principal economies under the classical gold standard. However, this method is less suitable in our time, when major exchange rates have been floating for two and one-half decades. There is no single recent year when everyone can agree that PPP held. Choosing any single base year is much more problematic, and different base years would yield a distressingly wide dispersion of PPP estimates.

Long-run Averaging

Fortunately, we don't have to use a single base year. Although nominal exchange rates are known to be close to (but not exactly) a random walk, empirical studies show that *real* exchange rates have the mean-reverting property. In other words, the nominal exchange rate and relative prices cointegrate. PPP tends to hold in the long run, and we have demonstrated that this occurs mainly because prices move to close the initial deviation from PPP created by an exchange-rate shock.

If so, a sufficiently long period can replace a single year as the base for estimating PPP even when exchange rates float. More precisely, θ in equation 9.10 is now

$$\theta = \frac{1}{T} \sum_{k=0}^{T-1} (e_{t-k} P_{t-k}^*/P_{t-k}),$$ (9.12)

where T is the number of years included in the base period. But how many years is a sufficiently long period? The base period should cover at least one medium-term exchange-rate cycle, which typically lasts several years. If the period taken is too long, however, the commodity basket may radically change, and price indices may suffer from small but cumulative biases due to quality change and the emergence of new products.[3] We consider a twelve-year moving average (inclusive of the current year) to be a reasonable choice in table 9.4.

Price Pressure Method

Instead of assuming an arbitrary base year or relying on long-run averaging, can we statistically estimate the unknown parameter θ from the entire sample period? By imposing structure on the data, we can extract various interesting information including the PPP exchange rate. However, the success of this more ambitious approach will depend on the validity of the assumed model.

One such attempt is the price pressure method developed in Ohno (1990). It is based on the model with two equations. On the one hand, the relative price equation posits that prices move to partially offset the international price gap in each period. The responses of profit-maximizing exporting firms to changes in competitiveness lead to this assumption. On the other hand, the relative cost equation assumes that the wage-setting behavior of labor and management partially alleviates the profit squeeze on the firm caused by overvaluation of the exchange rate.

By simultaneously estimating these equations, we can test the model specification and obtain information on the adjustment speeds of prices and costs as well as the absolute level of PPP. The confidence intervals of these parameters can also be calculated. PPP yen-dollar and mark-dollar rates have been successfully estimated by this method. However, this technique is not as robust as the simple long-run averaging. The data problem concerning the unit labor cost is particularly acute. The unit labor cost index is derived from wages, hours worked, and output, each of which has various alternative definitions. Furthermore, the index is strongly influenced by business cycles. It is also presented in table 9.4.

Price Survey

The methods described so far are useful only when direct price data are unavailable and researchers must resort to the commonly used price relatives. By far the best way to estimate PPP, however, is to compare the actual prices of identical goods sold in different countries. This "absolute" PPP estimation technique circumvents the base year problem entirely. Thanks to the emergence of the high yen problem in the late 1980s, the Japanese government annually compares Tokyo prices directly with those in New York, London, Paris, Berlin, and Düsseldorf using various baskets, and this estimate is reported in table 9.4.

Even the absolute estimation method is not free from technical problems, however. Constructing an identical basket is difficult when national tastes differ and popular national models of the same product have different product specifications. Department stores, specialty stores, and discounters offer various combinations of price, quality, selection, and consumer services. Although efforts are made to ensure international comparability (Ohno 1993b; Economic Planning Agency 1994; Research Institute 1994), in practice, adjusting for product specification gaps is a demanding task.[4]

Price Survey with Adjustment for Tradability

As a further extension of the absolute PPP method, Morrison and Hale (1987) and Hale (1989) devised a clever weight-adjustment technique to estimate PPP in tradables from the OECD price survey, which covers the entire domestic expenditure category. For major industrial countries, they modified the OECD data by purging nontradable goods and increasing the weights of tradable goods. (The new weights are derived from the common basket, reflecting the trade patterns of the United States, Japan, Germany, and the United Kingdom.) One drawback of the Morrison-Hale method is the inclusion of net indirect taxes in the original data. Some tradable goods, notably energy-related goods, have greatly different tax and tariff structures across countries. For example, energy is more heavily taxed in Japan and Germany than in the United States. For this reason alone, the Morrison-Hale estimate of the PPP yen-dollar rate in table 9.4 is biased upward.

Reliability of PPP Estimates

Because of price diffusion and PPP drift, PPP exchange rates are not invariant with respect to the basket and time. The results are also affected by the inclusion of indirect taxes and subsidies. However, when these factors are properly controlled, PPP can be estimated with relatively high statistical confidence even under the current floating exchange-rate system (table 9.4). Although PPP estimation is not a trivial exercise, it can be performed with scientific accuracy if certain care is taken with respect to data. Popular but misplaced agnosticism about PPP exchange rates should be dispelled.

10

Overcoming the
Syndrome: Toward a
United States–Japan
Commercial Compact and
Monetary Accord

Previous chapters have depicted a mutual policy trap: the syndrome of the ever-higher yen. For twenty-five years, ever since President Nixon effectively ended the postwar system of dollar par values for exchange rates in August 1971, the Japanese and American governments engaged in a mutually destructive battle over commercial and exchange-rate policies. Japan, stung by an ever-higher yen and the threat of trade sanctions, was overly reluctant to open up the protected segments of its economy to foreign competition. On the other hand, infuriated with apparently unequal market access, the United States used the wrong policy tools (dollar depreciation as well direct and indirect restrictions on Japanese exports) to reduce its trade deficit—which primarily reflected, and still reflects, abnormally low American private and public saving propensities (chapter 2).

Financial markets were also caught in the policy trap. Market participants expected that the yen would, on average, appreciate against the dollar in the longer term (over the next ten to twenty years)—as reflected in Japanese long-term interest rates being three to four percentage points lower than American. But they could not predict precisely *when* another appreciation episode would occur. Each of the great yen appreciations—1971–73, 1977–78, 1985–87, and 1993 to mid-1995—was associated with bilateral commercial tension as the trade gap widened and trade talks intensified. And, in the last two episodes, relative deflation in Japan turned into absolute deflation that caused damaging *endaka fukyo*, as explained in chapters 3 and 5.

To guard against this exchange risk and associated macroeconomic instability, producers, merchants, and investors must continually modify the currency composition of their asset portfolios lest their values be accidentally lost. After 1971, Japanese financial institutions, such as insurance companies, lending long in international markets suffered large foreign-exchange losses on their dollar assets. Those losses were particularly severe from early 1985 through mid-1995, whereas the huge bad debt positions of Japanese commercial banks arose mainly out of the collapse of the bubble economy in 1990–92 and its aftermath. (In chapters 3, 5, and 9, we argued that the beginning of the bubble economy itself was an indirect result of the Bank of Japan's resisting unwanted yen appreciation in 1986–87; then, to escape *endaka fukyo*, the Ministry of Finance actively promoted the increase in asset values in 1987–89 and so amplified the bubble.)

Correspondingly, financial flows from Japan to the capital-short United States have been destabilized—contributing to the U.S. credit crunch of 1991 (chapter 5), and to excessive interest-rate volatility in the industrial economies more generally (chapter 8). Despite the fact that Japanese interest rates have remained much lower than American ones, from 1994 through early 1996 (figure 1.5) private financial institutions remained unwilling to resume international lending sufficient to cover Japan's current-account surplus. The necessary finance came only through massive purchases of U.S. Treasury bonds by the BoJ.

How can this policy trap be sprung? First, the syndrome of the ever-higher yen must be correctly diagnosed—as in our earlier chapters—so as to better understand the financial consequences of commercial confrontations. Even if the syndrome has been in remission since mid-1995 (which is discussed in chapter 11), understanding how it developed in the past—this book's major objective—is necessary for preventing a relapse.

Second, once commercial confrontations end, policy convergence to a stable yen-dollar exchange rate must be carefully orchestrated. The relative deflation in Japanese money wages, prices, and interest rates must be ended without further destabilizing the natural flow of financial capital to the United States.

Ending commercial confrontations and achieving exchange-rate stability are closely related issues. We propose a new U.S.–Japan commercial compact for relaxing tensions on a permanent basis. Fortunately, after April 1995, the United States did (temporarily) relax its mercantile pressure on Japan, thus allowing the BoJ to reflate the Japanese economy with considerable incidental yen depreciation (see chapter 11). But this remission on the commercial side is very fragile and needs to be consolidated.

We also propose a full-scale monetary accord for securing the yen-dollar rate indefinitely in a new steady-state equilibrium. But transition to this virtual exchange-rate stability (*virtual* is defined later in this chapter) first requires convergence in some important macroeconomic variables. Thus, some months or years might be needed before national monetary policies can be safely harmonized. Let us consider these commercial and monetary proposals in turn.

10.1   A New U.S.–Japan Compact for Commerce and Trade

To relieve the commercial impasse between the two countries, we propose the following actions under the rubric of a bilateral commercial compact.

The American Side

First and foremost, the United States should unequivocally abandon any commercial use of exchange-rate policy. The Secretary of the Treasury and other high officials should declare that they will not try to manage the external value of the dollar for the purpose of reducing America's huge trade deficit—a futile, but nevertheless disruptive, exercise for a financially open industrial economy with a hard currency (see chapters 6 and 7). The U.S. trade (current-account) deficit is a serious problem that should be corrected by measures to boost domestic saving. Although trade negotiations may continue with Japan on sectoral access and individual items, they should be explicitly uncoupled from the macroeconomic issues of each nation's savings-investment balance or the bilateral exchange rate.

To ensure that this uncoupling takes place, the American president should forswear the use of—or at least leave in abeyance—the Super 301 amendment to the Trade Act of 1974. As analyzed in chapter 1, Super 301 enables the president to declare unilaterally that a particular country is guilty of an unfair trading practice, usually a country that just happens to have a trade surplus with the United States. Thus it naturally exacerbates pressure on the target country's exchange rate with the dollar. If the mechanism for settling disputes were played in a lower key, only narrow legal questions of undue protectionism by the industry in question would be at issue, rather than broad macroeconomic ones. And this microeconomic approach to dispute settlement is nicely encompassed under the multilateral auspices of the World Trade Organization (WTO). The U.S trade representative's June 1996 referral of the Kodak complaint against Fujifilm to the WTO is a welcome prototype for what American policy should be in the future (see chapter 11).

For settling commercial disputes between the two countries, our puta-tive Japan–U.S. commercial compact would require no new secretariat or bureaucracy—unlike, say, the elaborate dispute-settlement mechanism of the North American Free Trade Agreement (NAFTA). Rather, the world's two largest trading countries would simply agree to refer commercial dis-putes involving either government to the WTO, thus incidentally strength-ening that worthy organization.

Private protectionism, in the form of the innumerable private petitions brought under the American antidumping laws, is more difficult to deal with. Excessive litigation is an unfortunate aspect of the American legal system as a whole, and general tort reform in the United States could hardly be part of U.S.–Japan economic pact! However, exchange-rate volatility accentuates antidumping litigation. When the yen ratchets up sharply, most Japanese exporters appear to be dumping: the dollar prices of the goods they sell in the United States fall below the (dollar) prices of the same goods produced or sold in Japan. But if the yen-dollar exchange rate were stable so that the American and Japanese price levels for trad-ables became well aligned, then allegations of Japanese firms' dumping in American markets become more difficult to prove.

The Japanese Side

As a matter of highest national priority, Japan should commit itself to a comprehensive and concrete timetable for deregulating its hitherto pro-tected sectors, including construction, transportation, telecommunication, finance, distribution, health care (pharmaceuticals), and agriculture. The government should pledge an irrevocable commitment to a five-year de-regulation plan. To avoid the bureaucratic meddling and interest-group pressure characteristic of Japanese "developmentalism" (chapter 2), a task force directly reporting to the prime minister should be created to plan the program and monitor its progress.

Fortunately, the Japanese government has already begun such a program.

U.S. retailer Toys 'R' Us fired the opening shot in 1992, forcing the government to make some revisions in the Large-Scale Retail Store Law. The changes greatly simplified the approval process for opening or expanding large stores. In 1995, the government also exempted retail stores with a floor space of less than 1,200 square yards from the tortuously complicated procedures. Annual small-store open-ings roughly doubled as a result. More important, as more stores have opened, new competition forced the prices of things like beer, colas, and meats down sharply, sometimes by as much as 50%....

A 14-member panel of businessmen and experts [was] established in 1995 to advise Prime Minister Ryutaro Hashimoto on ways to hack away at the more than 10,000 antiquated, restrictive regulations covering virtually every area of Japan's manufacturing and service economy. Unlike other government-appointed panels, the Administrative Reform Committee has clout. Nominally, at least, its recommendations amount to a legal mandate to the prime minister (although such a scenario is unlikely in nonlegalistic Japan)....

However, in April 1996, the government issued a revised three-year deregulation package about half the size of the original package announced in 1995 that [had] targeted 1,091 items for deregulation. The new package has some teeth. It calls for an end of the government monopoly on salt and an end to the ban on self-service gas stations, as well as sweeping changes in foreign exchange procedures, easier listing requirements for over-the-counter companies and reductions in the minimum unit prices of commodity funds. Other measures include fewer restrictions on imported building materials and easier provisions for securing approvals of mobile phones. (*Barron's*, June 17, 1996, pp. 20–22.)

So, some progress in deregulating the Japanese economy is being made. But the current liberalization drive remains weak and vulnerable to bureaucratic resistance. Our commercial compact, coupled with the monetary accord—described below, with the United States could still be useful for promoting further liberalization. Agriculture is an area in which tight import quotas still remain, and the outright ban on rice imports is most notorious—although its impact on Japan's total trade is minuscule. The Japanese government is already committed to establishing and then gradually expanding the rice import quota.

The Importance of Exchange-Rate Stability for the Commercial Compact

Why are Japanese quota restraints on agricultural imports that compete with similar home-grown produce more difficult to jettison than similar quantitative restrictions protecting American agriculture? In the absence of quota protection, Japanese farmers are more vulnerable than American farmers to exchange risk because of the continued central role of the dollar in world commodity markets. International trade in standardized agricultural products is invoiced in dollars, with basing points in American locations along with centralized futures markets that are largely dollar denominated (McKinnon 1979). This asymmetry implies that fluctuations in the dollar's exchange rate against other currencies will initially have virtually a one-to-one impact on foreign-currency prices of standardized commodities, whereas their dollar prices are fairly immune.

Once the yen-dollar exchange rate is stabilized, however, we suggest that initial quotas covering a variety of Japanese agricultural products should immediately be converted to equivalent tariffs, which will be reduced over the next five to ten years to a low—but not necessarily zero—target level. With the removal of exchange risk, this tarification program should be easier to implement both economically and politically. For example, Japanese rice producers need no longer fear unexpectedly strong price competition from a sudden fall in the yen-dollar exchange rate, or from chronic yen overvaluation. Excess financial risk is thereby reduced—although Japanese farmers would, of course, remain vulnerable to ordinary commercial risk as relative commodity prices vary in world markets.

More generally, trade liberalization and exchange-rate stability go hand in hand. Stable exchange rates with properly aligned national price levels (see discussion of the monetary accord in the next section) provide a political as well as an economic impetus to opening markets, whereas exchange instability militates against it. Looking back over the last two centuries or so, periods of vigorous expansion of free trade have coincided with fixed exchange rates under a common monetary standard. Yet today, the economics profession often ignores the complementarity between free trade and exchange stability, in part because such a historical proposition is difficult to verify by modern econometric techniques.

As chapter 3 demonstrated, large deviations from purchasing power parity can easily wipe out hard-earned productivity gains, turn profits into losses, close factories, and lay off workers who are otherwise productive. With an overvalued currency, pressure from interest groups to protect domestic industries mounts, and the government finds it difficult to ignore. Once installed, however, protectionist measures are unlikely to be dismantled even when the exchange rate becomes undervalued. Thus, a ratchet effect drives up the level of protection with each major exchange-rate cycle (McKinnon and Fung 1993). And indeed, although import tariffs have continued to come down, protectionism in the form of nontariff barriers (NTBs)—import quotas, "voluntary" export restraints, administrative controls, and the like—has proliferated since the 1970s. Because they insulate domestic prices from exchange-rate fluctuations, these NTBs are more effective than tariffs in shielding domestic industries from sudden changes in international competitiveness when exchange rates are volatile.

Americans should be aware that there is increasing agreement in Japan that opening markets is inevitable and even desirable for Japan's own sake. With the collapse of the bubble economy and the emergence of Asia's newly industrializing economies as formidable rivals, Japanese people and enterprises have come to regard economic liberalization—that is, final abandonment of the developmentalist institutions—as a prerequisite for national survival. Why, then, was this collective determination not translated into real action until the 1990s? In the past, after all, Japan time and again demonstrated a remarkable capacity to adapt once a consensus for change was formed—for example, during the immediate postwar recovery of 1945–49, the high-growth era of 1950s and 1960s, and the oil shocks of the 1970s.

One reason for delaying deregulation until the 1990s was political weakness. But Japanese reluctance stemmed more fundamentally from the endless difficulties caused by the syndrome of the ever-higher yen. Although Japan was not really unwilling to open up on principle, occasional great overvaluations of the yen as well as the long-term prospect that the yen would continue to appreciate vis-à-vis the U.S. dollar inhibited bold actions to deregulate the economy. First, in a severe *endaka fukyo*, the government is so preoccupied with recovery measures that liberalization tends to be put aside. Second, the legitimate fear that market opening may subject a protected industry to an undue price disadvantage at the whim of financial markets engenders stiff resistance in the protected sector. When the yen is overvalued, the gap between international and protected domestic prices is too formidable to risk liberalization. Third, when Japan feels victimized by an engineered yen overvaluation, unilateral concession to the American demand of greater market access is politically infeasible.

At present, Japan wants a stable yen, and the United States wants broader market access. Each country is denying the wish of the other, and each remains frustrated. The new U.S.–Japan commercial compact, including an exchange-rate agreement, would force them to be generous toward each other and would break the deadlock in a manner that would satisfy the political needs of both countries.

But Americans should remember that even vastly improved access to Japanese markets will not itself reduce America's current-account deficit. Only increased American saving relative to investment will do that.

10.2   Monetary Accord in the Steady State

Once the political will is present, a Japanese-American economic pact to rationalize commercial policy is immediately feasible. Once American officials pledge not to use the exchange rate as a mercantile device to correct the American current-account deficit, the principal source of continual downward pressure on the yen-dollar exchange rate (i.e., upward pressure on the yen) would dissipate. But without further monetary cooperation, this action by itself would still leave the rate volatile. Monetary harmonization for keeping the rate within *hard* narrow bands, with a stable price level in common, would overcome the syndrome of the ever-higher yen once and for all.

However, such a monetary accord would likely require more time to implement than the putative commercial compact, for several reasons. First, such an accord really cannot be credible until commercial confrontations cease, as we demonstrated in chapter 1. Second, initial macroeconomic conditions at the time the accord is negotiated may or may not be favorable—depending on relative interest rates, the deviation of the yen-dollar exchange rate from purchasing power parity, and the comparative momentum in each country's domestic wages and prices.

Nevertheless, the BoJ and the Fed could begin working toward monetary convergence that would, some months or years hence, allow the yen-dollar rate to be stabilized within a narrow band. The threat of the yen rising ever higher into the distant future would be further alleviated at the outset. But for this transition to succeed, the rules of the game governing the behavior of the two central banks in the new steady state must be well defined.

This book's companion volume, *The Rules of the Game: International Money and Exchange Rates* (McKinnon 1996), lays out the alternative steady-state rules governing international monetary interactions from the late-nineteenth-century gold standard, through the postwar fixed- and floating-rate dollar standards, through the operation of the Plaza-Louvre Accords and the European Monetary System. Using this historical perspective on how a *consistent* set of rules could function under modern conditions, McKinnon then outlined (in the last chapter of that volume) a comprehensive proposal for stabilizing exchange rates and price levels among the major industrial countries in Asia, Europe, and North America. Despite its grand title, "A Common Monetary Standard for the 21st Century" (CMS21), the proposal elaborates and greatly tightens rules that have existed informally and loosely since the 1985–87 Plaza-Louvre Accords among the G7 industrial countries.

But the volatile yen-dollar relationship, marked by continual commercial pressure by the United States on Japan to appreciate its currency, was (and potentially still is) a major flaw in the Plaza-Louvre Accords. Therefore, a new monetary accord between Japan and the United States to stabilize the yen-dollar exchange rate would be fully consistent with

Monetary Accord between Japan and the United States:
New Rules of the Game for the Steady State

I. Announce a target zone for the yen-dollar exchange rate of ±5 percent. Base the central rate on the initial purchasing power parity rate that aligns wholesale price levels. Some years after confidence in the accord is established, narrow the band of exchange variation.

II. Intervene in concert to reverse short-run trends in the yen-dollar exchange rate that threaten to pierce zonal boundaries. Do not disguise these concerted interventions.

III. Practice free currency convertibility on current and capital account, and hold official exchange reserves symmetrically in each other's currencies. U.S. government should complete its buildup of reserves in yen, and possibly other convertible currencies.

IV. Don't fully sterilize the immediate monetary impact of interventions in the yen-dollar exchange market by the Bank of Japan or by the U.S. Federal Reserve Bank. Let short-term interest rates and each country's domestic monetary base adjust modestly (Bagehot's rule).

V. In case of a speculative attack that would require very sharp increases in short-term interest rates to defend the exchange rate, suspend rule I temporarily. But restore the "traditional" yen-dollar exchange parity as soon as practicable.

VI. Assign domestic central bank credit to anchor the price level of tradable goods—as measured by the WPI in Japan or the PPI in the United States—in the long run.

VII. Should under- or overshooting in either country's price-level target occur, do not rebase. Reflate or deflate gradually in subsequent periods as necessary to satisfy rule VI and to maintain traditional yen-dollar exchange parity.

VIII. Continue to play by the rules of the Plaza-Louvre Intervention Accords for limiting major fluctuations in the dollar's (and yen's) exchange rate against hard European monies.

Plaza-Louvre, and with any stronger and broader agreement for exchange-rate stabilization—such as CMS21—that might come later. Given the European preoccupation with monetary union (EMU), monetary harmonization between the United States and Japan—besides having great value itself—is also a possible first step in a broader exchange-rate agreement encompassing Asia as well as Europe.

In proposing new rules of the game between Japan and the United States for the steady state, we keep the spirit of CMS21. Because the bilateral Japan–U.S. relationship is less complex than the multilateral monetary arrangements envisioned in CMS21, the ongoing monetary interaction between the BoJ and the Fed requires fewer rules. Those rules are summarized in the accompanying box.

The historical rationale for each of these eight rules can be fully understood only by reading this book's companion volume. However, the main focus of the accord is to overcome, once and for all, the syndrome of the ever-higher yen—that is, to stabilize permanently the *nominal* value of the yen-dollar exchange rate within some narrow band (rule I). Yet, unless both central banks had already agreed on a price-level anchor for the new regime, announcing a hard target zone for the yen-dollar rate could be a mistake. Thus, rules VI and VII commit the BoJ and the Fed to aim for level (as distinct from rate-of-change) stability in the broadest index that we have for tradable goods prices: the wholesale price index (WPI) in Japan and its virtual equivalent, the producer price index (PPI) in the United States.[1]

Would these *domestic* price-level targets for each country be consistent with *external* exchange-rate stability? When the exchange rate was successfully fixed at 360 yen to the dollar in the 1950s and 1960s, figure 10.1 shows that price inflation in these two indexes was virtually the same (less than 1 percent per year) in Japan and the United States. Because they were highly diversified industrial economies, each producing thousands of (tradable) goods, international commodity arbitage—at the fixed exchange rate—was robust and, in the aggregate, terms-of-trade effects were minimal. And figure 10.1 also shows that, when the mark-dollar rate was fixed, this wholesale price-level alignment held with the industrially diversified German economy. (Between more specialized economies producing primary products, whose aggregate terms of trade are naturally variable, wholesale price levels need not line up so neatly.)

Conversely, if each country targeted a broad index including both tradables and nontradables, such as its own CPI or the GNP deflator, this index need *not* be consistent with exchange stability. Because of Japan's historically higher productivity growth in tradables (chapter 4), and because of greater protection for her nontradables sector—an aspect of Japanese developmentalism (chapter 2)—the Japanese CPI increased much faster than the American after 1950 (see figures 2.4 and 4.4). Therefore, if the BoJ were to set a level target for its CPI, and the Fed were to set a level target for the American CPI, exchange equilibrium might still require an (erratically) appreciating yen—precisely the syndrome from which we are trying to escape. Thus rule VI's emphasis on targeting the WPI or PPI.

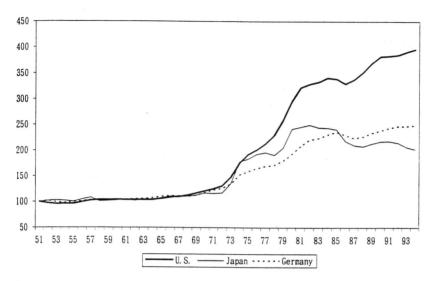

Figure 10.1
Wholesale price levels (1951 = 100).

Alternatively, if Japan continues to liberalize in the 1990s and so eliminates decades of excess protection of its nontradables (largely services)
sector, then the domestic prices of services could fall relative to commodities for a few transition years. This transition appears to be happening in
1995 and 1996: Japan's CPI is growing negligibly, while the WPI grows a
little more than 1 percent per year. This is all the more reason for the BoJ
to focus on stabilizing the level of the WPI, which remains relatively
immune to the large structural changes sweeping the service sectors of
the Japanese economy.

Suppose Japan and the United States each achieve a roughly level target for their WPI and PPI respectively, and their nominal interest rates—
particularly at long term—are fairly well aligned. Then the nominal exchange rate that just aligns the two national price levels—that is, the PPP
rate as per rule I, is fairly straightforward to estimate, establish, and then
maintain. Chapter 9's appendix discusses alternative methods for estimating purchasing power exchange rates. For the third quarter of 1996, table
9.4 shows that the relevant PPP rate was about 125 yen per dollar.

Once this official exchange parity is declared when the fundamentals
are right (how to determine the propitious moment is discussed further in
chapter 11), aligning the two countries' now stationary WPIs would normally require only modest levels of official intervention (rule II), and only

minor adjustments in *relative* short-term interest rates (rule IV), to keep
the market rate within ±5 percent or within some similarly narrow band.
The key is to have the two central banks signal strongly their intention to
maintain the new regime by overtly, and symmetrically, cooperating.
Kathryn Dominguez and Jeffrey Frankel in *Intervention Policy Reconsidered*
(1993) analyzed official interventions since the Plaza-Louvre Accords of
1985–87. They concluded that the major central banks were quite successful in ironing out extreme cyclical fluctuations in the yen-dollar and
mark-dollar exchange rates if official interventions were seen to be (1)
concerted and (2) highly visible or strongly signaled. Then, not much, if
any, supporting adjustment in domestic short-term interest rates was necessary: interventions could be largely sterilized in their domestic monetary impact and still succeed in stabilizing the exchange rate. Catte and
colleagues (1992) studied official interventions after 1985 to stop runs for
or against the dollar, in terms of marks or yen, and came to the same conclusions. Thus rule II emphasizes strong signaling by having both the Fed
and the BoJ intervene in undisguised concert to keep the yen-dollar rate
within its band.

10.3   Self-fulfilling Speculative Attacks: The European Experience

After macroeconomic convergence, central bank cooperation (as specified
in the rule box) can normally maintain exchange parity indefinitely. But
times aren't always normal. When the capital account is fully open, seem-
ingly firm parity commitments by central banks may be subject to speculative attacks: witness the traumatic breakdowns in the European Exchange
Rate Mechanism (ERM) in the early 1990s. Overwhelming capital outflows forced Britain and Italy to devalue and leave the ERM in September
1992, and Sweden abandoned its fixed exchange rate with the ecu later in
the same year. Similarly, in August 1993, hot money flows forced France
and the remaining countries around Germany to suspend their narrow
±2.25 percent bands in favor of meaninglessly wide ±15 percent bands.
Won't our putative monetary accord between Japan and the United States,
where international capital flows are unrestricted (rule III), also fall prey to
speculative attacks and possible collapse?

   Economic theory on the subject has been evolving. The "old" literature
on speculative attacks (Salant and Henderson 1978; Krugman 1979) presumed that the monetary fundamentals were not right for preserving a
fixed exchange rate. Indeed, Krugman began his analysis by assuming an

unsustainable expansion of central bank credit by one of the countries. Because a speculative attack was obviously inevitable if monetary conditions didn't change, the theoretical problem in the "old" crisis models was simply one of pinning down *when* it would occur. However, our monetary accord rules out precisely this kind of unlimited domestic credit expansion. Rules IV, VI, and VII restrict volitional credit expansion by the BoJ and the Fed to what is consistent with price-level and exchange-rate stability in the long run.

But the theoretical basis for the "new" crisis models—and for the corresponding deep pessimism over the viability of fixed exchange rates—is quite different. Writers in this new vein start with the presumption that monetary and current-account fundamentals could be more or less right, with no shortage of exchange reserves or credit lines for defending the fixed exchange rate. Even so, this new wisdom has it that any country with an independently circulating money may still be vulnerable to a *self-fulfilling* speculative attack[2] on its exchange rate in the short or medium runs.

Krugman (1996) neatly summarizes the essential elements of the new approach. Although the government normally would prefer to honor its commitment to a fixed exchange rate, in reality politicians need to minimize a more complex social loss function if they are to stay in office. For example, an unexpected cyclical downturn could lead both to an upsurge in unemployment when wages are sticky and to a burgeoning of the government's debt and deficit position, as with Sweden in 1990–92. A devaluation cum monetary expansion could be seen—as it indeed was in the Swedish case—as necessary to stimulate economic activity to mitigate unemployment and the fiscal deficit.

The higher the cost of remaining with a fixed exchange rate (the steeper the economic downturn), the greater the rate of depreciation that the markets come to expect. The defense of the exchange rate then requires an even sharper increase in nominal interest rates. But with domestic prices and wages fairly sticky, the consequential increase in real interest rates impedes recovery of the private economy. Public debt could then spiral upward because (1) the fall in net tax revenue increases the government's primary deficit, and (2) service charges on the public debt escalate as it is rolled over at the higher interest rates. As Krugman (1996) and the others point out, when everyone expects depreciation sooner or later, it becomes increasingly expensive *not* to depreciate. Although probing attacks against the currency to test the government's resolve need not be successful initially, the economic costs accumulate and eventually become overwhelming—whence a devaluation aided and abetted by self-fulfilling expectations.

Again, the Swedish experience nicely illustrates the new wisdom. After a boom that had overheated the economy by the late 1980s, the property crash and associated banking crises of 1990–91 provoked a downturn in the Swedish economy and uncovered larger than expected public-sector deficits. The basket peg for the krona exchange rate was subject to probing attacks over the period 1990–92. (Initially, the basket was weighted more toward the dollar, but after May 1991 it was centered on the ecu, with the mark getting a heavier direct and indirect weight than other European currencies.) By September 16, 1992, the government could only beat back a strong speculative attack by increasing overnight interest rates to an extraordinary 500 percent—now a very well-publicized landmark in the annals of international finance. But, by impeding Sweden's recovery and by increasing debt service costs, this high-interest strategy proved too costly. Thus, when another attack came on November 19, the government rather quietly gave up and floated the currency. By year's end, the krona had depreciated by 15 percent against the ecu, and by the end of 1993 it had depreciated another 9 percent.

What do proponents of the new theory of self-fulfilling speculative crises conclude? Without controls over international capital movements, and in the face of normal business-cycle fluctuations, no fixed exchange-rate regime can be sustained short of full-scale monetary integration. And much of the political push toward European Monetary Union (EMU) comes from the new belief that, where national monies remain in separate circulation, fixed nominal exchange rates are no longer feasible.

However, for our proposed monetary accord between Japan and the United States, we suggest that this new pessimism is largely unwarranted—as long as the two countries play by the steady-state rules sketched in the box above. We certainly do not propose a full-scale monetary union between Japan and the United States, nor do we believe it is necessary for achieving exchange stability. The dollar and yen would continue to circulate in largely separate domains.

What, then, makes the U.S.–Japan situation different from the European experiences of the early 1990s? First, the boom-and-bust cycles generated in a number of European countries in the late 1980s and early 1990s, culminating in devaluations against the mark, arose out of their asymmetrical positions with respect to Germany. While liberalizing their economies, Britain, France, Italy, Spain, and Sweden all opted to peg to the more stable-valued deutsche mark as an anchor for bringing down their higher rates of inflation. And it can be shown that, in the absence of capital controls, this method of disinflation can generate excessive capital inflows followed by a boom-and-bust cycle (Walters 1990; Pill 1995a; McKinnon 1996). In contrast, our U.S.–Japan monetary accord is crafted to keep the two countries symmetrically situated: each one must succeed in independently stabilizing its price level (rules VI and VII) before the yen-dollar rate is to be formally fixed.

Second, recent business cycles in Japan, and to a lesser extent in the United States, have themselves arisen out of the syndrome of the ever-higher yen. Indeed, the commercial and monetary accords proposed here are designed to overcome the syndrome, to put the two countries on a more symmetrical footing, and to allow Japan to avoid *endaka fukyo* while ameliorating U.S. credit crunches (chapter 5). Thus the accord could reduce the incidence and frequency of business cycles.

On the negative side, suppose that "random" business cycles, which are not themselves exchange-rate related, remain. After the monetary accord is established and a new official yen-dollar exchange parity has been declared, each country will experience cyclical fluctuations independently, or at least out of phase. For short- and medium-term macroeconomic management, might not these idiosyncratic cyclical fluctuations then occasionally require Japanese monetary policy to differ substantially from American?

For minor business cycles, having a band of ±5 percent gives substantial scope for differentiating short- and medium-term interest rates between the two countries for a year or two. Because of the mutual commitment to exchange-rate stability in the long run, however, long-term interest rates should remain much closer together.

For example, suppose a moderate cyclical downturn occurs in the United States, to which the Fed responds by temporarily easing monetary policy. U.S. short-term interest rates fall as the dollar depreciates to the bottom of the 10 percent band. As long as people anticipate that the dollar will gradually appreciate to the middle of the band, low short-term U.S. interest rates are consistent with foreign-exchange equilibrium. And these regressive expectations would be strengthened under a formal monetary accord that guaranteed the dollar's exchange rate in the long run. This regressivity makes it easier for the American monetary authorities to reduce short rates—thus dampening the cyclical downturn in the American economy—without reigniting inflationary expectations that would otherwise boost long-term interest rates. In either country, this commitment to price-level and exchange-rate stability in the long term (rules VI and VII) could make short-term countercyclical changes in monetary policy more effective.

However, isn't a self-fulfilling exchange-rate crisis still possible? Suppose some very large, and thus very unusual, macroeconomic shock occurred in one country. A good example is the sudden massive increase in government spending associated with reunification in Germany in 1990–92 (chapter 5). Because, at the same time, the Bundesbank was determined to fight inflation with a tight monetary policy, massive upward pressure on the mark developed in the foreign exchanges, leading to eventual sharp appreciation. Conversely, a sudden downturn in one of the two economies could provoke massive capital flight because speculators anticipate the need for an easier monetary policy, as in the case of Sweden in 1991–92. (We don't foresee any similar shocks in Japan or the United States once the syndrome of the ever-higher yen is overcome.) Can the rules of the game be established so that such speculative attacks, even when successful, are unlikely to fatally undermine our monetary accord?

10.4 Temporary Suspensions of Exchange Parities: The Restoration Rule

The behavior of countries under the international gold standard before 1914 is instructive. In the face of a liquidity crisis, a country would sometimes resort to the use of "gold devices"; that is, it would raise the buying price for gold or interfere with its exportation. This amounted to a minor, albeit temporary, suspension of the country's traditional gold parity. In more major crises, including wars, a few outright suspensions for some months or years occurred. In the long run, however, the gold standard was very successful in having countries adhere to their traditional exchange parities while anchoring the common price level. In early 1914, exchange rates and wholesale prices were virtually the same as they had been in the late 1870s.

What gave the pre-1914 gold standard its long-run resilience? After any short-run crisis forced the partial or complete suspension of a gold parity, the country in question was obliged to return to its traditional parity as soon as practicable. I have dubbed this unwritten obligation of the classical gold standard "the restoration rule" (McKinnon 1996, chapter 2). Because of the rule, longer-term exchange-rate expectations remained regressive with respect to the country's traditional gold parity. Although short-term interest rates fluctuated under the gold standard, long-term interest rates showed little volatility by modern standards, and, without significant interest-rate risk, their levels also remained low: about 3 percent in the United Kingdom and 4 percent in the United States (chapter 8).

The parallel for our monetary accord between Japan and the United States is clear. In some extraordinary upheaval in one of the two countries, which we cannot now imagine, the parity obligation could be suspended— as rule V permits. For example, if some very steep cyclical downturn required an extremely easy national monetary policy, the band of exchange-rate variation could be temporarily widened—or dropped altogether—to allow that country's currency to depreciate further.

However, that is not the end of the story. Any suspension of the exchange-rate parity would be only temporary. As soon as practicable after the speculative attack, rule V requires the central bank in the country experiencing the idiosyncratic shock to begin nudging the yen-dollar exchange rate back toward its traditional parity. Thus, expectations of an ever-higher yen (ever-lower dollar) could not develop.

In the 1990s, France provides the best modern example of a country following the restoration rule de facto. The massive speculative attack against the franc in September 1993 forced a virtual suspension of the ERM bilateral parity grid—the exchange margins were made ridiculously wide (± 15 percent). Yet, subsequently, the franc-mark exchange rate quickly returned to near its traditional level against the mark; and, unlike during the 1980s, French long-term interest rates have closely tracked German ones in the 1990s.

Allowing for temporary crisis-based suspensions of convertibility, followed by (gradual) restoration of the traditional parity, poses problems for speculators. They don't have any clear point at which to get out of their contracts (short in the weak currency) in order to realize speculative profits. In contrast, a more or less discrete devaluation in response to a speculative attack, with no attempt at restoration, makes it easy for speculators to get out safely. Thus, even though speculators know that temporary suspensions of convertibility are possible, speculative attacks may well be less likely if they also know in advance that the restoration rule is in place.

So, in response to a major speculative attack (but certainly not minor ones), a temporary parity suspension with some depreciation (or appreciation), coupled with the restoration rule, would have substantial advantages: (1) In the short run, the government in the country experiencing the shock isn't forced to increase interest rates sharply in a cyclical downturn—or isn't prevented from raising them sharply to prevent an inflationary explosion. (2) In the medium run when the errant exchange rate is nudged back up, the mercantile advantage from the unexpected competitive devaluation is dampened. (3) The promise of eventually returning to the traditional exchange parity and price-level target limits volatility in long-term interest rates.

The result is *virtual*, rather than absolute, exchange-rate stability in the new steady state. In our proposed monetary accord, the yen-dollar exchange rate would be more secure in the distant future than in the near term. Under this virtual exchange-rate stability, the expectation of an ever-higher yen would disappear, long-term interest rates would remain close together, and financial as well goods markets in both countries would become more stable.

10.5   Compact or Accord: A Concluding Note

However, a commercial compact must undergird the monetary edifice. Without at least a firm understanding that the yen-dollar exchange rate will not be subject to mercantile pressure or be used as an instrument to "correct" trade imbalances, ongoing monetary harmonization with financial stability in the two countries becomes impossible. Indeed, a U.S.–Japan commercial compact could stand by itself and still be of great value even if a formal monetary accord—however great its further value—proves too difficult to negotiate.

11 Is the Syndrome Over? The Fall of the Yen, 1995–96, and Its Implications for the Transition

Cecily, you will read your political economy in my absence. The chapter on the Fall of Rupee you may omit. It is somewhat too sensational. Even these metallic problems have their melodramatic side.

—Oscar Wilde, *The Importance of Being Earnest*, 1895

In concluding our study of the economic interaction between Japan and the United States, unlike Miss Cecily we dare not omit a chapter on the remarkable fall of the yen after April 1995. The main facts indicate that a break with the past is quite possible. Figure 11.1 shows rather dramatically a sharp V-shaped movement in the yen-dollar rate: from 112 in January 1994, to 100 by January 1995, to briefly touch 80 in April before recovering to 100 by December 1995. Completing the V, the yen fell even further, to about 110 to the dollar, in July 1996 and to 113 by the following December. This yen depreciation of more than 35 percent from its April 1995 trough is without parallel in Japanese financial history since exchange stabilization under the Dodge Plan of 1949.

As of early 1997, we don't yet know whether these events herald a permanent change in the exchange-rate regime—that is, that the yen is no longer expected to rise indefinitely. Alternatively, the 35 percent yen depreciation could be just a surprisingly large temporary remission, and the expectation of an ever-higher yen in the more distant future might remain intact.

Whether temporary or permanent, however, the fall itself provides new evidence about how mercantile pressure from the United States determines the yen-dollar rate. Because this hypothesis is so central to the book, let us first consider the precise sequence of events in 1995–96 that led to the changed behavior of the exchange rate.

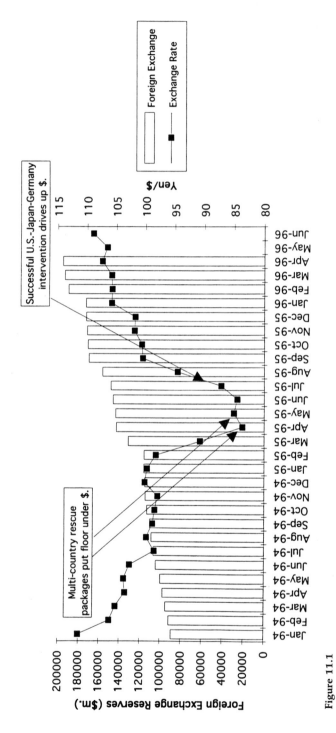

Figure 11.1
The yen-dollar exchange rate and Japanese foreign exchange reserves, 1994–96. *Source:* IMF, *International Financial Statistics.*

Then, we will analyze the likely consequences of the fall for interest rates and capital flows. This allows us to confront transition problems of how to escape from the syndrome. If Japan and the United States are indeed moving to a new steady-state equilibrium with virtual exchange stability (chapter 10), what monetary adjustments will be necessary to minimize financial volatility during the transition?

11.1   The Mercantile-Pressure Theory of the Yen-Dollar Exchange Rate: A Confirmation

Beginning in mid-1995, a major relaxation of American commercial and financial pressure on Japan allowed the Bank of Japan to mount a vigorous monetary expansion. By deliberately driving the yen-dollar rate back up toward purchasing power parity (PPP), the government of Japan halted what had become a disastrous deflationary spiral, and the Japanese economy showed significant increases in real output in 1996.

By contrast, in the decade before mid-1995, the United States had become increasingly aggressive in asserting trade grievances and then relying on "Super 301" negotiating authority to threaten Japan directly with sanctions (chapter 1), thus bypassing the World Trade Organization's (WTO's) multilateral dispute settlement mechanism. In the first four months of 1995, the dispute over opening Japan's domestic markets to imports of automobiles and parts, in which Americans demanded numerically specified targets, was particularly acrimonious and unsettling. From 100 to the dollar, the yen ratcheted up spectacularly to briefly touch 80 in April 1995. Japan's macroeconomy teetered on the brink of a major breakdown, with a fall in GNP, declining prices, and worsening bad debt positions of its banks, insurance companies, and so on. The yen was so high relative to its PPP (about 125 to the dollar—table 9.4) that domestic investment looked increasingly unprofitable and a further slump appeared to be in the offing. In retrospect, the syndrome became more acute than what had been experienced before or since.

Only in April 1995 did the American government finally realize that something had gone terribly wrong with its commercial and exchange-rate policies toward Japan. Besides imperiling Japan's economy, a collapse in the the Japanese financial system, bringing a great slackening of outflow of private financial capital, would make it more difficult for the U.S. Treasury to fund its own deficits. A potential capital shortage in the United States, reminiscent of the American credit crunch of 1991 (chapter 5), seemed uncomfortably close.

What was the American response? On the commercial side, U.S. officials abandoned further significant mercantile pressure on Japan. The dispute over automobile components was settled quietly in June 1995, without fixed numerical targets and with Japan promising only to simplify bureaucratic restraints on importation and to encourage dealers to stock a wider range of foreign vehicles and parts. Since then, new potential flashpoints for invoking Super 301 against Japan have been ignored for at least a year. Most important because of its great symbolism, the long-simmering dispute between Eastman Kodak and Fujifilm over Kodak's alleged inability to market its film freely in Japan (because of Fuji's alleged monopolization of the Japanese market) was defused and finally sent to the WTO after the U.S. government pointedly decided *not* to invoke Super 301:

In May of last year [1995], Kodak officials were brimming with confidence when their new Chairman, Mr. George Fisher, announced that the company had filed a complaint against Japan's Fuji with the US Trade Representative....

A year after the filing, the world's two photographic giants—having spent untold millions on lawyers, lobbyists, and public relations—have fought each other to a standstill. Yesterday the US Trade Representative's office announced not threats or sanctions in the usual US government fashion, but a decision to take Kodak's complaints to a multilateral forum—the World Trade Organization. (*Financial Times*, June 14, 1996)

For Japan's recovery in 1996 from the mid-1995 crisis, this relaxation of American commercial pressure was absolutely necessary. But it was not itself sufficient. In mid-1995, no formal commercial compact (of the kind proposed in chapter 10) ensured that the United States would tolerate a fall in the yen toward PPP over the coming year. The immediate signaling effect of this change in U.S. commercial policy was not strong enough.

A further unmistakable signal that the United States would tolerate substantial yen depreciation, incidental to the BoJ's reflating the Japanese economy, was required. In April and May 1995, a series of multicountry interventions in the foreign exchanges (figure 11.1) put a floor under the dollar. The one in late May was particularly well advertised to signal a change in U.S. foreign-exchange policy with respect to Japan:

The Clinton Administration and a dozen foreign countries took the foreign exchange markets by surprise today, buying billions of dollars in an intervention that appeared to have stopped yet another slump in the dollar.... Treasury Secretary Robert E. Rubin issued a statement this morning that described the currency market intervention as consistent with a commitment made in April by the United

States and six other leading industrial nations to bring about an orderly reversal of the dollar's fall this year.... American officials said privately that the administration also wanted to make it clear that it would not use a weak dollar as a weapon in the negotiations with Japan in the contentious trade dispute over American automobiles and auto parts. (*New York Times*, May 31, 1995)

Although undoubtedly very important in putting a floor under the dollar when it had slumped close to an all-time low of 80 yen, these joint interventions were not so different from the norm of concerted interventions that G7 governments have followed since the 1985–87 Plaza-Louvre Accords for ironing out the more extreme cyclical fluctuations in the dollar's collective exchange rate against other hard currencies (McKinnon 1996). But, valuable as they are, these accords were never strong enough to prevent secular yen appreciation. To revive the Japanese economy, American authorities needed to send a further strong signal that they would tolerate a substantial depreciation of the yen.

The concerted intervention at the beginning of August 1995 differed from a "normal" Plaza-Louvre–type intervention because the dollar had already recovered somewhat from its nadir of 80 yen. Both governments judged that, at 88 yen to the dollar, the yen was still far too high for the Japanese economy to revive and surmount its festering banking crisis. So on August 2 they cooperated in timing their intervention to (1) "ambush" the foreign-exchange markets to drive the dollar up directly, and (2) have the Japanese government simultaneously announce an elaborate set of rule changes to encourage further capital outflows and thus encourage sustained dollar appreciations.

The dollar soared to its highest level against the yen in nearly five months today [August 2] after the United States and Japan sold about $1 billion of yen and the Japanese government made it easier for institutions there to invest their yen abroad. With international markets flooded with yen, the dollar rose 3.3 percent against the Japanese currency, standing at 90.96 yen in late New York trading.... Today's intervention came when the dollar was already rising and when traders did not see an immediate need for the United States to support its currency.... Mr. Rubin's statement left the impression that the United States might take actions to push the dollar even higher. (*New York Times*, August 3, 1995)

The Japanese Ministry of Finance touted its surprise package of regulatory changes as a corrective for the overvalued yen, which is hurting economic growth by strangling Japanese exporters and making it tougher for domestic manufacturers to compete against imports.... "We want a strong dollar," said Eisuke Sakakibara, the director-general of the ministry's international finance bureau. The measures, he said, "will have a strong impact on markets for some months to come." ... Among the deregulatory steps taken by the ministry yesterday were an end to the ban on foreign currency loans by Japanese insurance companies, a lifting of the limit on insurers' participation in loans to overseas borrowers and a relaxation of restrictions on Japanese purchases of Euroyen bonds. The ministry also said that it would have the government's Import-Export Bank buy more foreign bonds. (*Wall Street Journal*, August 3, 1995)

Further joint official intervention on August 15, 1995, when the dollar was not under pressure, ambushed the market once more. The dollar was driven up even further, toward 97 yen, and not once on its erratic path to 113 yen by December 1996 did a responsible official in the American government complain that the dollar was too high. (However, some American economists outside the government complained, or predicted incorrectly, that the Japanese current-account surplus would get bigger.) Consequently, the BoJ felt uninhibited in expanding the Japanese money supply, often by buying foreign exchange, to nudge the yen down further. Figure 11.1 also shows the continual rise in Japanese foreign-exchange reserves (mainly U.S. Treasury bonds) over 1994 and into early 1996. Thus easy money and yen depreciation led to Japan's strong economic revival in 1996—in which real GDP grew at a remarkable 12.7 percent annual rate in the first quarter and more moderately throughtout the year.

The unusually large BoJ purchases of U.S. Treasury bonds over 1994–96, on the order of $100 billion, could also be viewed as a necessary substitute for private Japanese capital outflows, which had become inhibited by the huge foreign-exchange losses suffered by Japanese investors from 1985 to 1995 (see chapter 5).

So the striking events of 1995–96 confirm our theory that Japanese monetary policy, and macroeconomic policy more generally, have been (are) hostage to American mercantile pressure coming through the foreign exchanges. Only when that pressure was relaxed, allowing yen depreciation, could Japan escape from *endaka fukyo II* (1992–95), its longest and deepest postwar recession.

11.2   Exchange-Rate Expectations and the Great Interest-Rate Puzzle

Because expectations about the future course of the yen-dollar exchange rate remain all-important, the syndrome might not be over. Throughout the traumatic events of 1995 and the recovery of the Japanese economy in 1996, the wide differential between nominal interest rates in the two countries failed to narrow. Figure 11.2 shows that long-term rates on

Figure 11.2
Long-term interest rates. *Source:* IMF, *International Financial Statistics*, CD-ROM, March 1996.

dollar bonds were 3 to 4 percentage points higher than those on yen
bonds from 1994 through 1996—a differential that has prevailed, on
average, since 1978 (see figure 1.5 and chapter 4). At the more erratic and
government-manipulated short end of the market, figure 11.3 shows that
the differential widened to more than 5 percentage points in 1995–96
when the BoJ's frantic efforts to ease monetary policy drove the short rate
on government bonds to 0.5 percent: the virtual liquidity trap analyzed in
chapters 3 and 5.

Whence the great interest-rate puzzle. Suppose that financial markets
no longer believe that the yen will go ever higher—that is, they believe
that ongoing relative deflation in Japan has ended. Then the corresponding Fisher effect, the international arbitrage condition that forced Japanese
nominal interest rates below their American counterparts, should also be
over. Particularly at long term, Japanese nominal interest rates should
adjust upward to world levels, give or take a small risk premium. Long
rates prevailing in the United States and Germany were close to 7 percent
in the first half of 1996, while those in Japan remained at just 3.2 to 3.3
percent—with this interest differential persisting into 1997.

This persistent differential in nominal interest rates has at least two
interpretations. The first is simply that the syndrome is not over: the
financial markets continue to expect that the yen will rise. Its surprise fall

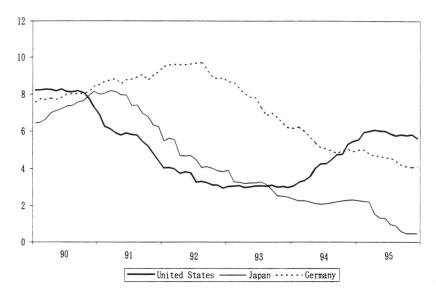

Figure 11.3
Short-term interest rates. *Source:* IMF, *International Financial Statistics*, CD-ROM, March 1996.

after mid-1995 is only an interlude in which the American authorities have finally recognized the severity of *endaka fukyo II* and the danger to their own economy from a collapse in the Japanese financial system. Once Japan stages a satisfactory cyclical recovery, however, political pressure within the United States will bubble up once more. American politicians will again "get tough" with Japan by talking the yen up and by demanding that Japan move faster in opening its economy to, say, semiconductors, or in bidding for domestic construction projects.

Although, throughout 1996, top officials in the American government did not complain, American industrialists were again showing concern with the "overvalued" dollar:

With the dollar near its highest level in nearly two and one half years, industrial leaders are beginning to express concern that the dollar's strong rebound may undermine American competitiveness against foreign rivals.... The latest and most explicit comment came today in Tokyo from Donald V. Fites, Chairman and chief executive of Caterpillar Inc., the earth-moving equipment company whose main competitor is Japanese.

"The recent dramatic weakness of the yen against the dollar is most worrisome and may demand attention from governments," said Mr. Fites, who is also chairman of the U.S.–Japan Business Council. "The yen at 111 to the dollar has the potential to erase and reverse the recent beginning of improvement in our bilateral trade balance." ...

Table 11.1
Government financial balances in Japan (as percentage of GDP)[a]

	1990	1991	1992	1993	1994	1995
Central government	−0.3	−0.2	−2.2	−2.9	−3.7	−3.9
Local authorities	0.3	−0.1	−1.1	−1.7	−3.4	−3.7
Central and local governments	−0.0	−0.3	−3.3	−4.6	−7.1	−7.7
Social security	3.6	3.8	3.4	3.5	3.5	3.5
General government	3.5	3.5	0.1	−1.1	−3.6	−4.2
Cyclical components	2.0	2.5	0.3	0.8	−0.9	−1.9
Structural components	1.6	1.0	−0.2	−1.9	−2.7	−2.3

Source: Ministry of Finance and EPA 1995.
a. Negative for deficit, positive for surplus.

Robert J. Eaton, chairman of Chrysler Corporation, brought up the dollar in a meeting with White House aides last month. The Big Three are worried that the stronger dollar will give Japanese car companies great ability to lower their prices. (*New York Times*, July 10, 1996)

Just understanding the American mercantile constraint on Japanese macroeconomic policy is not tantamount to ending the syndrome. Or, in the words of the baseball great, Yogi Berra, "It ain't over until it's over."

A second interpretation of the interest differential, more difficult to defend, is that most people agree that the syndrome is likely over. Japanese authorities are willing to risk substantial yen depreciation in the near term to secure economic recovery, and, in the longer term, they will not be constrained by the need to depress the yen-dollar exchange rate in order to placate American mercantile interests. No longer do people expect that the BoJ will tolerate (relative) deflation into the indefinite future. However, because of great inertia in the Japanese financial system, nominal interest rates on yen assets don't accurately reflect this new expectation that the yen-dollar rate is unlikely to move systematically one way or another.

This second interpretation becomes more plausible when one recognizes (1) the progress made in liberalizing Japanese markets for goods and services in the 1990s (chapter 10) with more such progress planned in the future, and (2) the massive Japanese fiscal deficits projected for the late 1990s (table 11.1), which, however unwise, will reduce Japan's current-account surpluses. On both counts, American mercantilists and politicians will have less to complain about.

Suppose one tentatively accepts the interpretation that the syndrome is over. What then could be the source of the inertia holding down Japanese nominal interest rates in 1995 into 1997? Because of the trauma of the 1992–95 recesssion, with its many false dawns, after mid-1995 the Japanese government engaged in a no-holds-barred monetary expansion by "sitting on" both short-term and nominal long-term interest rates in order to generate a persistent boom that would recoup the many quarters of lost output.

Consider first the short end of the maturity structure. Starting with a virtual liquidity trap (liquidity overhang) and the economy's deflationary momentum, in 1995–96 the BoJ could fairly easily cap the interbank lending rate by feeding in more base money at the official discount rate of 0.5 percent, the all-time postwar low (figure 11.3). Central banks the world over, including the U.S. Federal Reserve, can and do target short-term interbank lending rates for extended periods. As a result, many authors—notably Frankel (1995)—have shown empirically that short-term interest differentials have been poor predictors of exchange-rate movements.

The major puzzle concerns longer maturities. If the expectation of an ever-higher yen is over, why should Japanese long-term interest rates have remained so low since mid-1995—but particularly in 1996—relative to their American counterparts? After all, in countries with open capital markets, central banks typically exercise virtually no direct control over long rates. Indeed, the Fed seems to be driven by gyrations in long rates on U.S. Treasury bonds, rather than to control them. Is Japan different?

The BoJ is similar to the Fed in its ability to set interest rates only at the short end of the financial market—although not indefinitely. But, for both short and long maturities, Japan's Ministry of Finance has far more influence than does the U.S. Treasury—apart from any differences in regulatory powers between the two agencies. The Trust Fund Bureau of the finance ministry manages by far the biggest pool of financial assets in the Japanese economy: more than $2 trillion. This money is primarily the assets of the Postal Savings Bank and the Postal Insurance system. After the Japanese asset bubble burst in 1991, disintermediation from troubled Japanese commercial banks and stressed private financial institutions accompanied a "flight to safety" into postal savings. The proportion of household saving that flowed into the government-owned—and therefore safe—Postal Saving System rose from 10–15 percent before 1991 to an astonishing 50 percent from 1992 into 1996.[1]

With this huge flow of low-cost short-term funds at its disposal, the Ministry of Finance's Trust Fund opted to transform maturities on a massive scale. It lent long *directly* to the Japanese government and, occasionally, also bought Japanese government bonds in the secondary market. In addition, uncertainty in people's minds probably made it easier for a determined Japanese government to keep interest rates low and immobile from early 1995 into 1997. Thus the finance ministry could effectively cap long-term interest rates and determine the yield curve somewhat counter to the changed, but weakly held, private expectations on the future course of the yen-dollar exchange rate. This explains the surprising inertia in nominal interest rates on long-term yen bonds.

Once it becomes clear that the syndrome of the ever-higher yen is over because the yen no longer increases over an extended period, however, even the best combined efforts of the BoJ and the finance ministry to cap nominal interest rates at all maturities must eventually unravel. The likely forcing variable will again be the yen-dollar exchange rate, but this time because of the yen's becoming too weak! Unless nominal yields on yen assets rise toward those on similar dollar assets, massive capital outflows will eventually force a deep devaluation of the yen.

But deep yen depreciation would certainly provoke a mercantilist response from American business leaders. It would also undermine the American government's resolve, apparent since mid-1995, to secure Japanese economic recovery by benignly ignoring the yen's depreciation. The yen-dollar rate would again become the focus of political and commercial tension between the two countries. In a worst-case scenario, the expectation that the yen will go ever higher could be reestablished, together with an outbreak of protectionism in the United States.

11.3   The Right Timing for the Monetary Accord

How can such financial volatility be avoided? In the short and medium terms, continued U.S.–Japan cooperation to smooth exchange-rate fluctuations could be strengthened, particularly if the yen becomes excessively weak in the transition.

However, overcoming the syndrome also requires the *expectation* of exchange stability in the longer term. If and when a propitious moment arises, the BoJ and the Fed should be prepared to enter the full-scale monetary accord between Japan and the United States (see the set of proposed rules in chapter 10) in order to secure virtual exchange-rate stability indefinitely. But getting this timing right, when macroeconomic variables in the two countries are more or less correctly aligned, is all-important. Based on conditions prevailing in the two economies in 1996, this section sketches just one plausible scenario for a successful transition.

Consider first the problem of computing the starting PPP exchange rate on which to base the accord. While the syndrome still persists, causing ongoing relative deflation in Japan, the PPP exchange rate is a moving target. Figure 9.1 shows its clear downward drift from 1975 to 1995. So if some PPP rate, say 135, had been picked as the target at the end of 1992, drift could have pushed the PPP rate down to, say, 125 in 1997—well outside the putative target zone of ±5 percent specified in rule I (chapter 10). Thus it would have been wrong to fix the rate at 135 in 1992.

An important objective of our proposed U.S.–Japan commercial compact (chapter 10) is to allow Japan to reflate its economy—with some incidental yen depreciation. Relative deflation in Japan, and drift in the PPP exchange rate, would then slow and eventually halt. Because of the dramatic slackening of American mercantile pressure on Japan from mid-1995 through 1996, this process seems to be well under way. If the Japanese economic expansion in 1996 continues into 1997 and beyond, and if the yen depreciates toward the (drifting) PPP rate, the downward drift in the PPP exchange rate may itself end rather soon (unless an offsetting outburst of inflation occurs in the United States). This happy turn of events then makes it easier to find a sustainable PPP target rate, say roughly between 115 and 125 yen per dollar in 1997–98, on which to base a new accord.

The key problem in 1996 is the gap in nominal interest rates. As long as the BoJ and the Ministry of Finance cap rates on yen assets far below world levels in order to give the economy an extraordinary monetary stimulus, an exchange-rate accord is not feasible—and indeed is not desirable. If the accord eliminated long-term exchange risk but an interest differential of 3 to 4 percentage points between yen and dollar assets remained, capital outflows from Japan would become unmanageable.

The appropriate timing for implementing the accord thus hinges on when the Japanese government finishes its extraordinary monetary expansion associated with recovery from *endaka fukyo II*. An increase in Japanese nominal interest rates toward world levels would signal that the expansion is over and that Japan's economy is returning to more sustainable growth consistent with a stable WPI. If, in addition, the de facto 1995–96 commercial compact between the two countries continued to hold, rule I of the monetary accord could then be safely implemented. A new official parity for the yen-dollar exchange rate, which aligned their now-stable wholesale and producer price levels for tradable goods (rule VI, chapter 10), could be declared.

In the foreign-exchange market itself, the yen-dollar rate would be contained indefinitely within margins of ± 5 percent around this new parity. Within this 10 percent band, the two central banks would have leeway to differentiate their short-term interest rates in order to respond to purely domestic business cycles. (Years later they might even decide that monetary harmonization had progressed to the point where the band's width could be safely narrowed.) But, in the long run, the two countries would be bound together by having a common price-level target and a credible commitment to virtual exchange stability such that longer-term interest rates converged.

Once declared, this new exchange-rate parity should be defended vigorously so that, over time, it would become the new "traditional" yen-dollar rate. Then our virtuous circle is complete. Manufacturers, merchants, foreign-exchange dealers, the custodians of financial capital—such as banks and insurances companies—and politicians in Japan and the United States would no longer believe that the yen-dollar rate could be lobbied to their advantage (or disadvantage). The monetary authorities in each country would become better protected from untoward mercantile or political pressure. Syndromes like that of the ever-higher yen—or excess monetary and exchange-rate volatility more generally—if not vanquished altogether, would be more subdued.

Notes

Notes to Chapter 1

1. This early restraint on cotton exports, negotiated bilaterally between the United States and Japan, was the precursor of what in 1961 became the much more elaborate international multifiber textile agreement. All the industrial countries (now including Japan!) began collectively restricting their imports of textiles from developing countries. However, with the establishment of the World Trade Organization in late 1994, this multifiber agreement is slated to be phased out over ten years.

2. Start with the same catalog list price for any brand-name manufactured good in two countries. Then, if the exporting country's currency suddenly appreciates, it will be guilty of "dumping" even though the printed catalog prices remain unchanged—and indeed cannot feasibly be changed in response to the ebb and flow of exchange-rate fluctuations.

3. Since 1970, the only other country whose currency has appreciated against the dollar by a similar order of magnitude—although still less than that of the yen—is Switzerland. But, being small with a predominantly European trade orientation, Switzerland was never the focus of American trade policy. The Swiss franc's extraordinary appreciation can largely be explained by Switzerland's status as a haven for flight capital.

4. Fluctuations in the world's money driving the two great worldwide inflations of 1973–74 and 1978–79, and the great worldwide deflation of 1981–82, in the aftermath of the fixed-rate dollar standard, are explained in McKinnon (1996).

Notes to Chapter 2

1. A study by the World Bank (1993) characterizes Japan, along with other East Asian economies, as a country that attained high growth *and* relatively equal income distribution.

2. TFP compares output with an input index that summarizes the quantities of many inputs. The difference between output growth and the growth of the input index is defined to be improvement in productivity. TFP is usually calculated over the primary factor inputs such as labor, capital, and land. In contrast, our TFP is over labor and tradable materials as the primary "factors." Specifically, the cost function is specified as Cobb-Douglas in wage and materials prices, and the output price is defined to be a markup over input cost minus technical change.

3. Negative TFP growth does not necessarily signify technical backsliding if proper account is taken for quality improvement. Nonetheless, the fact of very low productivity growth in the United States up to 1990 is indisputable; see the technical appendix to this chapter.

4. These graphs are drawn in real terms, that is, after adjusting for inflation in each industry, with the base year of 1985 (Japan) or 1982 (United States). Because prices of machinery tend to decline over time relative to those of services and agricultural products, especially in Japan, failure to do this adjustment would obscure the enormous physical expansion of manufacturing industries. The U.S. data for 1990 are unavailable, and therefore 1989 data are substituted as the end of the series.

5. U.S. output data by industry are not available at the desired classification level for the earlier period.

6. In a survey conducted by the Prime Minister's Office on the "popular opinion on economic structural adjustment" (September 1988), respondents were asked if they were actually experiencing the richness of life associated with the highest income level of the world: 22.4 percent said they were, while 69.2 percent answered negatively. Another survey by the Economic Planning Agency, White Paper on the Life of the People (1990), asked whether the respondent found his or her life in general satisfying or not. The level of satisfaction was low (30 to 50 percent) among young and middle-aged people, whereas older groups were more content. Among all cohorts, males in their thirties living in Tokyo were least satisfied.

7. Under increasing returns to scale, larger production units are more efficient and able to underbid smaller rivals. If the market is left unattended over time, only one giant firm with complete monopoly power will emerge. Hence, the competitive environment—and with it the incentive to innovate—will disappear.

8. Statistical discrepancies in bilateral trade flows arise from different timing of recording (at shipment or customs clearance), inclusion or exclusion of cost, freight, and insurance associated with transportation, treatment of re-exports, false reporting (under- or overinvoicing), and estimation errors where direct data are not available.

9. Gross saving and investment include replacement of old structures and machinery to maintain the same level of capital stock as well as the "net" increase in such stock. The financial counterpart of replacement investment is called depreciation allowances of the corporate sector.

10. The accounts of the prefectural and local governments are consolidated with those of the central government. This reflects the fact that the expenditure, tax, and borrowing decisions of local governments in Japan are largely determined by the central government: Japan is not a federal state.

11. For example, in table 2.3, based on data from the U.S. Department of Commerce, gross investment (column 9) is the sum of private investment in residential structures, changes in inventories, and investment in plant and equipment—but it does not include government buildings, roads, and so on.

12. However, according to the similar OECD data, the gap in gross saving rates is proportionately much less: in 1993, the Japanese gross saving rate at 33.1 percent of GNP was "only" a bit more than twice as great as in the United States (14.3 percent).

13. Recent (and anticipated) improvement in U.S. public-sector saving under the Clinton budget program, coupled with Japan's aggressive fiscal expansion, may alter the relative saving positions of the two governments in the medium term. However, there is no sign at the moment of significant improvement in the low saving of the U.S. private sector.

14. Using a similar model, Ohno (1989b, 1991) studied the short-term export pricing behavior of Japanese and U.S. manufacturers. In these studies, export prices and domestic sales prices are separately analyzed. Here, with a focus on the long run, the Bank of Japan's overall wholesale price indices—i.e., the weighted average of domestic and export prices—are used.

15. If $\alpha_i = 0$, all inputs are tradable; if $\alpha_i = 1$, all inputs are nontradable. In general, α_i takes a value between the two extremes.

16. The model specification in terms of rate of change is justified because the Dickey-Fuller and augmented Dickey-Fuller tests on Japanese and U.S. prices, wages, and materials price and the real exchange rate do not reject the existence of unit roots in an overwhelming majority (65 out of 68 tests performed, which is about what one expects at the 5 percent significance level). To be exact, the notation for change in discrete data should be $\Delta \ln c$, $\Delta \ln w$, and so on. The dot is adopted here as a space saver.

17. This restriction is useful in analyzing bilateral competitiveness; see Ohno (1993b). The log likelihood ratio test rejects this constraint for food, paper, oil and gas, and ceramics industries but does not reject it for the remaining ten industries or for manufacturing industries as a whole. Because rejection occurs only in relatively unimportant industries for Japan–U.S. trade, the restriction is imposed throughout this section.

18. The real exchange rate variable (s_i) is replaced by its proxy (GNP-weighted and WPI-deflated exchange rates against other G7 countries).

19. Ohno (1989a) confirms this conclusion, especially for major machinery industries, which are the mainstay of Japanese exports.

20. Another possible reason for negative estimates is neglect of capital cost. However, low or negative sectoral productivity growth in the United States is also confirmed by other studies that take account of capital cost. For example, Jorgenson (1988) reports the sector-weighted technical change of 0.4 percent during 1960–79 and −0.7 percent during 1973–79 for all sectors. These are total factor productivity estimates including nonmanufacturing.

Notes to Chapter 3

1. The question of what constitutes the "correct" exchange rate is taken up in chapter 6. We shall argue that the only exchange rate that is consistent with free trade and capital mobility is the one that would equalize the price of a common broad basket of tradable commodities in each country, that is, tradable purchasing power parity. Chapter 7 shows that, in open industrial countries, a currency devaluation in pursuit of trade-flow adjustment is not only ineffective but highly disruptive to the entire economy.

2. In a provocative article, Krugman (1994) chastises politicians for their obsession with international competitiveness and argues that national welfare is hardly related to the trade balance (which is synonymous with competitiveness in his article). While he admits the (limited) political value of his admonition in the current U.S. debate over trade, shifting competitiveness as a source of economic dynamism and real structural change cannot be denied. We will also argue later that the linkage between competitiveness and the trade balance is more obscure than Krugman supposes.

3. For a mathematical presentation of this model, see the appendix to chapter 2.

4. The remaining (permanent) differentials in wage structure are almost fully explained by the characteristics of the workforce. The wage level in 1985 for each industry (in log) is

regressed on the percentage of female workers (*female*), average duration of service (*duration*), and average entering age (*enterage*), with the following result (standard errors are in parentheses):

ln wage = 7.06 − 0.508 *female* + 0.027 *duration* − 0.046 *enterage*
    (0.31) (0.208)   (0.015)   (0.007)

$N = 13$, $R^2 = 0.951$, SE = 0.061

After controlling for workforce characteristics, the high R^2 suggests that very little remains to be explained in the wage structure of Japanese manufacturing.

5. In the late 1980s, the movements of these price indices mostly reflected price pressure from exchange fluctuations, because global inflation was relatively low and stable. On this point, also see the next paragraph and table 3.1.

6. For Japan and Canada, the dollar exchange rate is the most important bilateral rate. Within Europe, intraregional trade is generally more important, but the European Exchange Rate Mechanism limited the variance of bilateral exchange fluctuations in the late 1980s. For these reasons the United States is chosen to be the common counterpart. Since U.S. producer prices react less and much more slowly to exchange-rate changes than those in the rest of G7 countries (see section 3.4), these regressions pick up mostly price reactions in countries other than the United States.

7. The French coefficient falls slightly short of the 5 percent critical value.

8. For example, Japan's Economic Planning Agency (1994) reports that the PPP yen-dollar rate measured by the consumer basket moved from 178 in November 1988 to 157 in November 1993.

9. For instance, using disaggregated export price data, Ohno (1989a) finds that the average pass-through of Japanese manufactured exports to the rest of the world is lower (0.78) than the almost complete pass-through of U.S. manufactured exports (0.95). In other words, the price of Japanese products in the United States is less sensitive to the exchange rate than is the price of U.S. products in Japan. However, after the bubble burst of 1991, Japanese manufacturers began to raise their export prices more readily as the yen appreciated.

10. Real growth is measured by annualized log-change in real GDP, except for Japan and Germany, for which real GNP (instead of GDP) is used. Early data on national income are incomplete for Japan, Germany, and France. Various statistics reported in the text are calculated by omitting missing observations.

11. For other countries, the growth rates in the first and second periods were as follows: 5.1 versus 2.4 percent for Germany, 5.3 percent versus 2.7 percent for France, and 2.9 versus 2.0 percent for the United Kingdom.

12. The *endaka fukyo* of the late 1980s and the early 1990s are examined further in chapter 5.

13. Here, for the purpose of exposition, we are treating the asset bubble, also observed in the rest of the industrialized world with varying timing and severity, as an independent shock. From a broader perspective, however, there are reasons to believe that the bubble was actually a manifestation of worldwide financial instability. Waves of dollar depreciation in 1971–73, 1977–78, and 1985–87 induced global liquidity gluts with a lag of one to two years. This appears to be a mechanism in the current international monetary system by which the lack of central (i.e., American) financial discipline is propagated to the rest of the world (Ohno 1991). In the first two periods, the world economy was faced with a commodity price inflation. In the third, for reasons yet unknown, asset price inflation ensued.

14. The combined effect of the exchange rate and asset bubble can be statistically verified. An ordinary least squares regression of operating profits of manufacturing industries on *bubble* (Nikkei stock index) and *pressure* (deviation from PPP) produces the following:

$$profits = -1.64 + 0.714 \; bubble + 1.255 \; pressure$$
$$\qquad\quad (0.40) \quad (0.096) \qquad\quad (0.206)$$

$$N = 44 \; (1984{:}Q1{-}1994{:}Q4), \quad R^2 = 0.532, \quad SE = 0.182, \quad DW = 1.29$$

Standard errors are in parentheses and all variables are in logarithms. Each of the reported coefficients is the sum of four coefficients on the current and one-to-three-quarters-lagged variable. A regression without lags generates a very similar result.

Notes to Chapter 4

1. Under the fixed-rate dollar standard, most industrial countries other than the United States maintained exchange controls on capital account.

2. Note, however, that labor productivity indices are subject to not insignificant measurement error. It is difficult to gauge heterogeneous labor input as well as a changing mix of real output. For example, labor productivity growth for Japanese manufacturing industries calculated from the indices of employment and hours worked (Ministry of Labor) and real output (Economic Planning Agency) is 7.5 percent per year during 1955–71—against the Japan Productivity Center estimate of 9.7 percent in table 4.1.

3. M1—coin and currency in circulation plus checking accounts in commercial banks—corresponds to line 34 of the IMF's *International Financial Statistics*.

4. This supply-side effect has often been misinterpreted as if the foreign income elasticity of demand for Japanese goods was unusually high—starting with the influential econometric work of Houthakker and MaGee (1969). If it was purely a demand-side effect based on a small number of products, then, to maintain external balance, one would expect the Japanese terms of trade and real exchange rate to continually appreciate. But this interpretation of high Japanese export growth in the 1950s and 1960s has been trenchantly criticized by Paul Krugman (1989a).

Notes to Chapter 5

1. The earlier worldwide inflations of the 1970s and the particularly painful disinflation in the United States in the early 1980s are worldwide phenomena associated with synchronized business cycles under "the floating-rate dollar standard" (McKinnon 1982, 1996; Ohno 1987). Because they are not particularly linked with the U.S.–Japan nexus, however, they are not systematically analyzed in this book.

2. We hesitate to say "cost of capital" because that general term has too many other dimensions—including taxes and the ease of issuing equities. We will return to these when considering Japan's bubble economy.

3. Courtesy of the *Bank Credit Analyst* (1995).

4. Strangely, Keynes (1936) does not associate liquidity traps in interest rates with expected appreciation of the foreign-exchange rate—or even with strong expectations of domestic deflation. Because these expectations effects are absent (or at least not explicit) in the standard textbook analysis of Keynesian monetary theory, which usually assumes the price level

to be fixed, it is not easy to apply the standard geometric or algebraic apparatus of Keynesian liquidity preference to the problem facing Japan.

5. Long-term capital flows are defined as direct and portfolio investments, including bank lending, in instruments greater than one-year duration.

6. If one accepts the hypothesis that domestic banks are special in that they serve smaller industrial enterprises where customer relationships and specific knowledge are important (Gertler and Gilchrist 1992), then any sudden diminution of normal lending could not immediately (in 1991) be offset by borrowing from other sources (e.g., by issuing commercial bills) at home or abroad. But in the longer run, many enterprises could escape from the banking crunch by turning to other sources of finance.

Notes to Chapter 6

1. In this chapter, we will not make the distinction between the trade balance and the current-account balance. Our concern here is theoretical, and at this level of abstraction we will ignore services, factor incomes, and unrequited transfers.

2. As Komiya (1994) put it, persistent trade surpluses and deficits lasting five, ten, or more years cannot be eliminated by exchange adjustment. His reason is twofold. First, these surpluses and deficits reflect long-term real propensities of the economies to save and invest, which are not mutable by exchange-rate changes alone. Second, real exchange rates are endogenous and cannot be viewed as a policy instrument or a cause in macroeconomic interaction. More on these points in chapter 7.

3. As the literature on the transfer problem shows (Jones 1975), the relationship between the relative price (i.e., the terms of trade) and the trade balance (i.e., the transfer of purchasing power) becomes ambiguous as one moves from a one-good economy to two-, three-, and N-good economies. This alone is a sufficient theoretical reason to deny a stable relationship between the exchange rate and the trade balance.

4. For example, in 1986, newspaper surveys of Japanese entrepreneurs found 200–220 yen to the dollar to be the rate consistent with their long-run normal profits. McKinnon (1988) regarded 200 yen as approximately the right yen-dollar rate (for more recent estimates, see chapter 9). The Japanese government was willing to tolerate yen appreciation only up to 160–180 yen; the U.S. government was for a while inclined to push the yen higher than that. Williamson (1986) estimated the proper rate to be 162, and an even higher yen is regarded as desirable by Bernstein (1986) and Krause (1986), whose estimates were 120 and 100, respectively. The actual yen-dollar rate in 1986 was 169. Such diversity in estimated "correct" rates is the rule rather than the exception because of the fundamental disagreement about exchange-rate policy, as discussed in the text.

5. This and the next sections are revised versions of the corresponding sections in McKinnon and Ohno (1988).

6. We assume (1) $0 < C' < 1$, (2) $-1 < B_1 < 0$, (3) $1 - C' + \alpha I' > 0$, and (4) $L_1 + \alpha L_3 > 0$. (1) and (2) confine the marginal propensities to consume and to import between 0 and 1. (3) guarantees a positive net marginal propensity to save as income increases. (4) is the condition that, in a boom where Y and p rise according to equation 6.5, the real demand for money increases rather than decreases. This is a reasonable assumption for countries with relatively low inflation (i.e., without hyperinflation).

7. Of course, international exchange of goods and services takes place between insular economies, enhancing efficiency and welfare relative to autarky. Resemblance to a closed economy is therefore with respect to macroeconomic balances only.

8. More precisely, rates of return tend to converge after expected movements of exchange rates and risk premia are taken into account (chapter 8). Later in this section, we will introduce simplifying assumptions that the expected changes in the exchange rates are 0 and that risk premia are also 0, while retaining the key assumption that interest rates are determined internationally.

9. In any economy the balance of trade is identical to the savings-investment (and income-expenditure) gap in the accounting sense. However, it is only when private capital is mobile internationally that firms and individuals can actively determine (collectively) the size of net foreign lending. In an insular economy the nation's net foreign-asset position is mainly under the control of the central bank.

10. Agents in our economy are rational in the sense that they do not make systematic errors in predicting future m and p relative to available information. They understand that, in the long run, monetary expansion is inflationary and PPP in tradables must hold. However, they do not know the structure of the economy in detail and cannot, therefore, reduce incoming information to probabilistic means (and variances) of future endogenous variables.

11. Lest we be accused of confusing an identity with causality, a few words of clarification are in order. Equality of the current account with the saving-investment gap is an identity, but this relationship does not provide a useful framework to study an insular economy that has no free capital mobility. It becomes a valid analytical tool only for an open economy where options to lend and borrow abroad are open to everyone—see also note 9. Then and only then, the real propensity to save or dissave will mainly determine the long-term trade balance, irrespective of the exchange-rate regime (chapter 7). This is an empirical statement, not mere repetition of an identity.

12. Somewhat surprisingly, one would get exactly the same signs for these variables if nominal money were fixed and the exchange rate appreciated so as to deflate the domestic price level.

Notes to Chapter 7

1. *Elasticity* is economic jargon for a measure of the percentage change in one variable with respect to a percentage change in another variable. In this case, the sensitivity of export and import volumes to a change in the real exchange rate is at issue. As the following note shows, these quantitative responses must be sufficiently large for the model prediction to be valid.

2. As in chapter 6, it is assumed that quantity responses of exports and imports are sufficiently large. Specifically, let trade be initially balanced ($pQ_x = ep^*Q_m$) and prices remain constant throughout. Then, totally differentiating the left and center sides of equation 7.3 and rearranging, we get $dT/de = (\eta_x + \eta_m - 1)pQ_x/e$, where η_x and η_m are price elasticities of export and import volumes (in absolute value). We assume that $\eta_x + \eta_m > 1$, and therefore $dT/de > 0$, when all other variables remain constant. This is the famous Marshall-Lerner condition.

3. The scope of fundamental variables is dependent on the model. For example, the simplest version of the Dornbusch overshooting model would consider income, interest rate, and prices—driven by a monetary shock—as fundamentals, whereas the standard portfolio approach equation would include relative prices, real interest rates, and the cumulative current account.

4. Ueda (1992) argues that the Bank of Japan eases too much and for too long when it wants to counter the appreciation of the yen, and that this tendency led to subsequent goods or asset inflations in 1973–74, 1977–80, and 1987–90. According to Ueda, the BoJ's pattern of overreaction stems from an overblown fear of *endaka fukyo* as well as from political pressures to ease from the Ministry of Finance and the U.S. government.

5. During the floating-rate period of 1974–93, *changes* in the two variables are significantly correlated (the correlation coefficient is 0.63) but not their *levels* (0.07), because of the opposite long-term trends in the real exchange rate and the trade balance. This vindicates Komiya's point that little correlation exists between the *structural* saving-investment balance and the real exchange rate. See note 11 below.

6. During the Bretton Woods years, an alternative mechanism for relative price adjustment was in place whereby differences in productivity growth or demand shifts across countries and industries were reflected in divergent movements in nominal wages and nontradable prices. Under this mechanism, the real exchange rate—defined as the overall tradable price level in country A relative to that in country B—did not have to change to secure the required adjustment (chapter 4).

7. This parameter, which will be estimated, is needed to translate relative PPP into absolute PPP; see chapter 9 and Ohno (1990). Price and exchange-rate data are normalized to have 1960 as the base year. This should affect the value of θ, but other estimation results should be unaffected.

8. The assumption of linearity seems reasonable for our data; see figure 7.1. Although a nation's borrowing behavior must satisfy an intertemporal budget constraint in the very long run, such a constraint is unnecessary for the length of time we are considering.

9. The yen-dollar exchange rate (annual average) is taken from the IMF's *International Financial Statistics*. U.S. real GDP (Department of Commerce) and Japanese real GNP (Economic Planning Agency) are deviations from the respective time trends. For prices, the U.S. producer price index and the Japanese overall wholesale price index are used.

10. Whereas the Japanese export price index starts in the 1960s, the corresponding U.S. index became available only recently. Trial estimation using Japan's export price index and the U.S. domestic producer price index does not lead to a meaningful convergence. Another estimation, pairing Japanese *domestic* WPI with American PPI, yields an even slower price adjustment of 5.2 percent per year, suggesting that adjustment speed is quite sensitive to the choice of the commodity basket.

11. In a similar spirit, Komiya (1994) argues that "monetary policy can affect the 'cyclic' parts of income (GNP), employment, the current account, etc. but its impact on 'trends' is simply that its stance determines the inflation rate. Monetary policy can hardly influence the 'trends' of various 'real' variables" (p. 179).

12. In theory, foreign-exchange intervention can alter the exchange rate by (1) a change in the monetary base; (2) the portfolio effect; and (3) the signaling effect. However, the first channel does not work for sterilized intervention, which seems to be the norm these days. The second channel works even if intervention is sterilized, but its calculated impact is usually minuscule. Since the Plaza Agreement of 1985, the impact of intervention has been attributed mainly to the third channel: intervention is a signal that there will be a change in domestic monetary policy in the future (Dominguez and Frankel 1993).

13. We are puzzled at calling this model "reduced-form." With the trade volume ratio on the left-hand side and real exchange rate and activity variables on the right-hand side, Cline's model should properly be called structural—it is a small, partial-equilibrium model with no

explicit consideration of the entire economy. Normally, a reduced-form model is one that expresses all endogenous variables as functions of only exogenous variables in the context of a simultaneous equations model. His right-hand-side variables are far from exogenous, and this is precisely the issue we take up in this section.

Notes to Chapter 8

1. Specifically, these countries were newcomers to the gold standard during the 1870s: Belgium, Denmark, France, Germany, Greece, Italy, Netherlands, Norway, Sweden, and Switzerland.

2. For an unconventional proof of this, see Sir Arthur Conan Doyle's *The Dancing Man* (1903): "'So, Watson,' said he suddenly, 'you do not propose to invest in South African securities?' I gave a start of astonishment. Accustomed as I was to Holmes' curious faculties, this sudden intrusion into my most intimate thoughts was utterly inexplicable." This and other Sherlock Holmes adventures demonstrate that individual purchases of foreign securities were not uncommon.

3. During 1952–70, average tradable inflation was 1 percent or less in the United States, Japan, Germany, and Italy. This is well within the margin of error arising from changes in quality and the product mix. In other words, the hypothesis that true tradable inflation was 0 cannot be rejected. British WPI inflation was proceeding at a higher rate of 2.3 percent, and French prices diverged upward in 1958 and 1968 due to social crises. But these occurrences did not spill over to other countries.

4. Again, the long-term dollar interest rate is no longer the lowest since the late 1970s. The Japanese ten-year government bond rate, which is not plotted because early data are not available, is much lower than the U.S. Treasury bond rate in the 1990s.

5. If, on the other hand, the center country is unable to provide such stability, it is likely that the fixed exchange-rate system will collapse sooner or later, because no countries in the periphery would like to give up monetary independence to import gyrating prices and interest rates. For the mechanics of an effective global nominal anchor, see chapters 9 and 10.

6. Japan momentarily returned to the gold standard in 1930 but left it in the following year. Our F dummy does not recognize this as a fixed-rate period because of its brevity.

7. Instrumental variable (IV) estimation is needed in the Alogoskoufis-Smith model because the lagged white-noise process driving the expected inflation may be correlated with π_{t-1}^F or π_{t-1}^{NF}. The instruments are a constant, F dummy, and the twice-lagged inflation rates. If, as we suspect, inflation does not persist during the fixed-rate period, π_{t-2}^F is not a good instrument for π_{t-1}^F. This means that the IV estimate of the coefficient of lagged inflation during the fixed-rate period is very imprecise with a large standard error—and this is exactly what we observe in table 8.1 and what Alogoskoufis and Smith also found.

8. One reason for the weaker or insignificant results for U.S. inflation is that the relation with Japan was not very important for the U.S. economy when Japan was a small, less developed country. Thus the fixity or nonfixity of the yen-dollar exchange rate is not an effective criterion for a regime shift in the U.S. monetary policy rules in the early years.

9. The formulas in equations 8.6 and 8.7 are defined only if λ and ϕ are both less than 1. If, on the other hand, the process of the short-term rate of inflation has a unit root (i.e., is a random walk), the variances of nominal interest rates will be infinite.

10. Although we mainly consider long-term financial instruments, the time horizon of international investors may be shorter than the maturity of the instrument implies. In that case, even though PPP tends to hold in the very long run, short-term deviation from it may well become a predominant concern for them.

Notes to Chapter 9

This chapter is based on a paper by Kazuko Shirono, "The Exchange Rate and Price Movements: A Causality Analysis of Yen Appreciation and Japanese Deflation after the Plaza Agreement" (1996). It was written in Japanese under the supervision of Kenichi Ohno. We would like to thank her for the original paper and for her statistical assistance.

1. In figure 9.1, the PPP estimate of the Research Institute for International Price Mechanism (1993) was the benchmark. Although other estimates of tradable PPP exist (see the appendix to this chapter), their use would not undermine our conclusion: the validity of PPP in the long term and its violation in the short run.

2. As Cassel (1921) notes, "When two currencies have been inflated, the new normal rate of exchange will be equal to the old rate multiplied by the quotient between the degrees of inflation of both countries" (p. 37).

3. When a compact disc player replaces an analog record player at the same retail price, how should that be reflected in the price index? If the former offers better quality, the price has fallen effectively. But the typical compiling procedure is to drop discontinued items from the survey list while adding new ones without due regard to either quality or the scope of consumption. Because of imperfect splicing, the price level may be overestimated in an economy with rapid technical change.

4. For example, MITI surveys three popular passenger cars by type (Research Institute 1994). For the 1,500-cc displacement and sedan type, the survey list includes Toyota Corolla, Honda Civic, and Ford Escort for the United States; Toyota Corolla, Nissan Sunny, and Honda Civic for Japan; and Mazda 323F, Ford Escort, and Opel Astra for Germany. In the past, cars sold in Japan tended to be more fully equipped than those sold in the United States. However, air bags, which are standard in the American market, have often been optional in Japan. Japanese car sales people are perhaps more polite. These differences—even for the same model—are difficult to quantify.

Notes to Chapter 10

1. The United States converted its general WPI into the new PPI in 1978 and ceased publishing the former. So U.S. historical data series, such as the "WPI" appearing in figure 10.1, splice the two indexes.

2. This new view seems to have had a long genesis. But recent statements of self-fulfilling exchange-rate crises—which include lengthy citations to other writers—are Obstfeld (1994); Eichengreen, Rose, and Wyplosz (1995); and Ozkan and Sutherland (1995).

Notes to Chapter 11

1. This analysis leans heavily on information provided by Dan Bernstein and Jeff Gardner, "Japanese MoF Purchases of JGBs," *Bridgewater Daily Observations*, June 11, 1996, pp. 1–5.

References

Alogoskoufis, George S. 1992. "Monetary Accommodation, Exchange Rate Regimes and Inflation Persistence," *Economic Journal*, May: 1–20.

Alogoskoufis, George, and Ron Smith. 1991. "The Phillips Curve, the Persistence of Inflation, and the Lucas Critique: Evidence from Exchange-Rate Regimes," *American Economic Review* 81(5): 1254–1275.

Balassa, Bela. 1964. "The Purchasing Power Parity Doctrine Reexamined: A Reappraisal," *Journal of Political Economy* 72:584–596.

Baldwin, Richard E. 1988. "Hysteresis in Import Prices: The Beachhead Effect," *American Economic Review* 78, no. 4: 773–785.

Baldwin, Robert E. 1988. *Trade Policy in a Changing World Economy*. Chicago: University of Chicago Press.

Bank Credit Analyst. 1995. "Interest Rate Forecast" 17, no. 5 (May).

Barro, Robert. 1987. "Budget Deficits: Only a Minor Crisis." *Wall Street Journal*, January 16.

Baumgartner, Ulrich, and Guy Meredith, eds. 1995. *Saving Behavior and the Asset Price "Bubble" in Japan: Analytical Studies*. Occasional Paper, no. 124. Washington DC: IMF.

Bayoumi, Tamim. 1990. "Saving-Investment Correlations." *IMF Staff Papers* 37(2): 360–398.

Bergsten, C. Fred. 1986. "The Outlook for the Trade Deficit and for America as a Debt Country." Statement before the Subcommittee on Trade of the House Committee on Ways and Means, September 24.

———, ed. 1991. *International Adjustment and Financing: The Lessons of 1985–1991*. Washington, DC: Institute for International Economics.

———. 1994. "Japan and the United States Should Take Lead in Introducing 'Target Zones': A Good Opportunity to Bring in a New System." *Japan Economic Journal*, October 14. In Japanese.

Bergsten, C. Fred, and William R. Cline. 1985. *The United States–Japan Economic Problem*. Policy Analyses in International Economics, no. 13. Washington, DC: Institute for International Economics.

Bergsten, C. Fred, and Marcus Noland. 1993. *Reconcilable Differences? United States–Japan Economic Conflict*. Washington, DC: Institute for International Economics.

Bernstein, Edward M. 1986. Statement of Edward M. Bernstein, Guest Scholar, Brookings Institution, to the Subcommittee on Commerce, Transportation, and Tourism of the House of Representatives, February 25.

Bhagwati, Jagdish. 1991. *The World Trading System at Risk*. Princeton, NJ: Princeton University Press.

—————. 1993. "U.S. Trade Policy at Cross Roads." In J. Bhagwati, *Political Economy and International Economics*. Cambridge, MA: MIT Press. First published in *The World Economy* 12, no. 4 (1989): 439–479.

Blinder, Alan. 1987. "The Market Wants the Dollar to Fall. Let It Happen." *Business Week*, October 19.

Boskin, Michael J., and Lawrence J. Lau. 1990. "Post-war Economic Growth in the Group-of-Five Countries: A New Analysis." Stanford University, CEPR Publication, no. 217, July.

Bosworth, Barry P., and Robert Z. Lawrence. 1982. *Commodity Prices and the New Inflation*. Washington, DC: Brookings Institution.

Branson, William H. 1985. "Causes of Appreciation and Volatility of the Dollar." In *The U.S. Dollar: Recent Developments, Outlook, and Policy Options*. Kansas City, MO: Federal Reserve Bank of Kansas City.

Bretton Woods Commission. 1994. *Bretton Woods: Looking to the Future*. Washington, DC, July.

Brown, A. J. 1985. *World Inflation since 1950: An International Comparative Study*. Cambridge: Cambridge University Press.

Bruno, Michael, and Jeffrey D. Sachs. 1985. *Economics of Worldwide Stagflation*. Cambridge: Harvard University Press.

Cassel, Gustav. 1918. "Abnormal Deviations in International Exchanges," *Economic Journal*, December.

—————. 1922. *Money and Foreign Exchange after 1914*. New York: Macmillan.

Catte, Dietro, Giampaola Galli, and Salvatore Rebecchini. 1992. "Exchange Rates Can Be Managed!" *International Economic Insights*. Sept./Oct.: 17–21.

Caves, Richard, Jeffrey Frankel, and Ronald Jones. 1996. *World Trade and Payments: An Introduction*. 7th ed. New York: Harper Collins.

Cline, William R. 1993a. "Japan's Current Account Surplus." Washington, DC: Institute for International Economics, July. Duplicated.

—————. 1993b. "Prices and Quantities in Projections of Japan's Trade." Washington, DC: Institute for International Economics, August. Duplicated.

—————. 1995. *Predicting External Imbalances for the United States and Japan*. Policy Analyses in International Economics, no. 41. Washington, DC: Institute for International Economics.

De Grauwe, Paul. 1994. *The Economics of Monetary Integration*. 2d ed. Oxford University Press.

Destler, I. M. 1992. *American Trade Politics*. 2d ed. Washington, DC: Institute for International Economics, with the Twentieth Century Fund.

Dominguez, Kathryn M., and Jeffrey A. Frankel. 1993. *Does Foreign Exchange Intervention Work?* Washington, DC: Institute for International Economics.

Dornbusch, Rudiger. 1987a. "Exchange Rates and Prices." *American Economic Review* 77, no. 1: 93–106.

―――. 1987b. "Heading toward 100 Yen: Why the Dollar Must Fall Another 30%." *New York Times*. May 8.

―――. 1988. *Exchange Rates and Inflation*. Cambridge: MIT Press.

Economic Planning Agency. 1994. *Price Report '94*. Tokyo: Economic Planning Agency. In Japanese.

―――. 1995. *Bukka [Price] Report '95*. Tokyo: Economic Planning Agency. In Japanese.

Eichengreen, Barry, Andrew Rose, and Charles Wyplosz. 1995. "Exchange Rate Mayhem: The Antecedents and Aftermath of Speculative Attacks." *Economic Policy* 21 (Oct.): 249–312.

Feldstein, Martin. 1986a. "Bailing Out Tokyo." *Wall Street Journal*, November 25.

―――. 1986b. "We Don't Need Protectionism to Close the Trade Gap." *Business Week*, September 15.

―――. 1987a. "Correcting the Trade Deficit." *Foreign Affairs* 65, no. 4: 795–806.

―――. 1987b. "A Self-Interested Way to Avoid Death in Venice." *Financial Times*, May 20.

―――. 1992. "The Case Against EMU." *Economist*, June 13.

Fisher, Eric O'N., and Joon Y. Park. 1991. "Testing Purchasing Power Parity under the Null Hypothesis of Co-integration." *Economic Journal* 101 (November): 1476–1484.

Frankel, Jeffrey A. 1984. *The Yen/Dollar Agreement: Liberalizing Japan's Capital Markets*. Policy Analyses in International Economics, no. 9. Washington DC: Institute for International Economics.

―――. 1995. *On Exchange Rates*. Cambridge: MIT Press.

Frenkel, Jacob A., Morris Goldstein, and Paul R. Masson. 1991. *Characteristics of a Successful Exchange Rate System*. IMF Occasional Paper, no. 82. Washington, DC: IMF.

Frenkel, Jacob, and Michael Mussa. 1980. "The Efficiency of Foreign Exchange Markets and Measures of Turbulence." *American Economic Review* 70, no. 2: 374–381.

―――. 1985. "Asset Markets, Exchange Rates and the Balance of Payments." Chap. 14 in R. W. Jones and P. B. Kenen, eds., *Handbook of International Economics*. Vol. 2. Amsterdam: North-Holland.

Friedman, Milton. 1953. "The Case for Flexible Exchange Rates." In *Essays in Positive Economics*. Chicago: University of Chicago Press.

―――. 1967. *The Balance of Payments: Free versus Fixed Exchange Rates*. Washington, DC: American Enterprise Institute.

Gertler, M., and S. Gilchrist. 1992. "Monetary Policy, Business Cycles, and the Behavior of Small Business Firms." New York University. Duplicated.

Golub, Stephen S. 1994. "The United States–Japan Current Account Imbalance: A Review." IMF Paper on Policy Analysis and Assessment, PPAA/94/8, March. Washington, DC: IMF.

Hale, Jeremy. 1989. *Dollar Exchange Rates: Powering Their Way to Purchasing Parity.* New York: Goldman Sachs.

Harrod, R. F. 1953. *International Economics.* Chicago: University of Chicago Press.

Helkie, William L., and Peter Hooper. 1988. "An Empirical Analysis of the External Deficit, 1980–86." Chap. 2 in R. C. Bryant, G. Holtham, and P. Hooper, eds., *External Deficits and the Dollar: The Pit and the Pendulum.* Washington, DC: Brookings Institution.

Hooper, Peter, and Catherine L. Mann. 1987. "The U.S. External Deficit: Its Causes and Persistence." Federal Reserve International Finance Discussion Paper, no. 316, November. Washington, DC.

Horiuchi, Akiyoshi. 1984. "The 'Low-interest Rate Policy' and Economic Growth in Postwar Japan." *Developing Economies,* December 22, 476–490.

Houthakker, Hendrick, and Stephen P. MaGee. 1969. "Income and Price Elasticities in World Trade." *Review of Economics and Statistics* 51:111–125.

Huizinga, John. 1987. "An Empirical Investigation of the Long Run Behavior of Real Exchange Rates." Paper presented at the Conference on the Dynamic Behavior of PPP Deviations, August, Cambridge, MA.

IMF (International Monetary Fund), *International Financial Statistics* (various years).

Isard, Peter. 1977. "How Far Can We Push the Law of One Price?" *American Economic Review* 67, no. 5: 942–948.

———. 1995. "Exchange Rates and National Price Levels." Chap. 4 in *Exchange Rate Economics.* Cambridge: Cambridge University Press.

Ito, Takatoshi. 1992. *The Japanese Economy.* Cambridge: MIT Press.

Itoh, Motoshige, with MITI. 1994. *Misperceptions of the Trade Surplus: What Is Wrong with the Japanese Economy?* Tokyo: Toyo Keizai Shimpo Sha. In Japanese.

Johnson, Chalmers. 1982. *MITI and the Japanese Miracle: The Growth of Industrial Policy, 1925–1975.* Stanford, CA: Stanford University Press.

Johnson, H. G. 1973. "The Case for Flexible Exchange Rates." In *Further Essays in Monetary Economics.* Cambridge: Harvard University Press.

Jones, Ronald W. 1975. "Presumption and the Transfer Problem." *Journal of International Economics* 5:263–274.

Jorgenson, Dale W. 1988. "Technological Innovation and Productivity Change in Japan and the United States." *American Economic Review* (May): 217–222.

Jorgenson, Dale W., and Masahiro Kuroda. 1991. "Productivity and International Competitiveness." MITI and Japan Industrial Policy Research Institute Conference Paper, no. 91–3–7, September.

Jorgenson, Dale W., and Mieko Nishimizu. 1978. "U.S. and Japanese Economic Growth, 1952–74: An International Comparison." *Economic Journal* 88 (Dec.): 707–720.

Kabashima, Ikuo. 1993. "Japan: There May Be a Choice." Chap. 10 in J. W. Morley, ed., *Driven by Growth: Political Change in the Asia-Pacific Region.* New York: M. E. Sharpe.

Kähkönen, Juha. 1995. "Movements in Asset Prices since the Mid-1980s." In Baumgartner and Meredith, eds., *Saving Behavior and the Asset Price "Bubble" in Japan: Analytical Studies.* Occasional Paper, no. 124. Washington, DC: IMF.

Katsu, Etsuko. 1994. *Economics of Yen, Dollar, and Mark: Reality of the 50 years of the Bretton Woods System.* Tokyo: Toyo Keizai Shimpo Sha. In Japanese.

Kawai, Masahiro. 1994. *International Finance,* Tokyo: Tokyo University Press. In Japanese.

Keynes, John Maynard. 1936. *The General Theory of Employment, Interest, and Money.* New York: Macmillan.

———. 1972a. "The Economic Consequences of Mr Churchill." 1925. Reprinted in *Essays in Persuasion: The Collected Writings of John Maynard Keynes.* Vol. 9. New York: Macmillan.

———. 1972b. "Positive Suggestions for the Future Regulation of Money." 1923. Reprinted in *Essays in Persuasion: The Collected Writings of John Maynard Keynes.* Vol. 9. New York: Macmillan.

Knetter, Michael M. 1989. "Price Discrimination by U.S. and German Exporters." *American Economic Review* 79, no. 1: 198–210.

Komiya, Ryutaro. 1994. *Economics of Trade Surpluses and Deficits: Absurdity of Japan–U.S. Friction.* Tokyo: Toyo Keizai Shimpo Sha. In Japanese.

Komiya, Ryutaro, Masahiro Okuno, and Kotaro Suzumura, eds. 1988. *Industrial Policy of Japan.* New York: Academic Press.

Krause, Lawrence B. 1986. "Does a Yen Valued at 100 Per Dollar Make Any Sense?" January 31, University of California, San Diego. Duplicated.

Kravis, I. B. 1986. "The Three Faces of the International Comparison Project." *World Bank Observer* 1, no. 1. Washington: DC.

Kravis, I. B., A. Heston, and R. Summers. 1978. *International Comparisons of Real Product and Purchasing Power.* Baltimore: Johns Hopkins University Press.

Krueger, Anne O. 1995. *American Trade Policy: A Tragedy in the Making.* Washington, DC: AEI Press.

Krugman, Paul R. 1978. "Purchasing Power Parity and Exchange Rates," *Journal of International Economics* 8:397–407.

———. 1979. "A Model of Balance-of-Payments Crises." *Journal of Money Credit and Banking* 11:311–325.

———. 1987. "Pricing to Market When the Exchange Rate Changes." In S. W. Arndt and J. D. Richardson, eds., *Real-Financial Linkages among Open Economies.* Cambridge: MIT Press.

———. 1989a. "Differences in Income Elasticities and Trends in Real Exchange Rates." *European Economic Review* 33:1031–1054.

———. 1989b. *Exchange-Rate Instability.* Cambridge: MIT Press.

———. 1991. *Has the Adjustment Process Worked?* Policy Analyses in International Economics, no. 34. Washington, DC: Institute for International Economics.

———. 1994. "Competitiveness: A Dangerous Obsession," *Foreign Affairs* (March/April).

————. 1996. "Are Currency Crises Self-Fulfilling?" Paper presented at NBER Macro Annual Conference, March 8–9.

Krugman, Paul R., and Richard E. Baldwin. 1987. "The Persistence of the U.S. Trade Deficit," *Brookings Papers on Economic Activity* 1. Washington, DC: Brookings Institution.

Krugman, Paul, R. and Maurice Obstfeld. 1994. *International Economics: Theory and Policy.* 3d ed. New York: Harper Collins.

Kuroda, Masahiro. 1992. "Economic Growth and Structural Change in Japan: 1960–1985." Keio Economic Observatory Discussion Paper, Keio University, Tokyo, February.

Kuznets, Simon. 1971. *Economic Growth of Nations.* Cambridge: Harvard University Press.

Levich, Richard. 1986. "Gauging the Evidence on Recent Movements in the Value of the Dollar." In *The U.S. Dollar: Recent Developments, Outlook, and Policy Options.* Kansas City, MO: Federal Reserve Bank of Kansas City.

Lindbeck, Assar, ed. 1979. *Inflation and Unemployment in Open Economies.* Amsterdam: North-Holland.

MacDonald, Ronald. 1995. "Long-Run Exchange Rate Modeling," *IMF Staff Papers* 5(3): 437–489. Washington, DC: IMF.

Maddison, Angus. 1989. *The World Economy in the 20th Century.* Paris: OECD.

Mann, Catherine L. 1986. "Prices, Profit Margins, and Exchange Rates." *Federal Reserve Bulletin* 72, no. 6. Washington, DC.

Manning, Linda M., and Dimitri Andrianacos. 1993. "Dollar Movements and Inflation: A Cointegration Analysis." *Applied Economics* 25:1483–1488.

Marston, Richard C. 1985. "Stabilization Policies in Open Economies." Chap. 17, R. W. Jones and P. B. Kenen, eds., *Handbook of International Economics.* Vol. 2. Amsterdam: North-Holland.

————. 1987. "Real Exchange Rates and Productivity Growth in the United States and Japan." In S. W. Arndt and J. D. Richardson, eds., *Real-Financial Linkages among Open Economies.* Cambridge: MIT Press.

————. 1991. "Pricing Behavior in Japanese and U.S. Manufacturing." In P. Krugman, ed., *Trade with Japan: Has the Door Opened Wider?* Chicago: University of Chicago Press.

McKinnon, Ronald I. 1979. *Money in International Exchange: The Convertible Currency System.* New York: Oxford University Press.

————. 1980. "Exchange Rate Instability, Trade Imbalances, and Monetary Policies in Japan and the United States." In P. Oppenheimer, ed., *Issues in International Economics.* Oxford: Oriel.

————. 1981. "The Exchange Rate and Macroeconomic Policy: Changing Postwar Perceptions." *Journal of Economic Literature* 19, no. 2: 531–557.

————. 1982. "Currency Substitution and Instability in the World Dollar Standard." *American Economic Review* 72, no. 3: 320–333.

————. 1984. *An International Standard for Monetary Stabilization.* Policy Analyses in International Economics, no. 8. Washington, DC: Institute for International Economics.

—————. 1987. "Interest Volatility and the Dollar Exchange Rate: An Interpretation of Recent Financial Instability in the World Economy." Stanford University, Stanford CA, October. Duplicated.

—————. 1988. "Monetary and Exchange Rate Proposals for International Financial Stability: A Proposal." *Journal of Economic Perspectives* 2, no. 1: 83–103.

—————. 1990. "Interest Rate Volatility and Exchange Risk: New Rules for a Common Monetary Standard." *Contemporary Policy Issues* 8, no. 2: 1–17.

—————. 1993. "The Rules of the Game: International Money in Historical Perspective." *Journal of Economic Literature* 31 (March): 1–44.

—————. 1994. "A Common Monetary Standard or a Common Currency for Europe? Fiscal Lessons from the United States." *Scottish Journal of Political Economy* 41 (Nov.): 337–357.

—————. 1996. *The Rules of the Game: International Money and Exchange Rates.* Cambridge: MIT Press.

McKinnon, Ronald I., and K. C. Fung. 1993. "Floating Exchange Rates and the New Interblock Protectionism: Tariffs versus Quotas." In D. Salvatore, ed., *Protectionism and World Welfare.* Cambridge: Cambridge University Press.

McKinnon, Ronald I., and Kenichi Ohno. 1988. "Getting the Exchange Rate Right: Insular Versus Open Economies." *Seoul Journal of Economics* 1, no. 1: 19–40.

—————. 1989. "Purchasing Power Parity as a Monetary Standard." Chap. 7 in O. Hamouda, R. Rowley, and B. Wolf, eds., *The Future of the International Monetary System: Change, Coordination, or Instability?* Aldershot, England: Edward Elgar.

Meade, James E. 1951. *The Balance of Payments.* London: Oxford University Press.

—————. 1955. "The Case for Variable Exchange Rates." *Three Banks Review* 27 (September): 3–27.

Mecagni, Mauro, and Peter H. Pauly. 1987. "Recursive Band Spectrum Analysis of Purchasing Power Parity." Paper presented at the Conference on the Dynamic Behavior of PPP Deviations, August, Cambridge, MA.

Meese, Richard A., and Kenneth Rogoff. 1983. "Empirical Exchange Rate Models of the Seventies: Do They Fit out of Sample?" *Journal of International Economics* 14, no. 1/2: 3–24.

Meredith, Guy. 1993. "Revisiting Japan's External Adjustment Since 1985." IMF Working Paper WP/93/52, June. Washington, DC: IMF.

Ministry of Finance and EPA. 1995. "Annual Report on National Accounts and OECD as reported in the *Financial Times*," December 28.

Miyagawa, Tsutomu, and Joji Tokui. 1994. "*Economics of Yen Appreciation: Changing International Competitiveness and the Problem of Current Account Surplus.* Tokyo: Toyo Keizai Shimpo Sha. In Japanese.

Miyashita, Takao. 1994. "On Exchange Risk Hedging." In *The Future Prospects of the International Monetary System.* Tokyo: Japan Center for International Finance. In Japanese.

Modigliani, Franco. 1987. "The Real Trade Issue: In the Shadow of the Budget Deficit." *New York Times*, March 1.

Morrison, David, and Jeremy Hale. 1987. "The Search for Equilibrium Exchange Rates." London: Goldman Sachs, *The International Economics Analyst*, February.

Mundell, Robert A. 1987. "New Deal on Exchange Rates." Paper presented at Japan–United States Symposium on Exchange Rates and Macroeconomics, January, Tokyo.

Murakami, Yasusuke. 1992. *Anti-Classical Political Economy*. 2 vols. Tokyo: Chuo Koron Sha. In Japanese.

Niskanen, William. 1987. "A Lower Dollar vs. Recession." *New York Times*, October 27.

Obstfeld, Maurice. 1994. "The Logic of Currency Crises." In *Cahiers économiques et monétaires*. Vol. 43. Paris: Bank of France.

———. 1995. "International Currency Experience: New Lessons and Lessons Relearned." *Brookings Papers on Economic Activity* 1:119–187. Washington, DC: Brookings Institution.

Ohno, Kenichi. 1987. "The Exchange Rate and Prices in Financially Open Economies." Ph.D. diss., Stanford University, Stanford, CA.

———. 1989a. "Export Pricing Behavior of Manufacturing: A U.S.-Japan Comparison." *IMF Staff Papers* 36, no. 3: 550–579. Washington, DC: IMF.

———. 1989b. "Testing Purchasing Power Parity and the Dornbusch Overshooting Model with Vector Autoregression." *Journal of the Japanese and International Economies* 3, no. 2: 209–226.

———. 1989c. "Trade Balance and Exchange Rates: The Debate of 1987." Paper presented at the McGill Economics Centre Conference, March, Montreal.

———. 1990. "Estimating Yen/Dollar and Mark/Dollar Purchasing Power Parities." *IMF Staff Papers* 37, no. 3: 700–725. Washington, DC: IMF.

———. 1991. *International Monetary System and Economic Stability*. Tokyo: Toyo Keizai Shimpo Sha. In Japanese.

———. 1993a. "Dynamism of Japanese Manufacturing: Evidence from the Postwar Period." Institute of Socio-Economic Planning, University of Tsukuba, Japan, January.

———. 1993b. "International Price Differentials of Manufactured Products: Measurement and Implications," Special Research Project on the New International System Discussion Paper, no. 2, University of Tsukuba, Japan, January.

Okimoto, Daniel I. 1989. *Between MITI and the Market: Japanese Industrial Policy for High Technology*. Stanford, CA: Stanford University Press.

OECD (Organization for Economic Co-operation and Development). 1992. *Purchasing Power Parities and Real Expenditures: ESK Results 1990*. Vol. 1. Paris: OECD.

———. 1995. *OECD Economic Surveys: Japan*. Paris: OECD.

Ozkan, F. Gulcin, and Alan Sutherland. 1995. "Policy Measures to Avoid a Currency Crisis." *Economic Journal* 105 (March): 510–519.

Papell, David H. 1994. "Exchange Rates and Prices: An Empirical Analysis." *International Economic Review* 35, no. 2: 397–410.

Pill, Huw. 1995a. Financial Liberalisation and Financial Management in the Open Economy." Ph.D. diss., Stanford University.

————. 1995b. "Target Zones & the European Monetary System: A Reconciliation." CREG Memo, no. 313, Stanford University, February.

Research Institute for International Price Mechanism. 1993. *A Comparison of Competitiveness among Japan, the United States, and Germany*. Tokyo: Research Institute for International Price Mechanism. In Japanese.

————. 1994. *Study Report on Living Costs at Home and Abroad*. Tokyo: Research Institute for International Price Mechanism. In Japanese.

Robinson, Joan. 1937. "The Foreign Exchanges." Pt. 3, chap. 1 in *Essays in the Theory of Employment*. New York: Macmillan.

Salant, Stephen, and Dale Henderson. 1978. "Market Anticipation of Government Policy and the Price of Gold." *Journal of Political Economy* 86:637–648.

Sekimoto, Tadahiro. 1994. "Japan-U.S. Economic Friction and the Ptolemaic Theory." *ESP*, Economic Planning Agency, no. 271, November. In Japanese.

Shirono, Kazuko, 1996. "The Exchange Rate and Price Movements: A Causality Analysis of Yen Appreciation and Japanese Deflation after the Plaza Agreement." Tsukuba University. Duplicated.

Summers, Lawrence. 1987. "In the Wake of Wall Street's Crash." *New York Times*, October 21.

Summers, Robert, and Alan Heston. 1988. "A New Set of International Comparisons of Real Product and Prices: Estimates for 130 Countries." *Review of Income and Wealth* 34, no. 1: 1–25.

Suzuki, Yoshio. 1986. *Money, Finance, and Macroeconomic Performance in Japan*. New Haven, CT: Yale University Press.

————. 1989. *Japan's Economic Performance and International Role*. Tokyo: University of Tokyo Press.

Takagi, Shinji. 1991. "Exchange Rate Expectations: A Survey of Survey Studies." *IMF Staff Papers* 38, (March): 156–183.

Takahashi, Josen, and Noriko Hama. 1992. *Will the Dollar Revive? The Lessons of the Rise and Fall of the Dollar*. Tokyo: Nihon Hyoron Sha. In Japanese.

Takenaka, Heizo. 1991. *Economics of Japan U.S. Friction*. Tokyo: Nihon Keizai Shimbun Sha. In Japanese.

Taniguchi, Tomohiko. 1993. *Japan's Banks and the "Bubble Economy" of the Late 1980s*. Monograph Series, no. 4. Princeton, NJ: Center of International Studies Program on U.S.–Japan Relations.

Tavlas, George S., and Yuzuru Ozeki. 1992. *The Internationalization of Currencies: An Appraisal of the Japanese Yen*. Occasional Paper 90. Washington DC: IMF.

Taylor, John B. 1992. "Discretion versus Policy Rules in Practice." Center for Economic Policy Research Publication, no. 327. Stanford University, November.

Tyson, Laura D'Andrea. 1992. *Who's Bashing Whom? Trade Conflict in High Technology Industries*. Washington, DC: Institute for International Economics.

Ueda, Kazuo. 1992. *Monetary Policy under Balance-of-Payments Disequilibrium.* Tokyo: Toyo Keizai Shimpo Sha. In Japanese.

————. 1995. "Japanese Monetary Policy, Rules or Discretion? Part II." Paper presented at the Bank of Japan's Seventh International Conference, October 26–27, Tokyo.

Walters, Alan. 1990. *Sterling in Danger.* London: Institute for Economic Affairs and Fontana Press.

Ward, Michael. 1985. *Purchasing Power Parities and Real Expenditures in the OECD.* Paris: OECD.

Williamson, John. 1985. *The Exchange Rate System.* Policy Analyses in International Economics, no 5. Washington, DC: Institute for International Economics.

————. 1986. Memorandum from John Williamson to Lawrence B. Krause. February 26.

Williamson, John, and Randall Henning. 1994. "Managing the Monetary System." In P. B. Kenen, ed., *Managing the World Economy: Fifty Years after Bretton Woods.* Washington, D.C.: Institute for International Economics.

Woo, Wing T. 1984. "Exchange Rates and the Prices of Nonfood, Nonfuel Products." *Brookings Papers on Economic Activity*, no. 2. Washington, DC: Brookings Institution.

World Bank. 1993. *The East Asian Miracle: Economic Growth and Public Policy.* New York: Oxford University Press.

Yoshino, Naoyuki. 1995. "Changing Behavior of Private Banks and Corporations and Monetary Policy in Japan." Chap. 6 in K. Sawamoto, Z. Nakajima, and H. Taguchi, eds., *Financial Stability in a Changing Environment.* New York: St. Martin's Press.

Yoshino, Naoyuki, and Masaharu Yoshimura. 1995. "The Exogeneity Test of Monetary Policy Instrumental Targets and Money Supply." Bank of Japan Monetary Research Institute. Duplicated. In Japanese.

Index

Aggregation problem, 54–55
Agriculture, 209
Alogoskoufis, George S., 168–171
Antidumping duties and suits, 7–8, 12
Arrow-Debreu dilemma, 67–68
ASEAN countries, 68–69, 126
Asset bubble
  collapse of, 45, 71, 93, 97, 108–110, 193,
    210
  dollar-yen exchange rates and, 69
  endaka fukyo and, 117–118
  escape hatch, 115–118
  productivity gap and, 32
  syndrome of the ever-higher yen and,
    93–94
Asymmetrical policy shocks, 90
Asymmetric real shocks, 73–74, 87–92
Automobile industry, 9–10, 71

Balassa-Samuelson effect, 33, 80–81, 179
Bank of Japan (BoJ)
  appreciation of yen and, 15, 71, 148, 206
  call rate and, 192
  commercial pact and monetary accord and,
    233
  discount rate and, 192
  domestic credit expansion by, 2, 52–53, 82
  Domestic Wholesale Price Index of, 188
  easy money policy and, 148, 157
  endaka fukyo and, 19, 118
  exchange rates and, 75, 82–83, 149, 177
  Export Price Index of, 188
  Federal Reserve and, 83, 158, 171
  Import Price Index of, 188
  interest rates and, 111, 114, 232
  monetary reaction function of, 190–194
  overvalued yen and, 94, 116

policy of Japan and, monetary, 15, 84
policy reaction function of, 194–199
syndrome of the ever-higher yen and,
  17–18
Barron's, 208–209
Basle Accord, 119–120
Baumgartner, Ulrich, 104–105
Bergsten, C. Fred, 6, 129, 133, 150
Bhagwati, Jagdish, 6, 7
Bilateral productivity gap, 27–28, 32, 77,
  83–84
Blumenthal, Michael, 15–16
BoJ. See Bank of Japan
Bond market, 95, 97–102, 120–122, 228
Bretton Woods international dollar
  standard, 2, 15, 87, 151, 164, 166
Britain. See United Kingdom
Bundesbank policy, 91, 158, 220
Bush administration, 9, 119
Bush, President George, 119

Call rate, 192
Capital, 44, 106. See also Transfer of capital
Capital flows
  international, 52, 95
  short- versus long-term, 103–107
  in United States, 119
Carter administration, 85
Carter dollar rescue package, 16
Cassel, Gustav, 62, 178–181, 201
Cassel-Keynes method, 201–202
Catch-up model of Japan
  completion of, 21–22
  delayed graduation from, 28–35
  dismantling of, 21
  implications for prices, 28–35
  remnants of, 31

Catch-up model of Japan (cont.)
upgrading of industrial infrastructures and,
29
Catte, Pietro, 216
Causality
dollar-yen exchange rates and, 188–189
existing test, 182
in long-term purchasing power parity,
178–183
in monetary reaction function of Bank of
Japan, 190–194
policy implication of assumptions about,
182–183
in price levels, 177, 183–189, 199–204
proving, 64
Cheap-dollar policy, 155, 157
China, 103, 126
Classical dichotomy assumption, 172–173
Cline, William R., 129, 146–151, 158–161
Clinton administration, 226–227
Clinton boom, 122
Clinton, President William, 91
CMS21, 212–214
Cobb-Douglas with technical change, 46
Commerce Department, 8, 41
Commercial disputes, Japan–United States,
2, 4–10, 71
Commercial pact and monetary accord,
Japan–United States, 205–222
American side, 207–208, 211
Bank of Japan and, 233
European experience and, 216–220
exchange-rate stability and, 209–211, 222
Federal Reserve and, 233
Japanese side, 208–209, 211
policy trap and, 205–206
restoration rule and, 220–222
in steady state, 211–216
timing of, 233–235
"A Common Monetary Standard for the
21st Century" (CMS21), 212–214
Consumer price index (CPI)
of Japan, 214–215
tradable goods and, 80
of United States, 32, 63
wholesale price index and, 31–32, 80, 195
Cotton textiles, 7
CPI. See Consumer price index
Credit crunch of 1991 (United States), 93,
118–122
Current-accounts
deficits, 7, 37, 83, 118

multilateral versus bilateral, 44–45
partial-equilibrium model of, 147
surplus, 8, 12–13, 106, 120, 206

Daylight saving time argument for flexible
exchange rates, 57, 73, 88
Deficits, trade, 7, 12–13, 36–37, 133–134,
159–161
Deflation
in Japan, 13, 18, 83–86, 93, 99–100, 152,
205
price, 53, 177, 183–189
De Grauwe, Paul, 88
Depreciation. See Devaluation
Deregulation, 209, 211
Devaluation
divergent views of, 127
of dollar, 8, 17, 83–86
price effect of, 127
real, 137
trade balance and, 125, 147, 155
Developmental authoritarianism, 5, 29–30,
81, 208
Developmentalism, 5, 29–30, 81, 208
Diminished giant syndrome, 6–7
Discount rate, 192
Dodge Plan (1949), 6, 77–78
Dollar. See also Exchange rates, dollar-mark;
Exchange rates, dollar-yen
appreciation of, 63, 141
devaluation of, 8, 17, 83–86
overvaluation of, 15–16, 231
run on, from 1977–78, 86
Domestic Wholesale Price, 188
Dominguez, Kathryn, 216
Dornbusch overshooting model, 163, 187
Dornbusch, Rudiger, 129, 180
Durbin's h statistics, 196, 199
Dynamism, economic, 22–23, 54–57

EAG model. See External adjustment with
growth (EAG) model
East Asian economies, 29
Eastman Kodak complaint against Fujifilm,
207, 226
Eaton, Robert J., 231
Elasticities approach, 12–13, 47, 143–147,
156
Electronics industry, 7
EMU. See European monetary union (EMU)
Endaka fukyo
appreciation of yen and, 149–150

asset bubble and, 117–118
Bank of Japan and, 19, 118
capital flow and, international, 52
deflation causing, 18, 205
demand for bank credit during, 111–114
described, 126
economy of Japan and, 22
exchange rates and, 68–71
in future, 71
historical perspective, 68–71, 108–110,
    205
liquidity traps and, 114
overvaluation of yen and, 52, 92
predicament of Japanese monetary
    authorities in dealing with, 94
recovery from, 107, 228, 234
severe, 211
status of, current, 19
term of, 18, 93
I, 71, 108, 117, 193
II, 71, 108–110, 117–118, 193, 234
ERM. *See* European Exchange Rate
    Mechanism (ERM)
European Exchange Rate Mechanism (ERM),
    216, 221
European experience, 88–89, 216–220
European Monetary System, 68, 212–213
European monetary union (EMU), 213, 218
Exchange policy trap, 157–158
Exchange rates, 51–71, 125–141, 143–161
    as adjusting variable, 181
    adjustments to, 4, 47, 75–81
    asymmetry, 62–64
    Bank of Japan and, 75, 82–83, 149, 177
    determinants of, 147–150
    dollar-mark, 60, 63, 214
    dollar-yen
        American officials' view of, 11–12
        appreciation of yen and, 14–18
        asset bubble and, 69
        causality and, 188–189
        commercial disputes and, Japan–United
            States, 4–5
        deficit and, U.S., 12
        deflation in Japan and, 100
        determination of, 4–5, 135
        devaluation of dollar and, 17
        as forcing variable, 2, 181, 190
        historical perspective, 2
        mercantile pressure and, 225–228
        parity for, 234–235
        percentage deviation of, 69

policy and, monetary, 2
spot movements in, 16–17
trade flow adjustment and, 128
economic efficiency and, 163
elasticities approach and, 143–147
endaka fukyo and, 68–71
expectations, 15–18, 53, 220, 228–233
Federal Reserve and, 75, 149
fiscal rigidity in, 147–150
fixed, 79–80, 87–92
flexible, 51, 57, 73, 87–92, 125
floating, 52–53, 60, 64–68, 87–92, 166,
    177, 179
fluctuations in, 4, 62, 68–69, 73
as forcing variable, 2, 135, 181, 190
as forward-looking variable, 135, 181
Germany and, 60, 63
gross domestic product and, 161
in hard-currency countries, 4
instability, 52–53
insular economy and, 127–134
interest rates and, 163
lagged, 60–61
long-term drift of, 53, 136
management of, 145
markup of, 47
misalignment of, 52–53, 66, 68
monetary perversity in, 147–150
noise, 66–67
nominal bilateral, 61
nonneutrality of, 57–62, 71
no-par floating, 10
open economy and, 13, 127, 129, 134–141
par values for, 8, 83
pass-through, 62–64, 126, 159
populist pressure in, 14
price levels and, 177, 183–189, 199–204,
    214
purchasing power parity and, 127–128,
    177, 180–181
real, 4, 146–147, 150–155, 161, 196
reduced-form model and, 158–161
reducing risk of, 122–123
relative price effect and, 125–127
shocks, 86, 193, 196
slowdown and, economic, 66–68
in soft-currency countries, 4
speculative attacks, self-fulfilling, 216–220
stability for, 209–211, 222
structural changes in, correct signals for,
    53–57
theory and, 155–158

Exchange rates (cont.)
  trade balance and, 4, 125–129
  trade flow adjustment and, 127–128
  trade gap and, structural, 150–155
  trade liberalization and, 210
  views of "right," 127–129
  volatility of, 15, 52, 66, 68, 163
Expected returns, 163
Export Price Index, 60, 188
Exports, 143–147. See also Trade balance
  to Japan, 7–8
  from Japan, 5, 62–63
External adjustment with growth (EAG)
  model, 146–147

Fall of yen, 223–235
  endako fukyo II and, 71
  exchange-rate expectations and, 228–233
  historical perspective, 68–69
  impact of, 223–225
  interest-rate puzzle and, 228–233
  mercantile pressure and, 2, 71, 223, 225–
    228
  timing of United States–Japan commercial
    pact and monetary accord and, 233–235
Federal Reserve
  Bank of Japan and, 83, 158, 171
  commercial pact and monetary accord and,
    233
  easy money policy and, 121, 157
  exchange rates and, 75, 149
  inflation rate and, 2, 15
  interest rates and, 232
  lending rate and, 232
  monetary targets of, intermediate, 178
  multicountry model and, 147
  policy of United States and, monetary, 36,
    171, 219
  price levels and, common, 82–83, 234–235
Feldstein, Martin, 129
Financial markets, 17, 95–97, 120, 156, 166,
  205–206
Financial Times, 226
Fiscal rigidity in exchange-rate
  determination, 147–150
Fisher effect, 99, 115, 172–175
Fisher equation, 172
Fisher, George, 226
Fisher, Irving, 172
Fites, Donald V., 230
Foreign Exchange and Trade Control Law of
  1980, 95

Foreign pressure on price levels, 33
Frankel, Jeffrey, 17, 216, 232
Friedman, Milton, 57, 73, 88, 155, 169
Fujifilm, Kodak complaint against, 207, 226

G5 countries, 65–66
G7 countries, 41, 127, 227
Gaiatsu (foreign pressure), 33
GATT. See General Agreement on Tariffs
  and Trade (GATT)
GDP. See Gross domestic product
General Agreement on Tariffs and Trade
  (1947), 6
Gensaki market, 95, 111
Germany
  dollar appreciation and, 63
  European Exchange Rate Mechanism and,
    216
  exchange rates and, 60, 63, 214
  government expenditure increases and, 91
  growth in, 65
  interest rates in, 229
  reunification costs, 91, 120, 220
Global competition. See International
  competitiveness
GNP, 43, 80, 225
Gold standard, classical international, 164–
  166, 220
Gold window, 84
Golub, Stephen S., 145
Goods
  multiplicity of, devaluation and, 127
  nontradable, 33, 54, 58, 80, 179
  tradable (I and II), 53–54, 58, 61–62, 75,
    79–80, 179
Granger causality test, 182–183
Gross domestic product (GDP)
  exchange rates and, 161
  of Japan, 39, 45, 82, 91, 228
  of United States, 36–37, 41, 44–45, 63, 82,
    91, 119

Hale, Jeremy, 204
Hard-currency countries, 4, 60
Harrod, R. F., 58
Hashimoto, Ryutaro, 209
Helkie, William L., 147–149, 181
Hicksian aggregation of wages, 54–55
High yen–induced recession. See Endaka
  fukyo
Hooper, Peter, 147–149, 181
Houthakker, Hendrick, 159

IIE. *See* Institute for International Economics
  (IIE)
IMF. *See* International Monetary Fund (IMF)
Import Price Index, 188
Imports, 143–147. *See also* Trade balance
  Japanese, 62–63, 209
  tariffs on, 9–10
  United States, 62–63
Indonesia, 103
Inflation
  from expansionary domestic monetary
    policy, 126
  global, 75
  hedges, 174
  indexes, 196
  Korean War and, 77–78
  long-term, 173
  national price, 4
  persistence, 168–171, 174
  price, 15, 79, 175
  protectionism and, 8
  rate, 2, 15
  Scandinavian model of, 79–80
  short-term errors in, 155
  Taylor's rule and, 178
  unemployment and, 155
  in United States, 99
  wholesale price and, 99
Institute for International Economics (IIE),
  158
Instrumental variables (IV) estimation, 170,
  182
Insular economy, 127–134
Insurance industry, 205–206
Interest rates, 163–175
  Bank of Japan and, 111, 114, 232
  behavior of, overview of, 164–168
  exchange rates and, 163
  expectation theory of terms structure of,
    172
  Federal Reserve and, 232
  Fisher effect, 172–174
  Fisher equation of, 172
  gap in nominal, 234
  in Germany, 229
  global economic regimes and
  independent versus forced monetary
    accommodation, 171–172
  inflation persistence, 168–171
  in Japan, 97–102, 111, 114, 191, 229, 232
  long-term, 15–18, 97, 121, 166–168, 172,
    174, 191, 229

  lowering, 53
  puzzle, 228–233
  risk for international investors and, 174–
    175
  short-term, 15–16, 97, 114, 166–168,
    172–173, 178
  Taylor's rule and, 178
  in United States, 16–17, 97–102, 111,
    120–121, 229
  volatility of, 68, 163, 166–168, 172–174
Internal price divergence, 31–32
International competitiveness, 73–92
  adjustments to exchange rates and, 75–81
  deflation in Japan and, 83–86
  fluctuations in exchange rates and, 73
  policy of Japan and, monetary, 81–83
  price adjustment, under fixed rate dollar
    standard from 1951–71, 75–81
  unfair, by Japan, 5–6, 14
  wage adjustment and
    breakdown of, after 1971, 83–86
    idealized, 86–87
    under fixed-rate dollar standard from
      1951–71, 75–81
  yen appreciation and, 75–81
International finance, study of, 2
International Monetary Fund (IMF), 75, 106
  Article 8, 7
International monetary system, 166
Investors, international, 163, 174–175
Ito, Takatoshi, 190–191
IV estimation. *See* Instrumental variables (IV)
  estimation

Japan. *See also* Commercial pact and
    monetary accord, Japan–United States
  agriculture in, 209
  capital outflow from, 120–121
  catch-up model of
    completion of, 21–22
    delayed graduation from, 28–35
    dismantling of, 21
    policy, monetary, 21–22, 28–35
    remnants of, 31
    upgrading of industrial infrastructures
      and, 29
  commercial disputes between United States
    and, 2, 4–10, 71
  consumer price index of, 214–215
  deflation in, 13, 18, 83–86, 93, 99–100,
    152, 205
  dependent policy of, monetary, 10

Japan (cont.)
  deregulation of economy of, 209, 211
  dualism in, economic, 29, 31
  economic interaction between United
    States and, 1–4, 62–64, 223
  economy of, 22–28
  exports from, 5, 62–63
  exports to, 7–8
  financial markets in, 95–97
  GNP, 43, 225
  gross domestic product of, 39, 45, 82, 91,
    228
  high-growth era of, 23–27
  imports from, 62–63, 209
  interest rates in, 97–102, 111, 114, 191,
    229, 232
  as international creditor, dollar-based, 44,
    95, 102–108
  labor market in, 90
  Liberal Democratic Party in, 30–31
  macroeconomics in, 71
  money growth in, 81–83
  policy of, monetary
    Bank of Japan and, 15
    dependent, 10
    future, 15
    international competitiveness and, 81–83
  price levels in, 183–189
  productivity in, 5, 14, 22–23, 45–49, 57,
    74, 76
  protectionism in, trade, 5–7, 13, 80–81
  recessions in, 68–69
  savings rates in, 13, 41–44, 91, 93
  stock crash in, 120
  wage and price adjustment under fixed-rate
    dollar standard, 75–81
  wages in, evolution of, 54–55
  wholesale price index, 13, 15, 75–76, 85–
    86, 99, 152
  world-banker route for, 107
Japan Offshore Market, 95–97
Japan Productivity Center, 76
J-curve effect, 126

Kabashima, Ikuo, 30
Kaihatsushugi (Developmentalism), 5, 29–30,
  81, 208
Kawai, Masahiro, 126, 136–137
Keynes, John Maynard, 201–202
Kodak complaint against Fujifilm, 207, 226
Komiya, Ryutaro, 157
Krueger, Anne, 9

Krugman, Paul R., 57, 127, 145–146, 182,
  216–218
Kuznets inverted U-curve phenomenon, 30
Kuznets, Simon, 23

Labor market, 54, 89–90
Land prices, 69, 109, 117
Large-Scale Retail Store Law, 208
LDP, 30–31
Liberal Democratic Party (LDP), 30–31
Liquidity traps, 15, 53, 93–94, 110–114
Long-run averaging, 202–203
Long-term drift of exchange rates, 53, 136
Lucas critique, 168

Macroeconomics
  economic interaction between Japan and
    United States and, 1–2
  fluctuations of exchange rates and, 4, 62
  insular economy and, 127–134
  in Japan, 71
  no-par floating exchange rates and, 10
  open economy and, 127, 134–141
  syndrome of the ever-higher yen and, 18,
    108–110
  yen appreciation and, 71
MaGee, Stephen P., 159
Mark, deutsche, 60, 91
Markup, 47
Marshall-Lerner elasticities conditions, 125,
  131, 133
Marshall Plan (1948), 6
Marston, Richard C., 183
"Mass. Ave." model, 145–146
McKinnon, Ronald I., 58, 86, 212
MCM. See Multicountry model (MCM)
Meese, Richard A., 135
Mercantile pressure
  appreciation of yen and, 2, 17–18
  exchange rates and, 225–228
  fall of yen and, 2, 71, 223, 225–228
  historical perspective, 7
  Nixon shock and, 36
Meredith, Guy, 104–105, 145
Mexican financial crisis, 71
Microeconomics, 4, 10, 62, 89
Ministry of Finance, 116–117, 206, 227,
  232–233
Misalignment of exchange rates, 52–53, 66,
  68
Missing markets in Arrow-Debreu dilemma,
  67–68

Miyagawa, Tsutomu, 126
Miyashita, Takao, 66–67
Morrison, David, 204
Morrison-Hale estimation, 204
Multicountry model (MCM), 147
Mundell-Fleming model, 148
Murakami, Yasusuke, 29–30

NAFTA. *See* North American Free Trade
    Agreement (NAFTA)
Naigai kakakusa (price diffusion), 33, 58–62,
    69
Newly industrializing economies (NIEs),
    68–69, 210–211
New York Times, 227, 230–231
NIEs. *See* Newly industrializing economies
    (NIEs)
Nikkei stock index, 69, 117
Nixon, President Richard, 8, 10, 84–85
Nixon shock, 11, 36
Noland, Marcus, 6, 150
Nonneutrality of exchange rates, 57–62, 71
Nontariff barriers (NTBs), 210. *See also*
    specific types
Nontradable goods, 33, 54, 58, 80, 179
No-par floating exchange rates, 10
North American Free Trade Agreement
    (NAFTA), 208
NTBs. *See* nontariff barriers (NTBs)

OECD. *See* Organization for Economic
    Cooperation and Development (OECD)
Ohno, Kenichi, 181–182, 203
Oil prices, 32, 63, 65–66
OLS estimation. *See* Ordinary least squares
    (OLS) estimation
Omnibus Trade and Competitiveness Act of
    1988, 9
OPEC, 65–66
Open economy, 13, 127, 129, 134–141
Ordinary least squares (OLS) estimation,
    170, 182, 195
Organization for Economic Cooperation and
    Development (OECD), 32–33, 41, 43,
    81, 159, 169, 204
Ozeki, Yuzuru, 94–96, 103, 106

Partial-equilibrium current-account model,
    147
Par value system, 8, 83
Pass-through exchange rates, 62–64, 126,
    159

Perversity in exchange-rate determination,
    147–150
Phillips curve, 155, 168–169, 171
Plaza Agreement of 1985, 60, 168, 182, 188,
    192, 199
Plaza-Louvre Accords, 212, 227
Policy, monetary
    asymmetrical shocks and, 90
    catch-up model and, 21–22, 28–35
    causality assumptions and implications for,
        182–183
    cheap-dollar policy, 155, 157
    determinants of, 4
    dollar-yen exchange rate and, 2
    economic interaction between Japan and
        United States and, 21–22
    economies of Japan and United States and,
        22–28
    financial responsibility of United States
        and, restoring, 35–37
    of Germany, 91, 158
    inflation from expansionary domestic, 126
    international competitiveness and, 81–83
    of Japan
        Bank of Japan and, 15
        dependent, 10
        future, 15
        international competitiveness and, 81–83
        Lucas critique of, 168
        populist behavior and, 12–15
        productivity in Japan and United States
            and, 45–49
    savings rates and, 37–45
    traditional approach to, 4
    of United States
        determinants of, 14–15
        effect of, on rest of world, 35–37
        Federal Reserve and, 36, 171, 219
        goal of, 22
        independent, 10, 171–172
        periods of, 35
Policy trap, 156, 205–206
Postal Saving System, 232
PPP. *See* Purchasing power parity
Price deflation, 53, 177, 183–189
Price diffusion, 33, 58–62, 69
Price divergence, 175
Price inflation, 175
Price levels
    adjustments, under fixed-rate dollar
        standard from 1951–71, 75–81
    causality in, 177, 183–189, 199–204

Price levels (cont.)
devaluation of, 127
domestic, 214
domestic versus foreign-exchange
determination of, 183–189
exchange rates and, 177, 183–189, 199–
204, 214
fair foreign, 8
food and service, 33
foreign pressure and, 33
gaps in, international, 53–54
in Germany, 63
in Japan, 183–189
land, 69, 109, 117
mercantile pressure and, 36
misalignments of, 83
oil, 66
pricing-to-market effect and, 183–184
purchasing power parity and, 32–33
relative, 177
target, common, 234–235
Price pressure, 58–60, 203
Price survey, 203–204
with adjustment for tradability, 204
Pricing-to-market effect, 183–184
Productivity
deviations from purchasing power parity
and, 210
gaps, bilateral and, 27–28, 32, 77, 83–84
in Japan, 5, 14, 22–23, 45–49, 57, 74, 76
policy and, monetary, 45–49
reduced, 49, 66
total factor productivity and, 23
in United States, 22–23, 27–28, 45–49, 57,
74, 77
Protectionism, trade
inflation and, 8
in Japan, 5–7, 13, 80–81
nontariff barriers, 210
old GATT and, 36
private, 208
tariffs, 9–10, 210
trade deficit and, 134
in United States, 6–11, 36
Pseudo-nontradable goods, 80–81
Purchasing power parity (PPP), 177–204
causality in long-term, 178–183
deviations from, 151–155, 210
Dornbusch's view of, 180
drifting, 62, 234
estimating tradable, 200–204

exchange rates and, 127–128, 177, 180–
181
formulation of, 178–179
long-term, 178–183
monetary reaction function, of Bank of
Japan, 190–194
Morrison-Hale estimate of, 204
percentage deviation of dollar-yen
exchange rate from, 69
policy reaction function of Bank of Japan,
194–199
price deflation and, 177
price levels and, 32–33
short-term, 179
tradable goods and, 61–62
trade flow adjustment and, 140
traditional view of, 180
yen rise and, 225

Reagan administration, 11, 16–17
Real estate prices, 69, 117
Recession, in Japan, 68–71. See also Endaka
fukyo
Redistribution, 30
Reduced-form model (RFM), 158–161
Relative price effect, 57, 125–127
Research Institute for International Price
Mechanisms, 69
Restoration rule, 220–222
RFM. See Reduced-form model (RFM)
Ricardian equivalence, 45
Rogoff, Kenneth, 135
Rubin, Robert E., 226–227
"Rust bowl" in American Midwest, 68

Savings rates
gap, Japan-United States, 43–44
in Japan, 13, 41–44, 91, 93
policy and, monetary, 37–45
postal, 232
statistical issues, 37–41
in United States, 7, 13, 37–45, 91, 93
Scandinavian model of inflation, 79–80
Sims test, 182–183
Slowdown, economic, 66–68, 119
Smith, Ron, 168–171
Smithsonian Agreement, 84
Soft-currency countries, 4
Southeast Asia, 126
Static trade models, 54
Summers, Lawrence, 129

Super 301, 9, 207, 225–226
Supply shocks, 66
Suzuki, Yoshio, 108
Sweden, 217–218
Syndrome of the ever-higher yen, 1–19
  asset bubble and, 93–94
  Bank of Japan and, 17–18
  commercial disputes between Japan and
    United States and, 4–10
  described, 10–15
  economic interaction between Japan and
    United States and, 1–4
  end of, impact of, 233
  exchange-rate expectations and, 15–18
  financial markets associated with, 17
  investments and, 108–109
  liquidity traps and, 15, 110–114
  long-term drift of exchange rates and, 136
  macroeconomics and, 18, 108–110
  overcoming, 18–19
  policy trap and, 205
  propagation of, 10–11
  transfer of capital and, 93–94
  understanding, 206

Takagi, Shinji, 135
Taniguchi, Tomohiko, 117
Tariffs, 9–10, 210
Tavlas, George S., 94–96, 103, 106
Taylor, John B., 178
Taylor's rule, 178
Technical change, 45–49, 57
TFA. See Trade flow adjustment (TFA)
TFP. See Total factor productivity (TFP)
Theory, economic, 155–158
Theory-to-reality feedback, 155
3SLS method. See Three-stage least squares
  method
Three-stage least squares (3SLS) method, 47
Tokui, Joji, 126
Total factor productivity (TFP), 23
Toys 'R' Us, 208
Tradable goods (I and II), 53–54, 58, 61–62,
  75, 79–80, 179
Trade Act of 1974, 207
Trade balance, 125–141, 143–161
  appreciation of yen and, 149–150
  bilateral, 150–155
  devaluation and, 125, 147, 155
  elasticities approach to, 12–13, 143–147
  exchange rates and, 4, 125–129
  expectations, 155–158

fiscal rigidity and, 147–150
insular economy and, 127–134
monetary perversity and, 147–150
open economy and, 13, 127, 129, 134–141
policy, 155–158
reduced-form model and, 158–161
theory and, 155–158
trade flow adjustment and, 144
trade gap and, structural, 150–155
Trade deficits, 7, 36–37, 133–134, 159–161
Trade flow adjustment (TFA), 127–128, 133,
  140, 144
Trade flow, study of, 2
Trade gap, 150–155, 205
Trade liberalization, 210
Transfer of capital, 93–123
  asset bubble and
    collapse of, 93, 108–110
    escape hatch, 115–118
    syndrome of the ever-higher yen and,
      93–94
  credit crunch of United States (1991) and,
    93, 118–122
  financing, 94–107
  liquidity traps and, 93–94, 110–114
  problem, 122–123
  syndrome of the ever-higher yen and,
    93–94
Trust Fund, Ministry of Finance, 232–233
t-statistics, 199
Tyson, Laura D'Andrea, 5–6

Ueda, Kazuo, 194
Unemployment, 155
Unilateralism in trade law, 9
United Kingdom, 7, 65, 106, 164
United States. See also Commercial pact and
    monetary accord, Japan–United States
  budget deficit, 133, 141
  capital flows in, 119
  Clinton boom and, 122
  commercial disputes between Japan and, 2,
    4–10, 71
  consumer price index, 32, 63
  credit crunch of 1991 in, 93, 118–122
  diminished giant syndrome and, 6–7
  economic interaction between Japan and,
    1–4, 62–64, 223
  economy of, 22–28
  exports, 62–63
  financial responsibility of, restoring, 22,
    35–37

United States (cont.)
GNP of, 43
gross domestic product, 36–37, 41, 44–45, 63, 82, 91, 119
imports, 62–63
independent policy of, monetary, 10
inflation in, 99
interest rates in, 16–17, 97–102, 111, 120–121, 229
as international banker, 44, 103
labor market in, 90
policy of, monetary
  determinants of, 14–15
  effect of, on rest of world, 35–37
  Federal Reserve, 36, 171, 219
  goal of, 22
  independent, 10, 171–172
  periods of, 35
productivity in, 22–23, 27–28, 45–49, 57, 74, 77
protectionism in, trade, 6–11, 36
saving-investment gap in, 44
savings rates in, 7, 13, 37–45, 91, 93
trade deficit, 12–13, 133–134
wage and price adjustment under fixed-rate dollar standard, 75–81
wages in, 57
wholesale price index, 13, 63, 85–86
United States Commerce Department, 8, 41
United States Federal Reserve. See Federal Reserve
United States Trade Representative (USTR), 9
Uruguay Round in the GATT, 10
USTR. See United States Trade Representative

VAR. See Variable autoregression (VAR)
Variable autoregression (VAR), 182–183
VERs. See Voluntary export restraints (VERs)
VIEs. See Voluntary import expansions (VIEs)
Volatility
  of exchange rates, 15, 52, 66, 68, 163
  of interest rates, 68, 163, 166–168, 172–174
Voluntary export restraints (VERs), 7–8, 12
Voluntary import expansions (VIEs), 9

Wage adjustment
  breakdown of, after 1971, 83–86

idealized, 86–87
under fixed rate dollar standard from 1951–71, 75–81
Wall Street Journal, 227–228
Wholesale price index (WPI)
  consumer price index and, 31–32, 80, 195
  Domestic, 188
  export prices and, 63
  Fisher effect and, 99
  inflation and, 99
  Japan, 13, 15, 75–76, 85–86, 99, 152
  overall, 152
  United States, 13, 63, 85–86
Wilde, Oscar, 223
World Trade Organization (WTO), 10, 207–208, 225–226
WPI. See Wholesale price index
WTO. See World Trade Organization (WTO)

Yen. See also Exchange rates, dollar yen; Fall of yen
  appreciation of, 2, 10–11, 13–18, 53, 69, 71, 75–81, 148–150, 205–206
  overvaluation of, 52, 92, 94, 116, 126–127
  recession and high, 68–71
  rise of, 225
Yoshimura, Masaharu, 194, 199
Yoshino, Naoyuki, 194, 199